Anderson Zaca

FIRE ISLAND INVASION

Day of Independence

History

It all started in the summer of 1976. A group of friends, including Cherry Grove icon, Teri Warren, took a water taxi over to Fire Island Pines for dinner at The Botel. What should have been a lovely evening quickly took a fateful turn.

When the Botel's owner, John Whyte, noticed that Teri was dressed in full drag, he immediately dispatched his maître d' to handle the situation. With all the other patrons watching, the maître d' declared in a booming voice that The Botel was a "family restaurant" and that the group was not welcome. It was a humiliating spectacle.

1976 also marked the 200th birthday of the United States. New York's Bicentennial celebration included a massive flotilla in the Hudson River that was a media sensation. With all this patriotic hype in the air, it occurred to me and my friends that we could create our own July 4th "flotilla" in a grand act of defiance. Earlier that season, I'd been crowned the first Homecoming Queen of Cherry Grove, an honor intended only to celebrate our community's campy, joyous culture. In the wake of Teri's rebuke at The Botel, the big joke became that I would lead a revolutionary invasion of our own: the Queen of Cherry Grove would lead an "invasion" of her colony, The Pines, on July 4th.

And so The Invasion of The Pines began as a symbolic act, a playful surprise attack by water taxi. The idea was simple: each queen or lesbian would dismount ceremoniously, one by one, and I, the newly crowned Queen of Cherry Grove, replete in a flowing pink cape and crown, would be The Invasion's grand finale. When the boat arrived, packed with our entourage, passersby on the boardwalk started to gather, asking, "Why is she here? Why is she here?" One of my dear friends (and the sister of my first true love), Amelia Migliaccio, was helping us all off the boat in our heels. She heard the buzz and turned to me to whisper, "Tommy, everyone wants to know why you're here."

At that moment, an answer just came to me. Dramatically, I told her, "Tell them I'm here to bless the harbor." Amelia smiled and turned to the woman behind her. "She's here to bless the harbor." That woman turned to the group of people behind her, repeating, "She's here to bless the harbor!" As we watched my spontaneous proclamation spread like a wave through the crowd, the legend and purpose of The Invasion was born.

Glancing up, I noticed that The Botel had three stories. I decided our entourage would seize the third-floor balcony, where I could properly bless the harbor. "Let's go!" I commanded. From my perch on the balcony, I waved and blew kisses to the growing crowd, I made the sign of the cross, and I blessed the harbor. Then, I turned to the other queens and told them that it was time to leave and go home. Everyone was having so much fun, and they much preferred to stay, but I said, "This is the time to go. Let's leave them on a high note, and let's go home now." So, we boarded our water taxi and returned to Cherry Grove, concluding the first Invasion.

There were seven queens and two lesbians in the first year, a group of twenty-seven in the second, and it grew and grew over the years. The peak was in the 1990s with 352 queens. Over time, small boats wouldn't hold the entire entourage anymore, and Rose Levine almost fell into the bay one year, but we packed onto more and more boats in our heels anyway and did our thing. The rooftops and yachts of The Pines were always packed with spectators, eager to witness us queens in all our glory. Eventually, in the '80s, Ken Stein of Sayville Ferry joined the festivities, supplying us invaders with a "battleship that could accommodate us all."

In the early days, John Whyte would call and demand angrily that we not come. He would say, "How dare you come and disrupt The Pines!" And of course, we would go anyway. Eventually, John welcomed us. From then on until he passed, he would have champagne and roses waiting for every invader. This became our tradition, our ritual, a statement of our right to be there. Yes, The Invasion is a day of joy and celebration. However, it was also a loud and proud statement against homophobia and transphobia in our own LGBTQIA+ community.

My friend, Zondra Fox, first introduced me to Anderson Zaca at The Invasion in 2007. I cherish the way Zaca's images capture the grace of The Invasion in a way I hadn't seen before. Through these stunning portraits, his work immortalizes the magic of that first Invasion, along with the vibrant energy that has followed every year since.

This book will allow you to feel the pulse of the celebration, just as we lived it.

Panzi

MAKE UP

The day begins early, with every house of drag queens up by 7 am. By 8 am, preparation is in full swing. Queens dress and paint each other while sipping champagne, setting the stage for a morning that is equal parts chaos and camaraderie. Music pulses through the air as queens rush around, shaving, fixing hair, perfecting makeup, and laughing at the occasional misstep.

At 10 am, Panzi makes her rounds, bullhorn in hand. "Get ready, girls - paint!" Her sharp humor, peppered with teasing and funny insults, keeps everyone on their toes. By 11:30 am, she is out on the boardwalk, tossing out her signature irreverent lines to signal that it is nearly time for the main event.

For the newer queens, this is a moment of transformation. The veterans guide them through the rituals of drag, from applying makeup to mastering the art of walking in heels. This challenge always draws plenty of laughter. Amidst the mayhem, a playful tradition has unfolded.

Judges wander through the houses and nominate the best looks, groups, and styles. The categories are improvised, which adds a lighthearted competition to the morning's preparations. As the queens later make their way down the red carpet, sashes are draped over the winners to honor the creativity and spirit that defines The Invasion of The Pines.

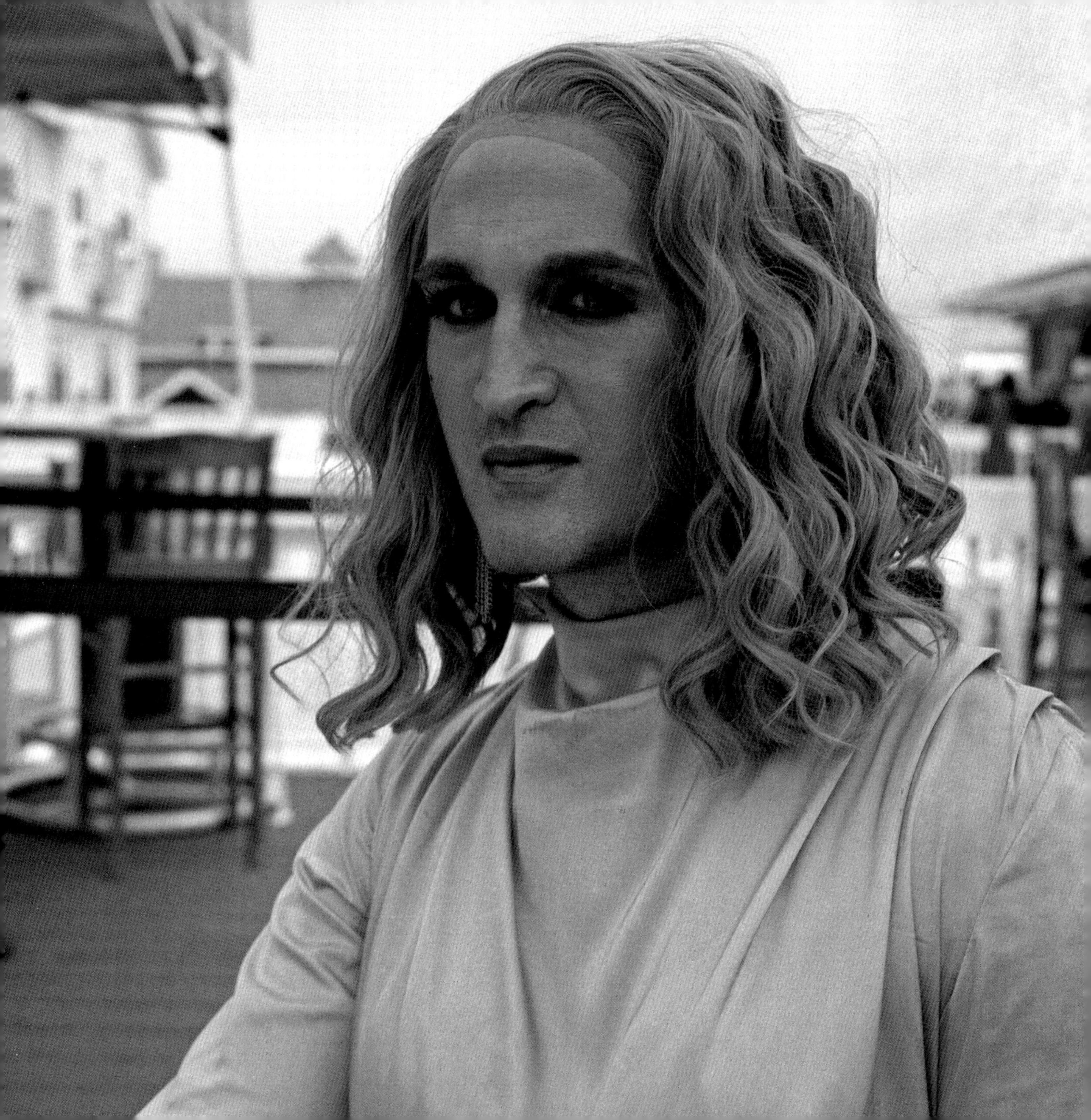

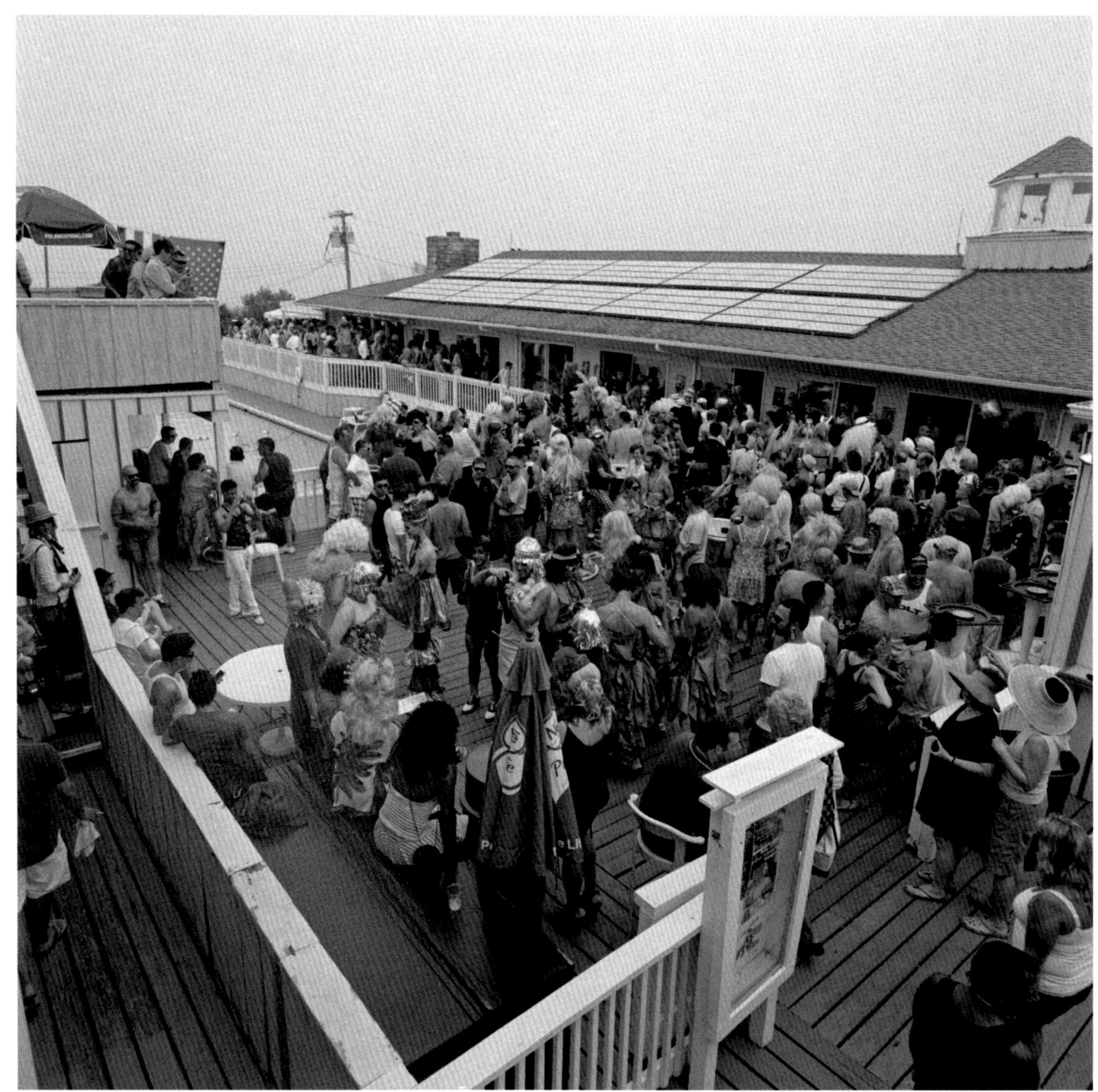

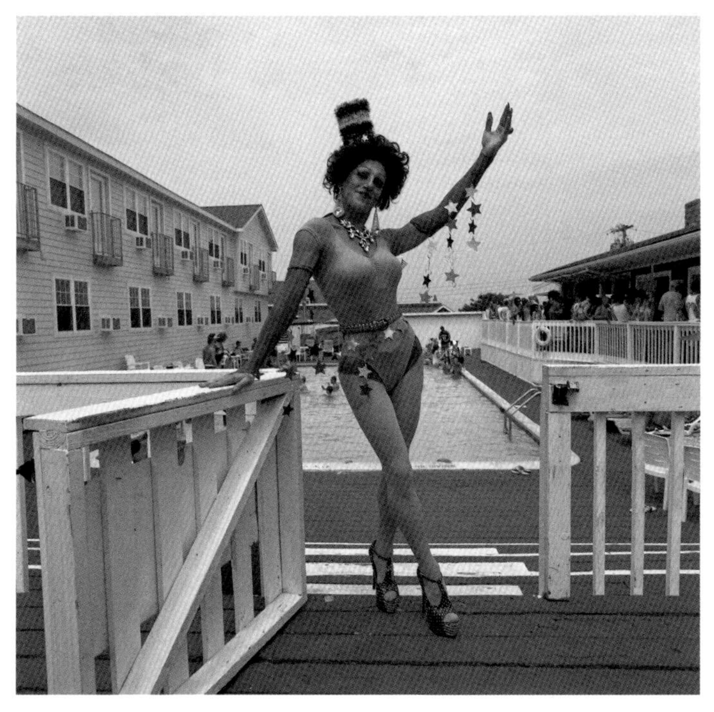

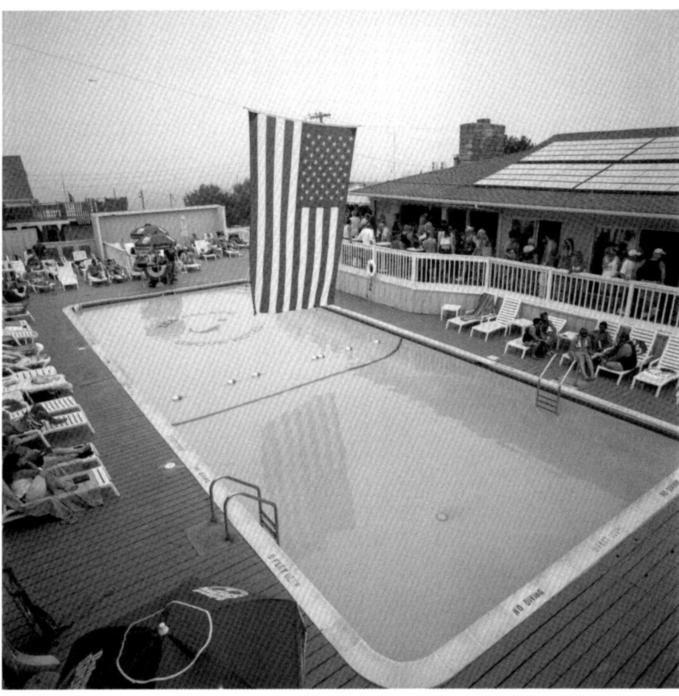
NO DIVING

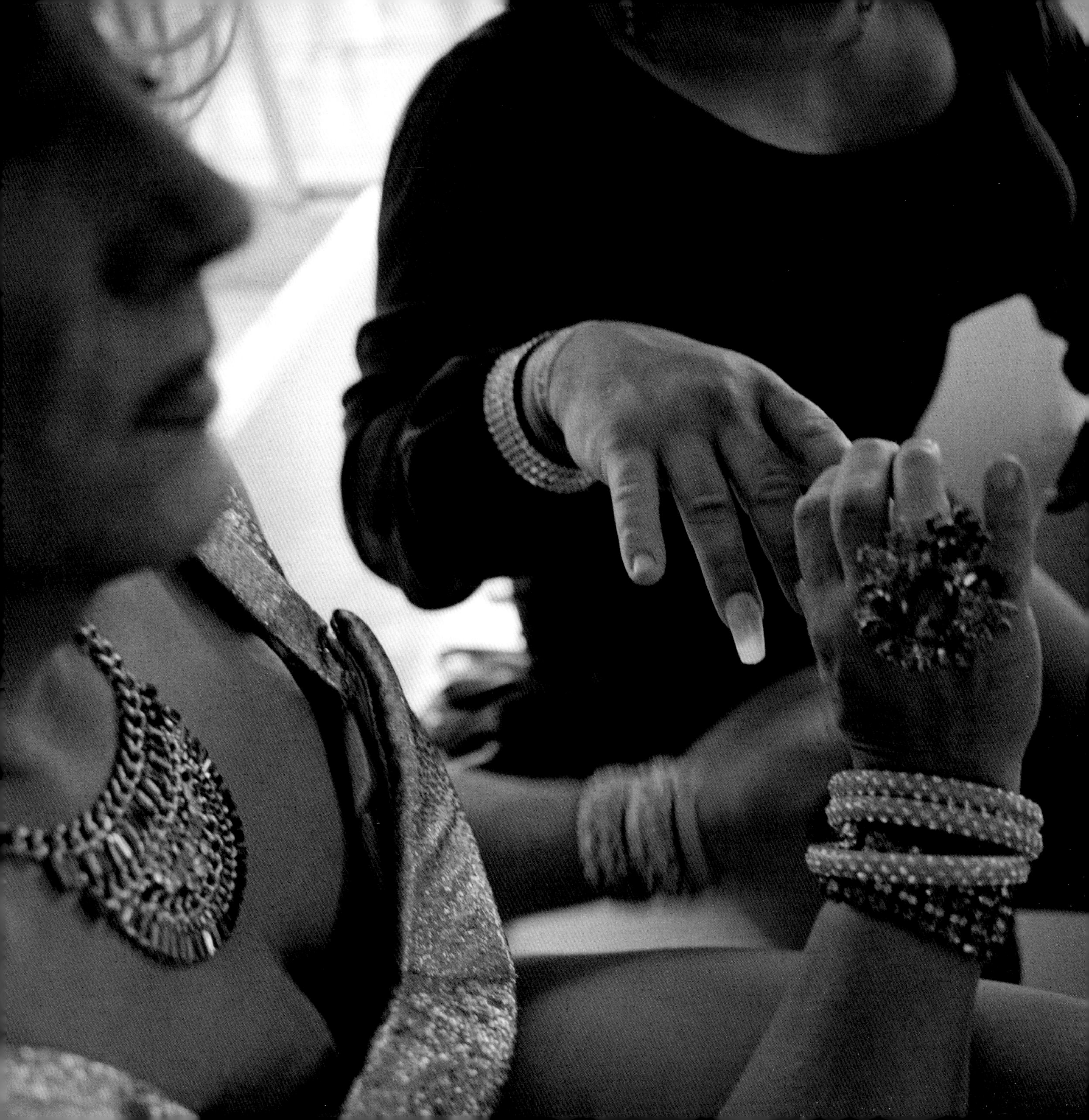

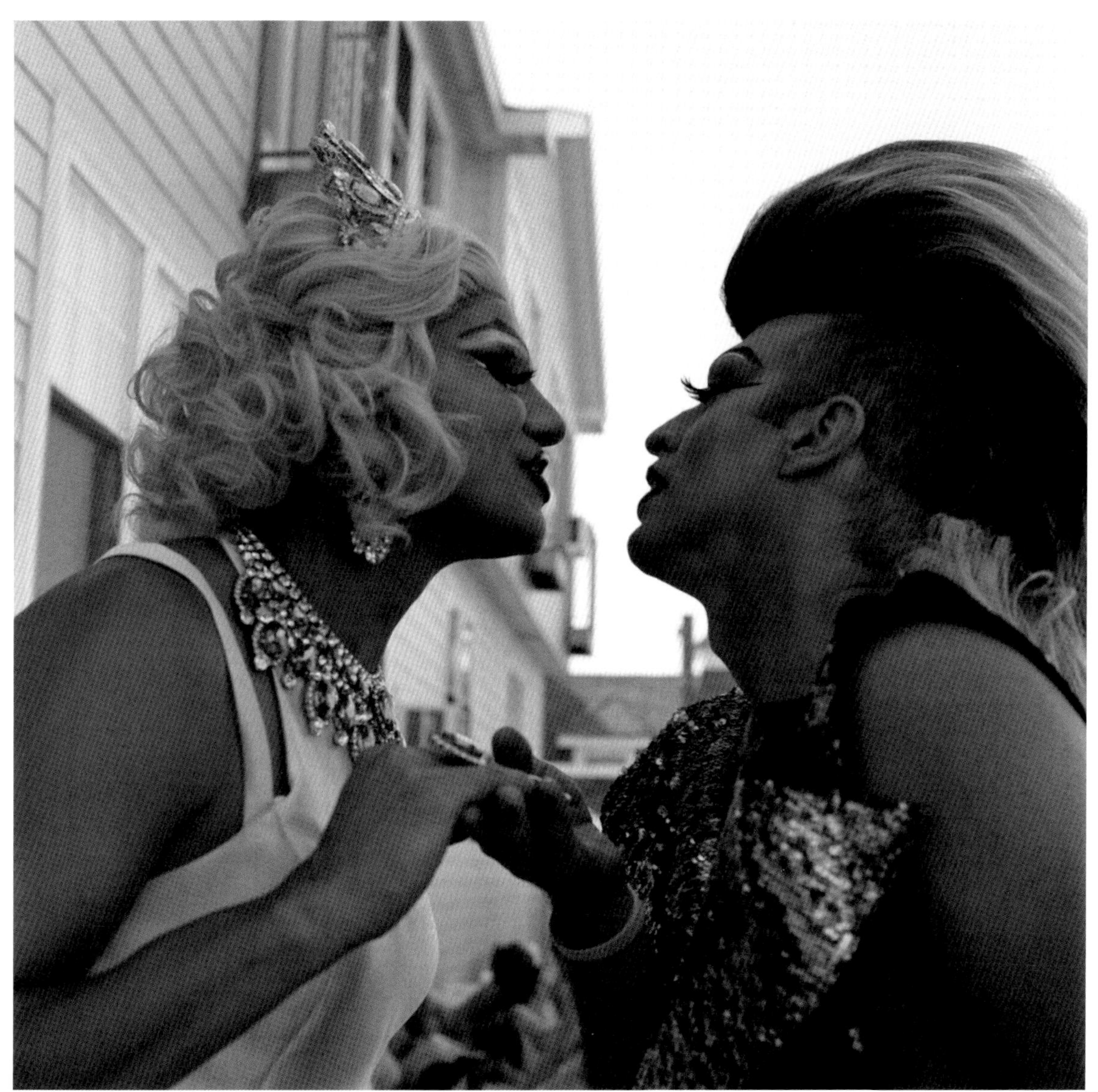

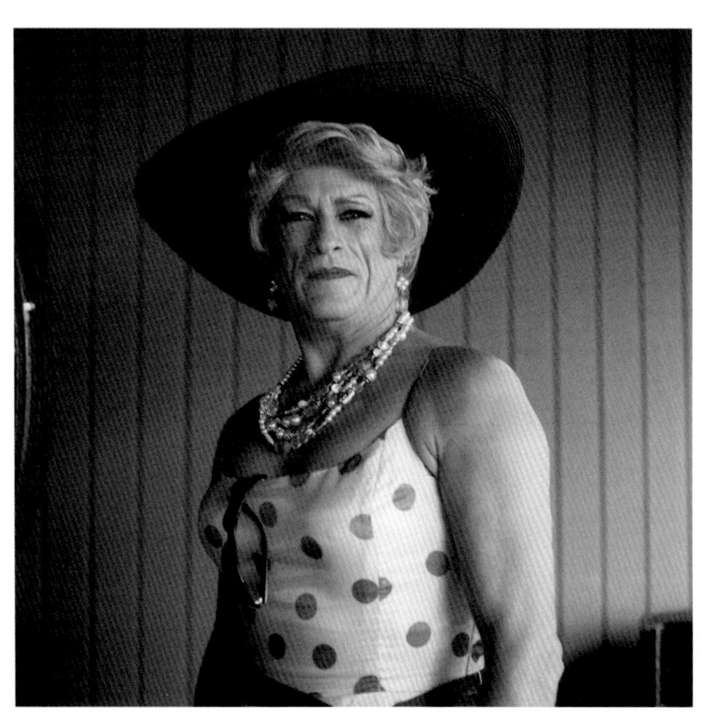

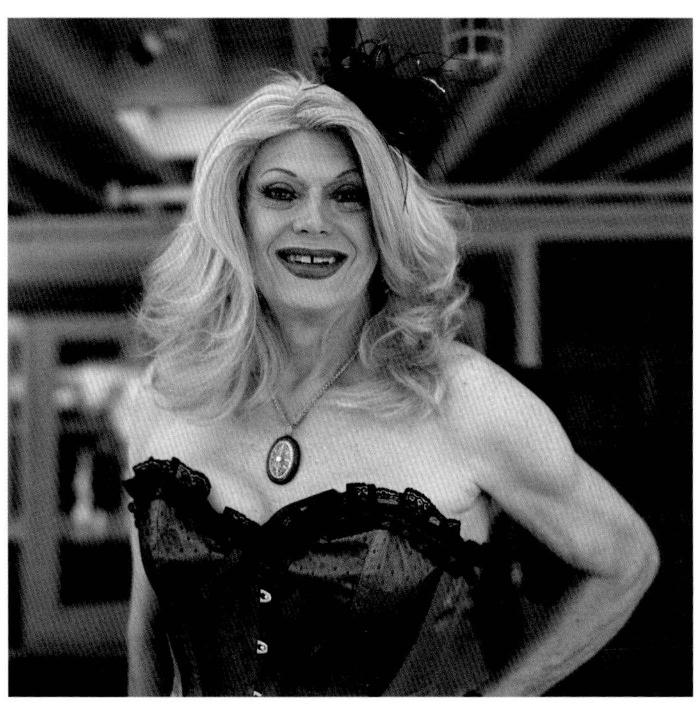

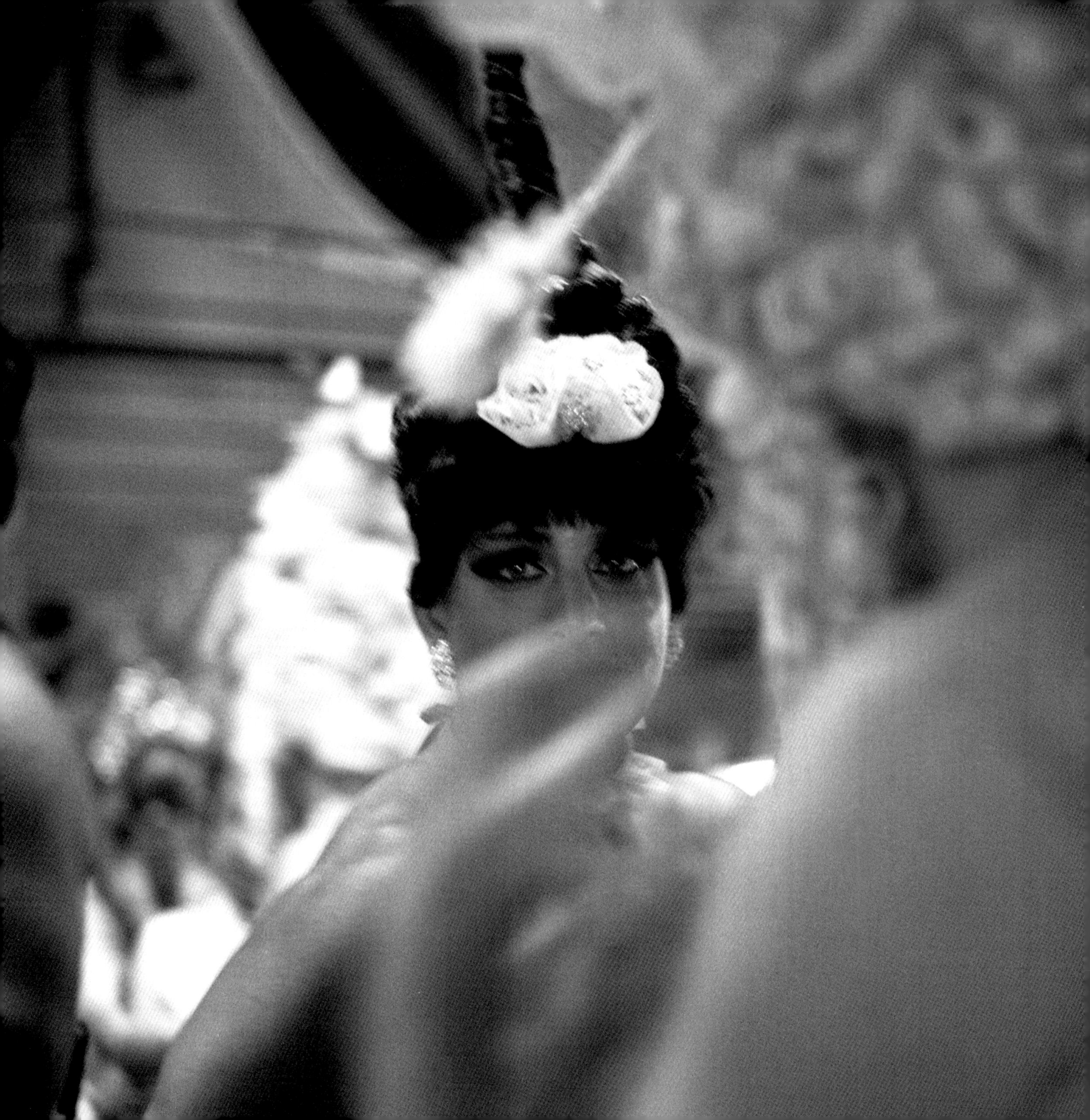

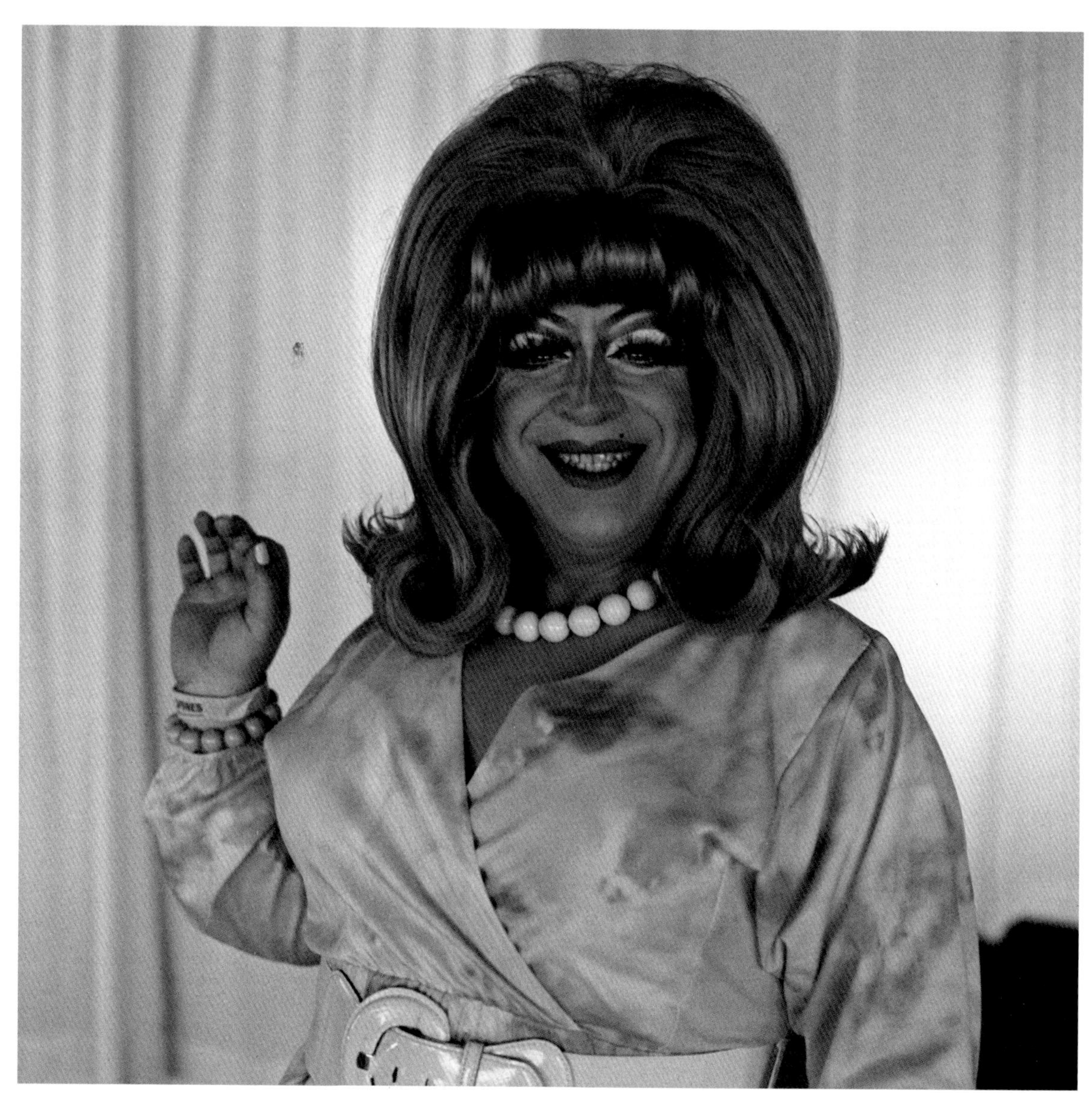

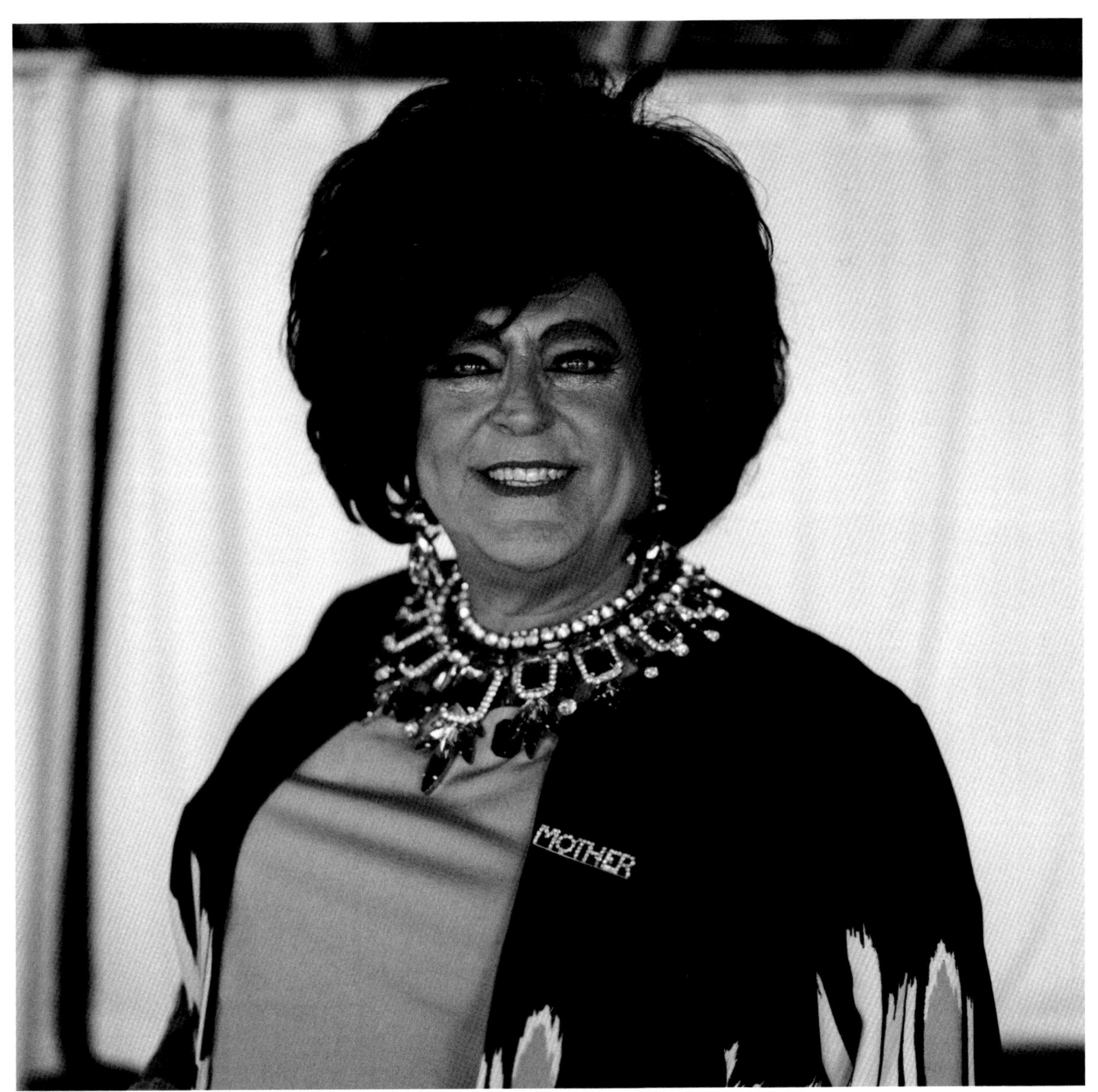
MOTHER

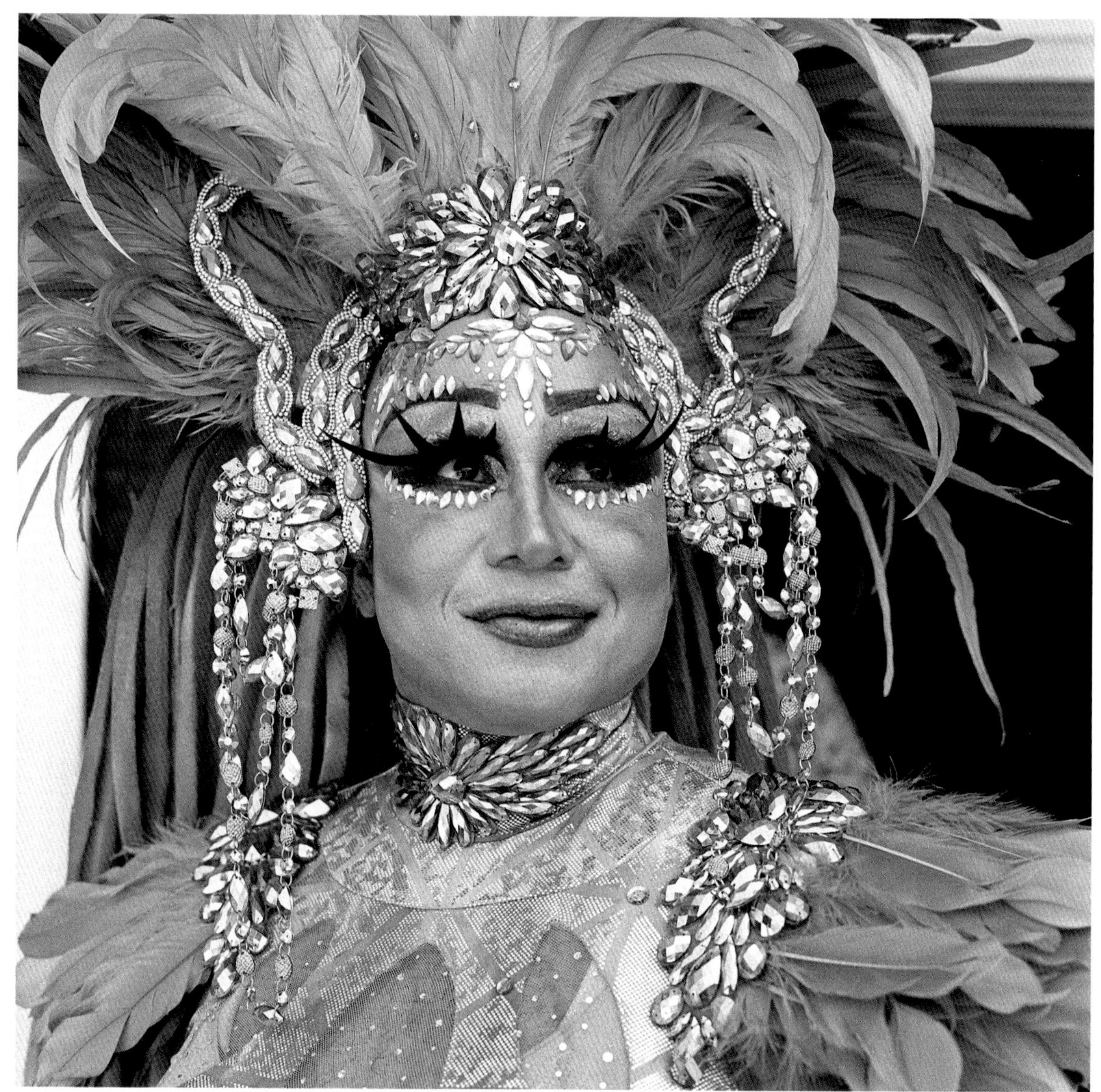

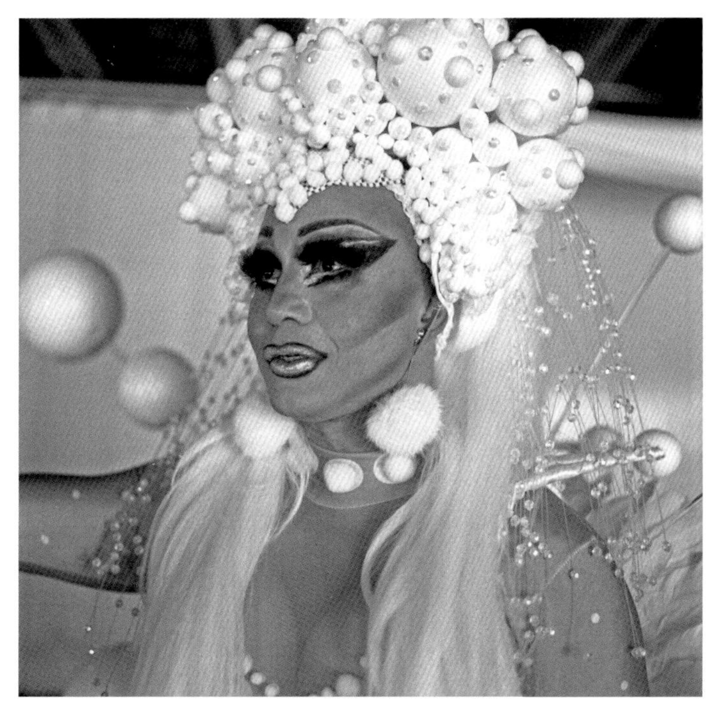

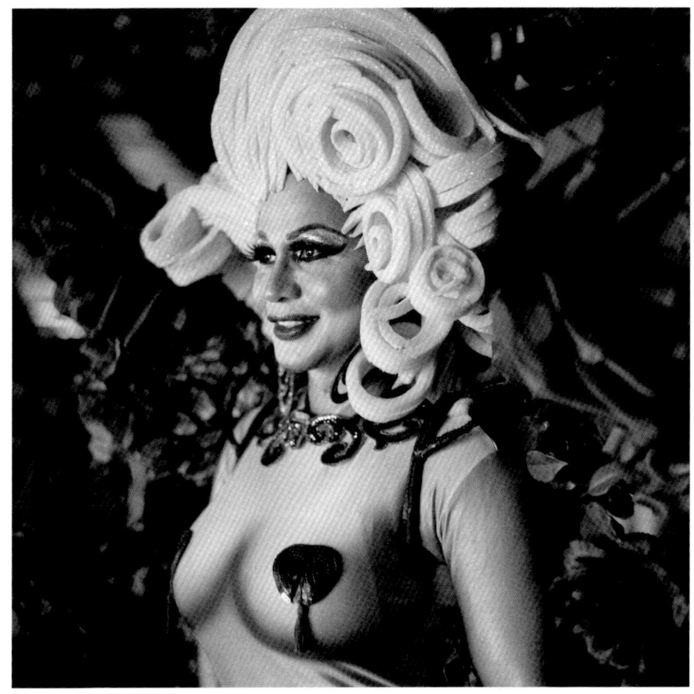

"A place where I can experience and play with different sides of myself without being judged "

Peter Ciriola

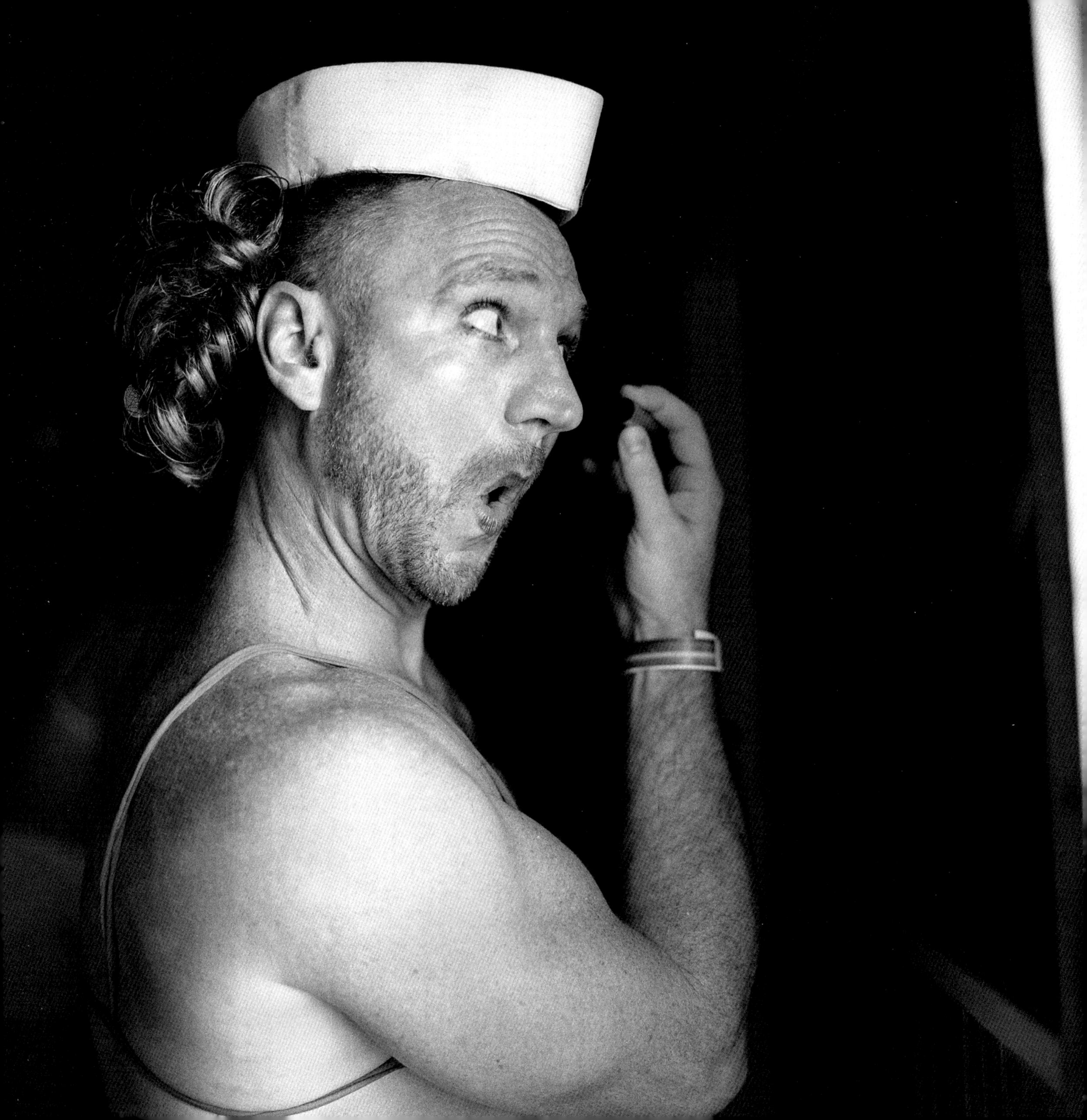

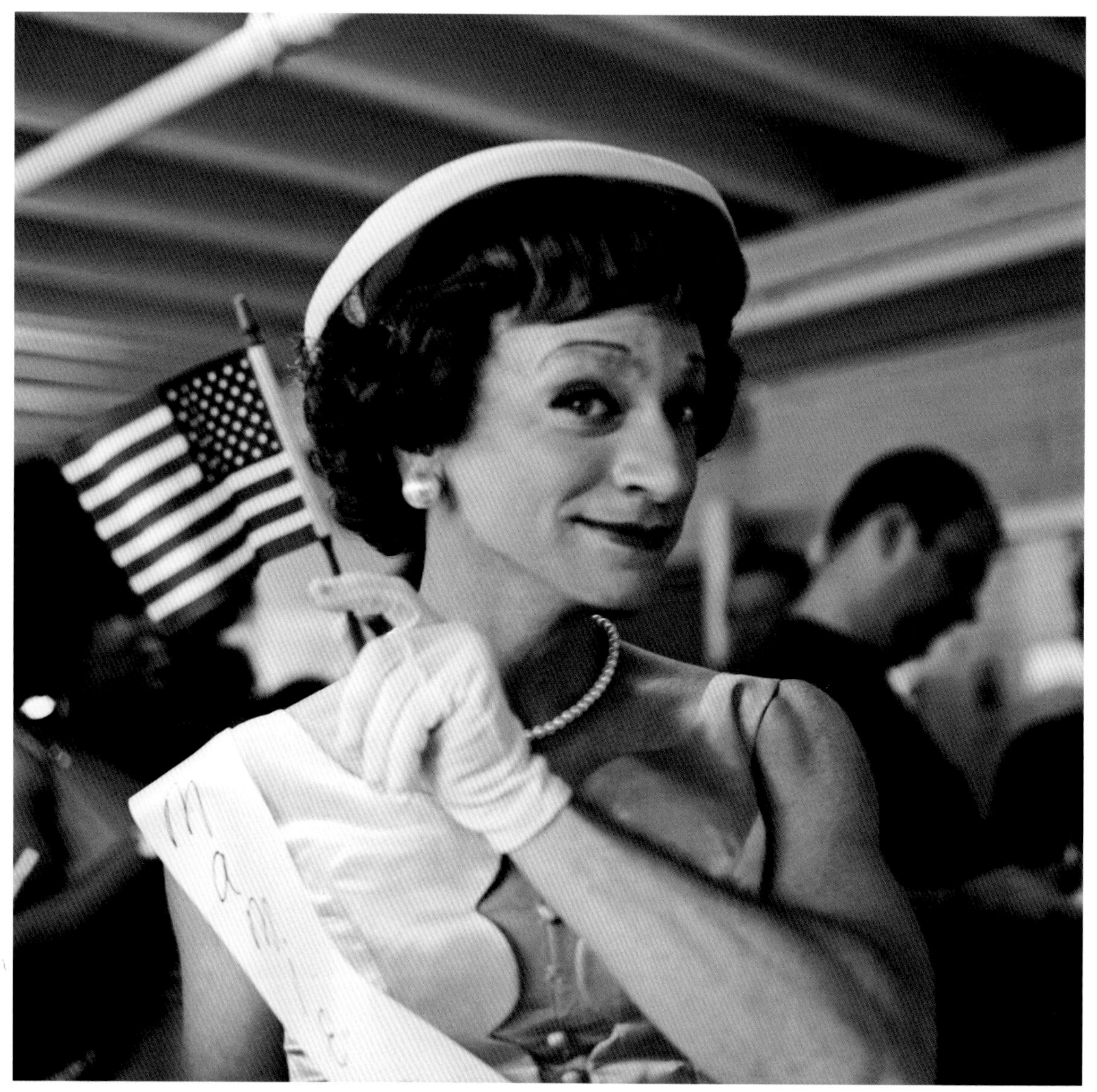

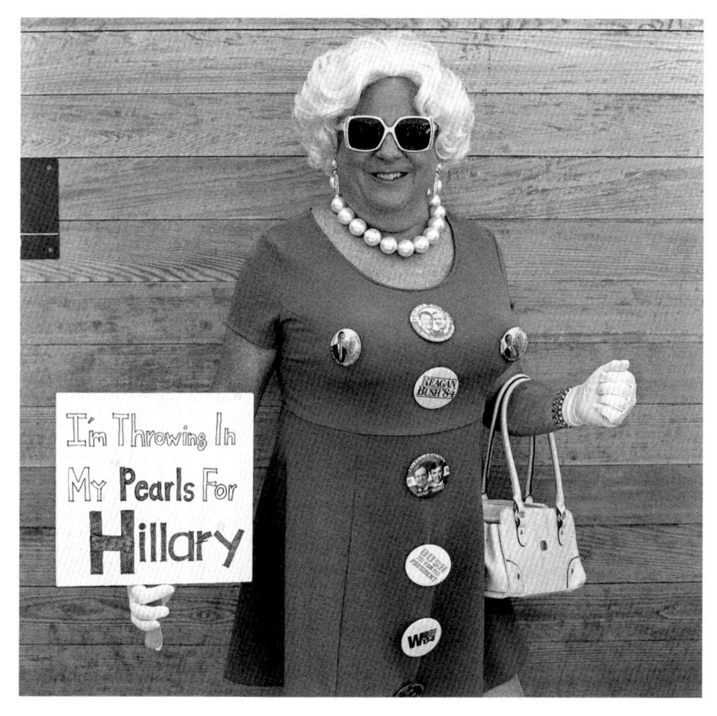
I'm Throwing In
My Pearls For
Hillary
REAGAN
BUSH'84

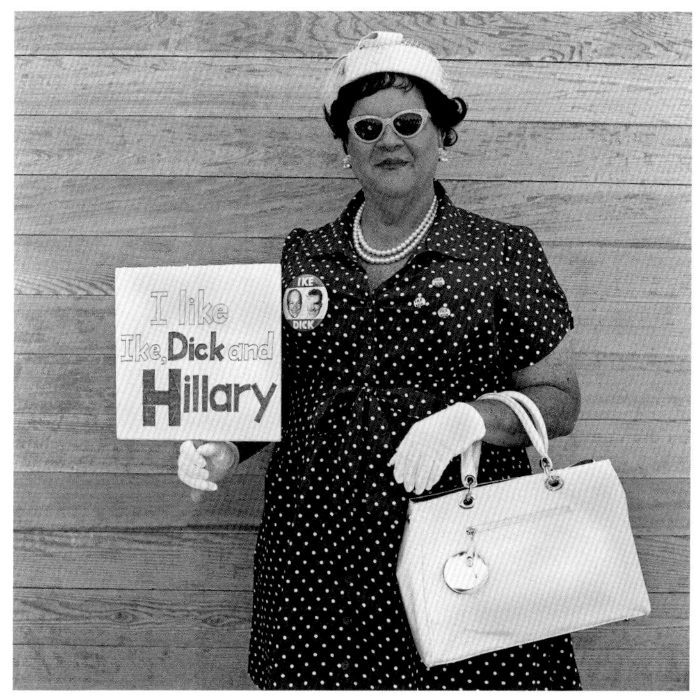
I like
Ike, Dick and
Hillary
IKE
DICK

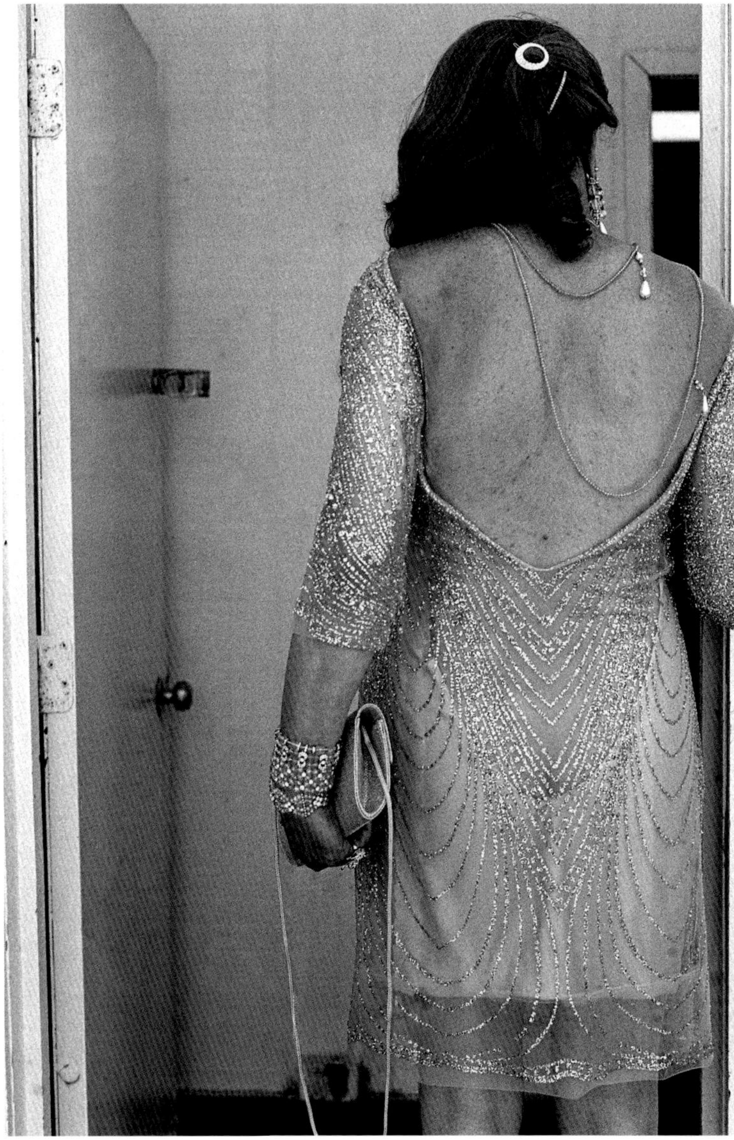

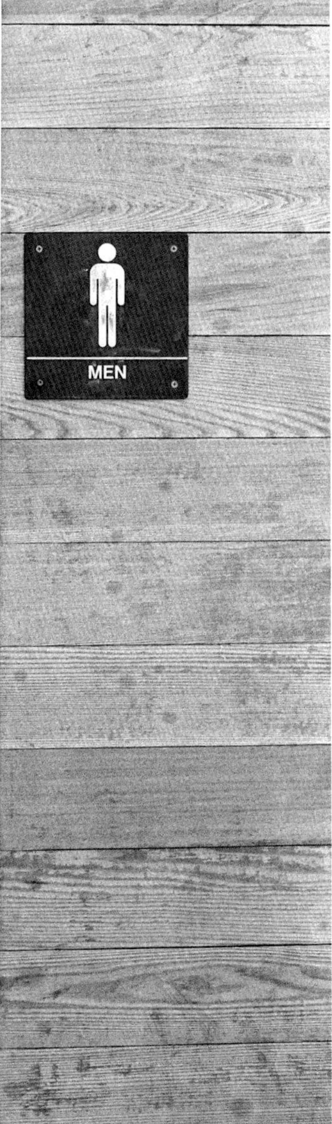
MEN

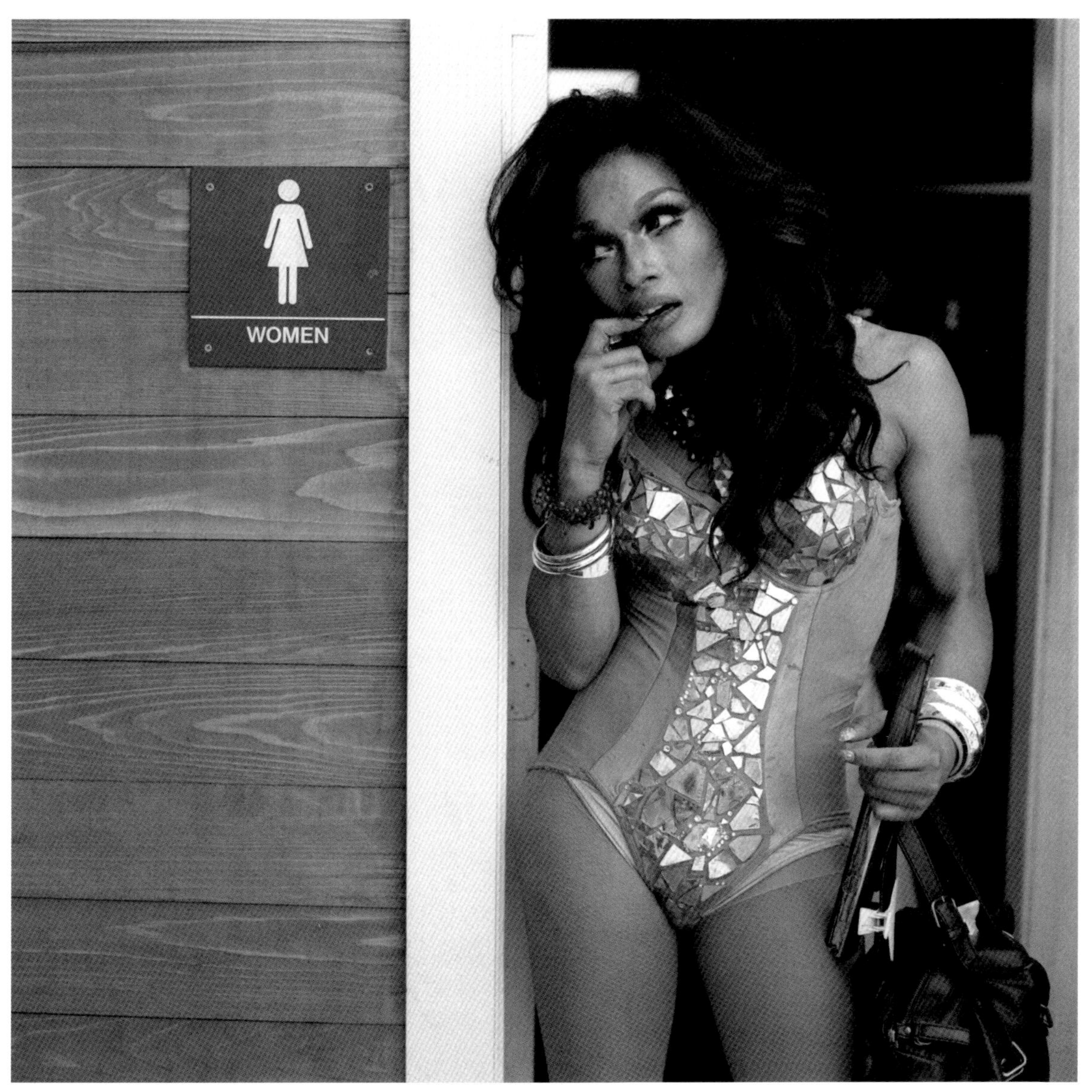
WOMEN

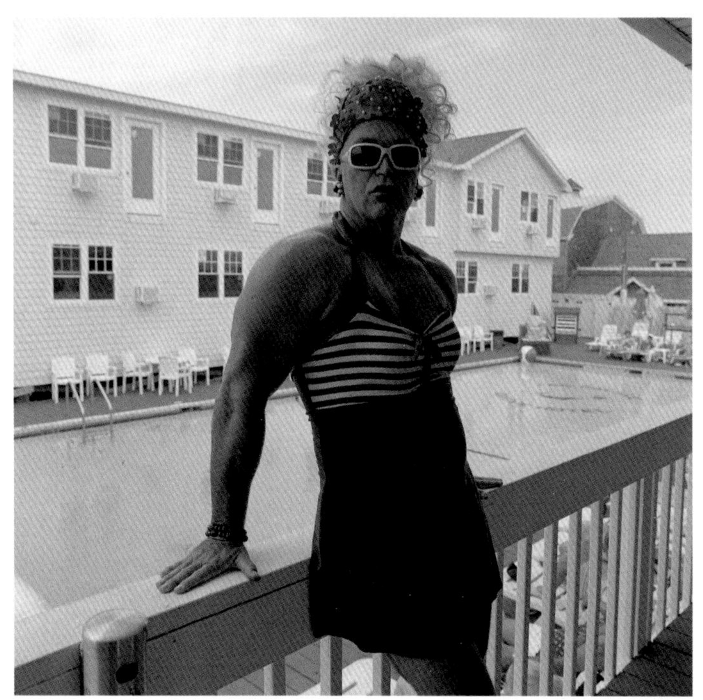

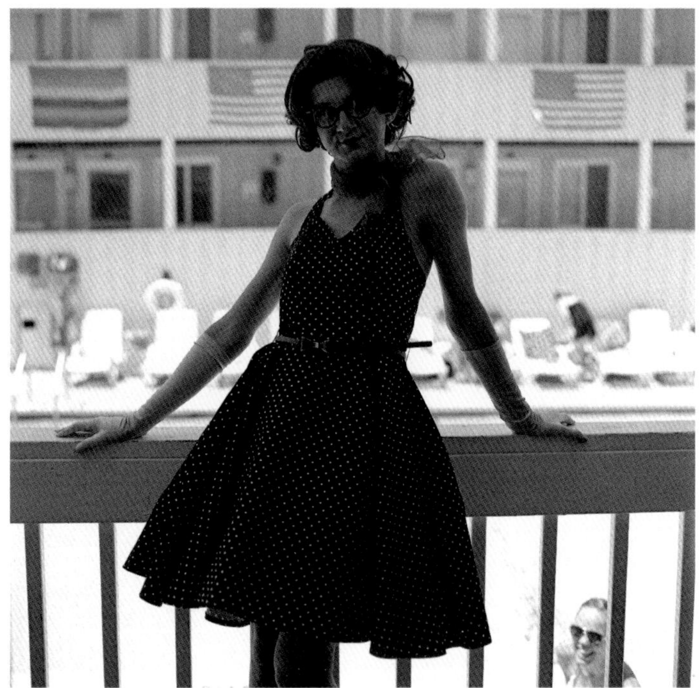

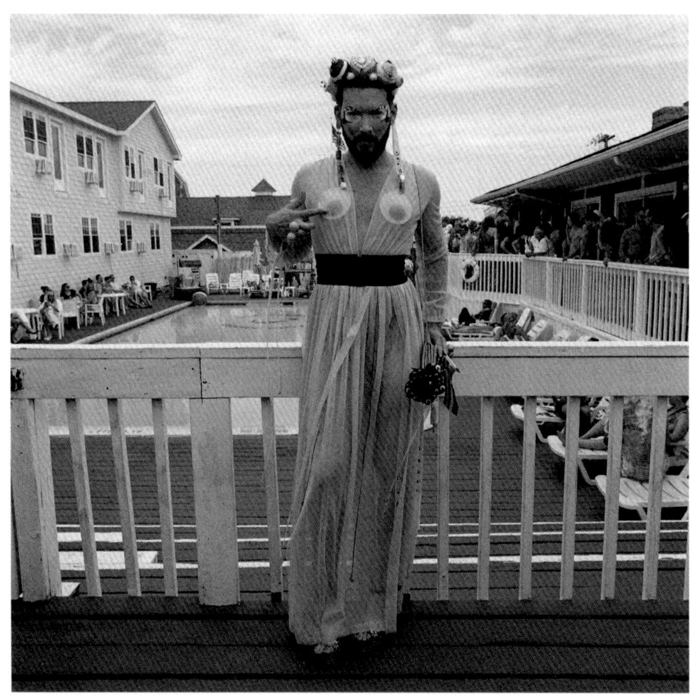

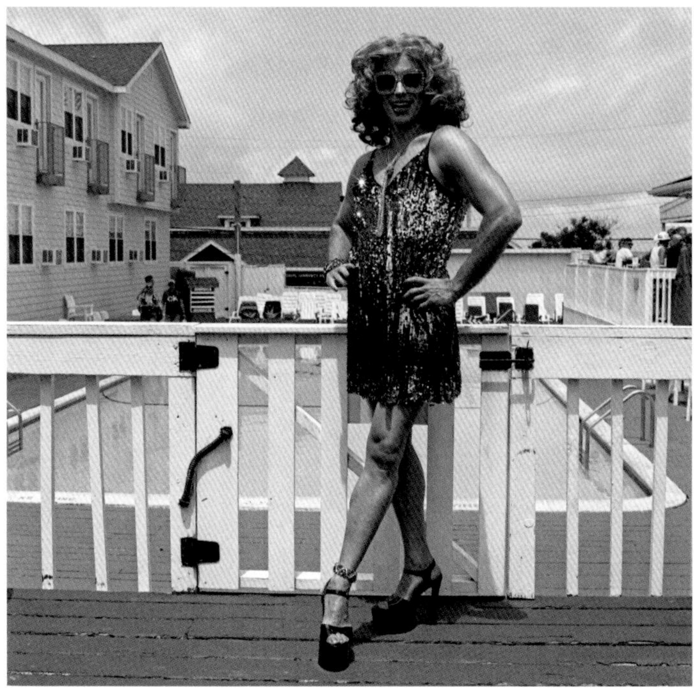

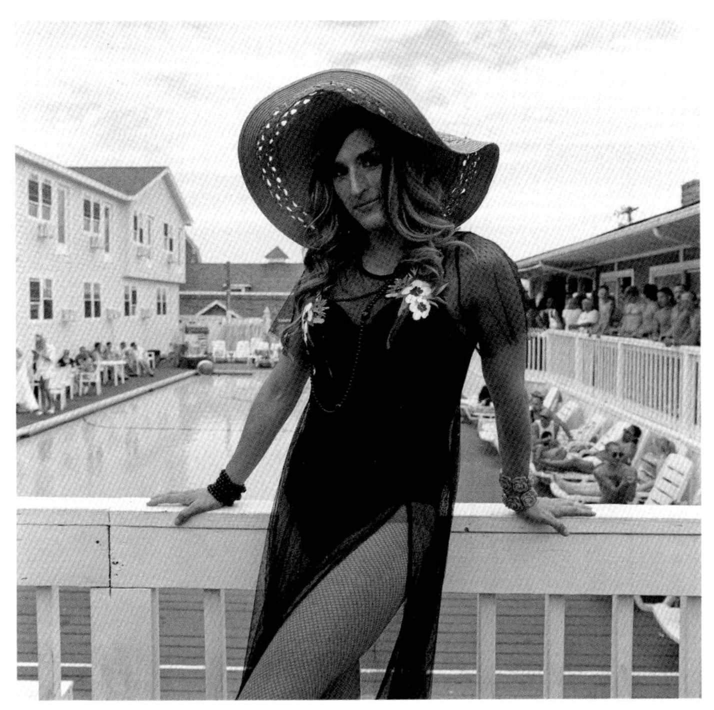

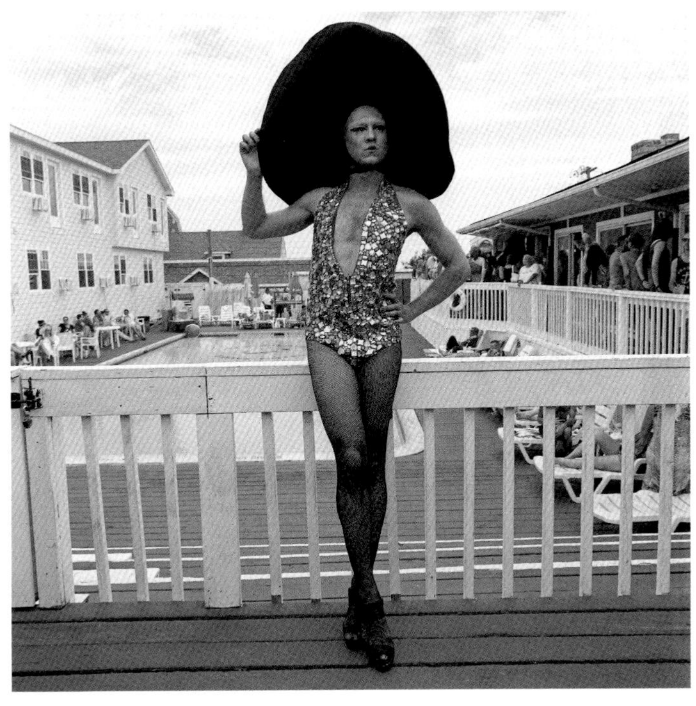

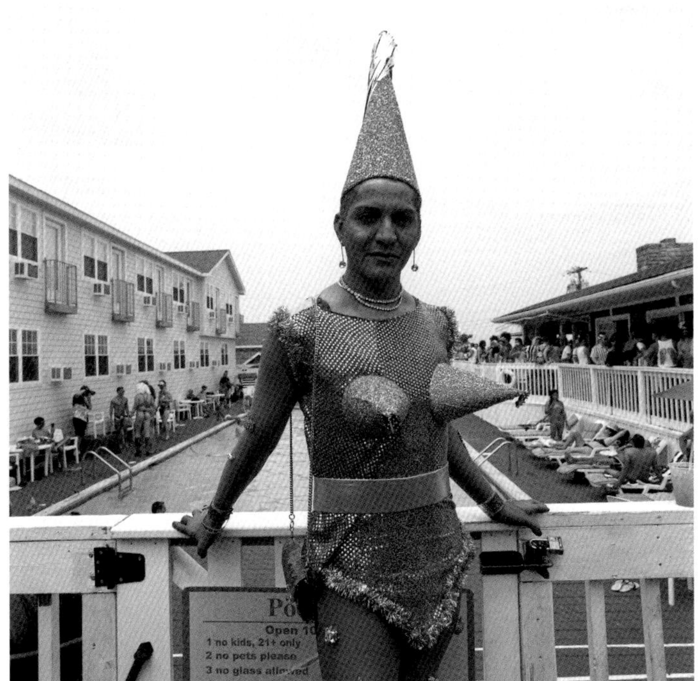
Po
Open 10
1 no kids, 21+ only
2 no pets please
3 no glass allowed

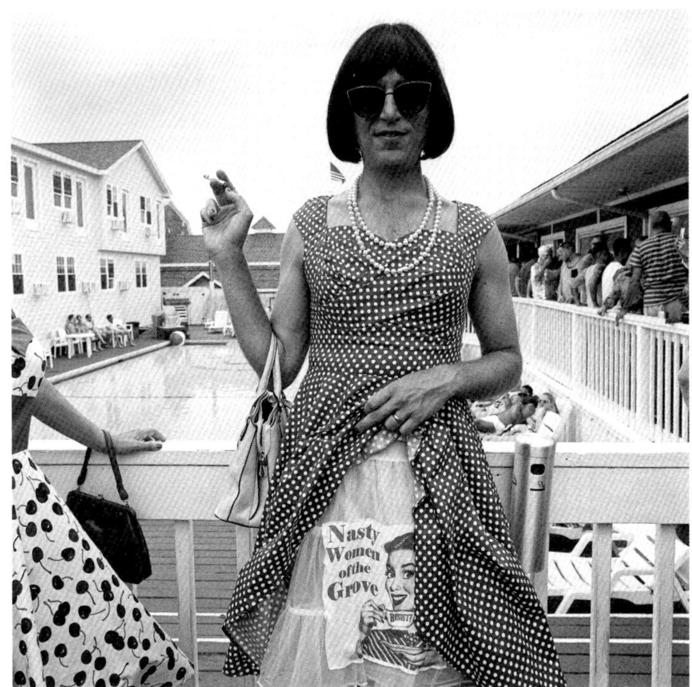
Nasty Women of the Grove

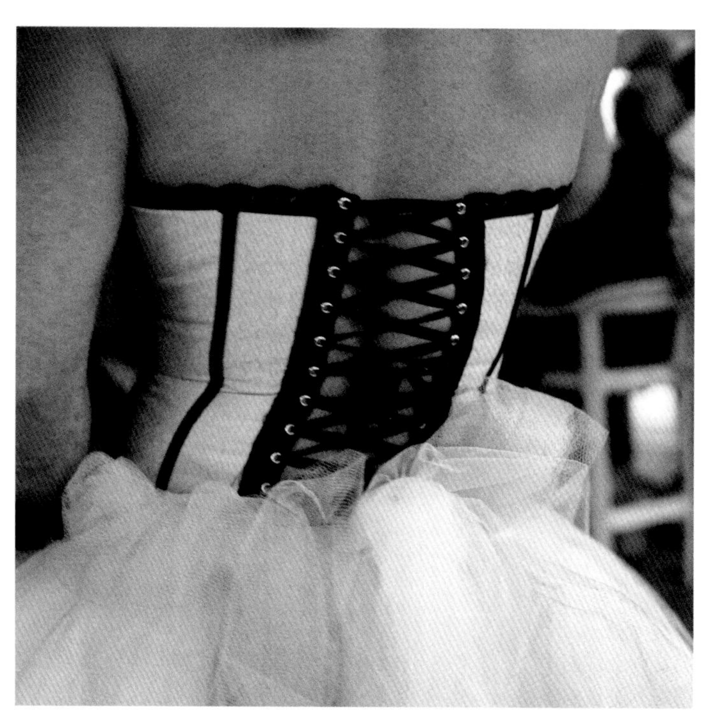

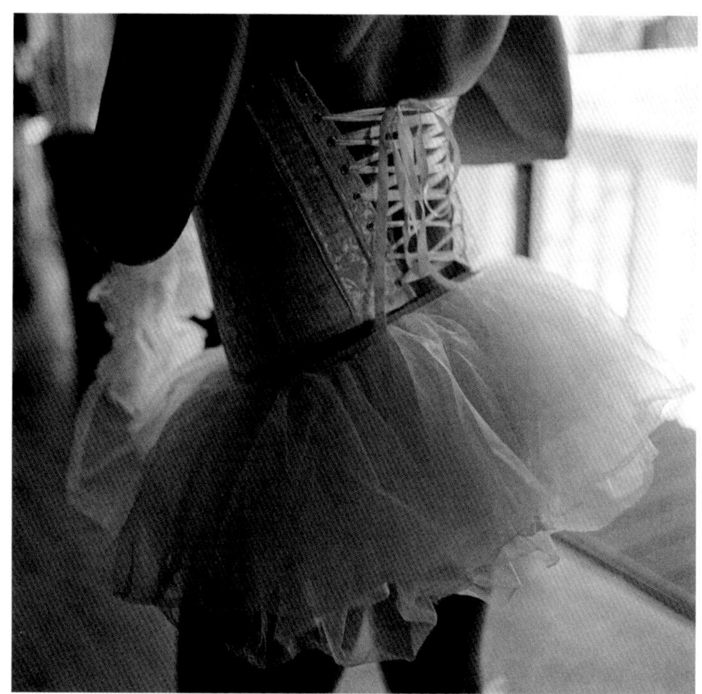

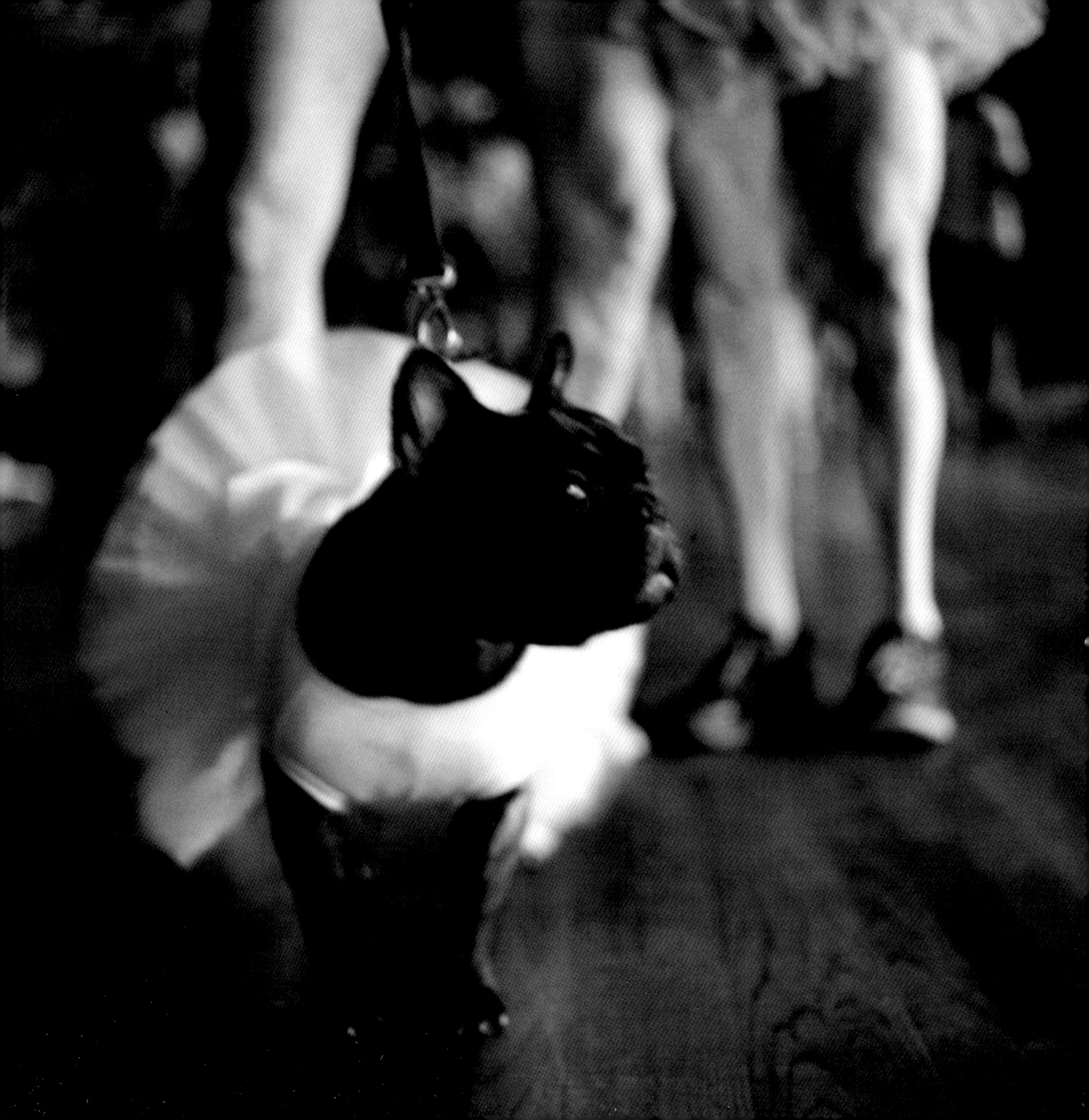

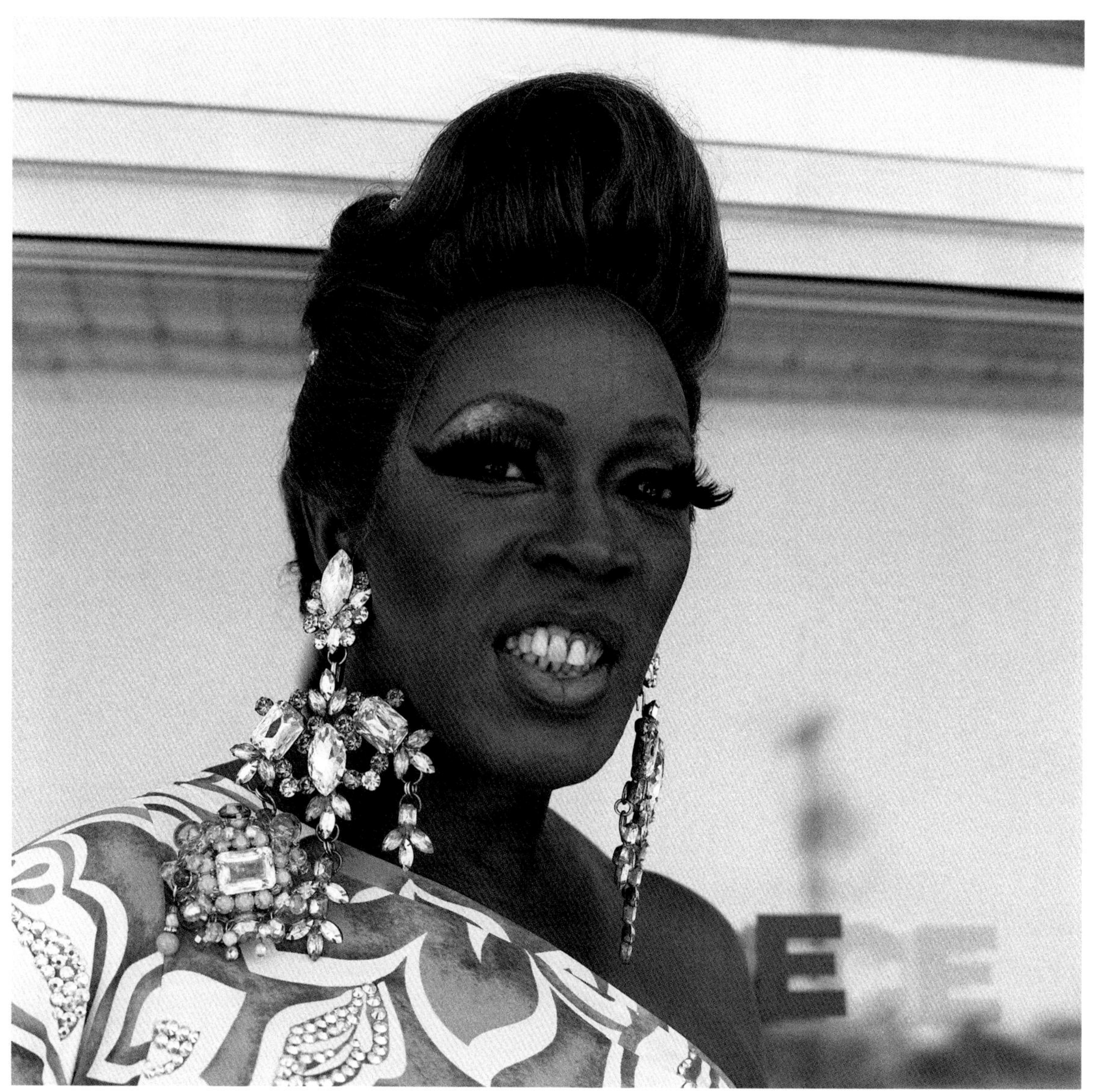

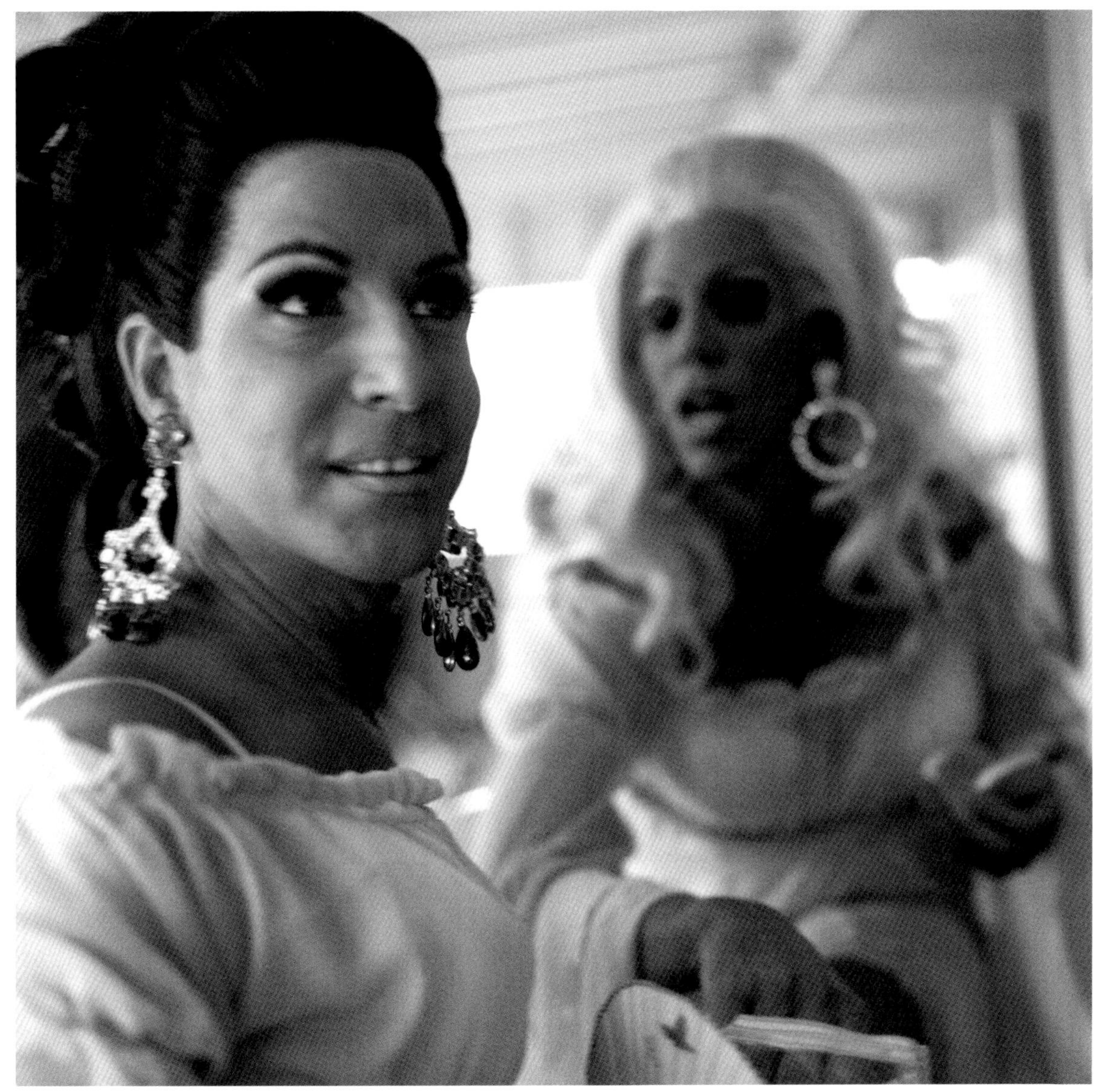

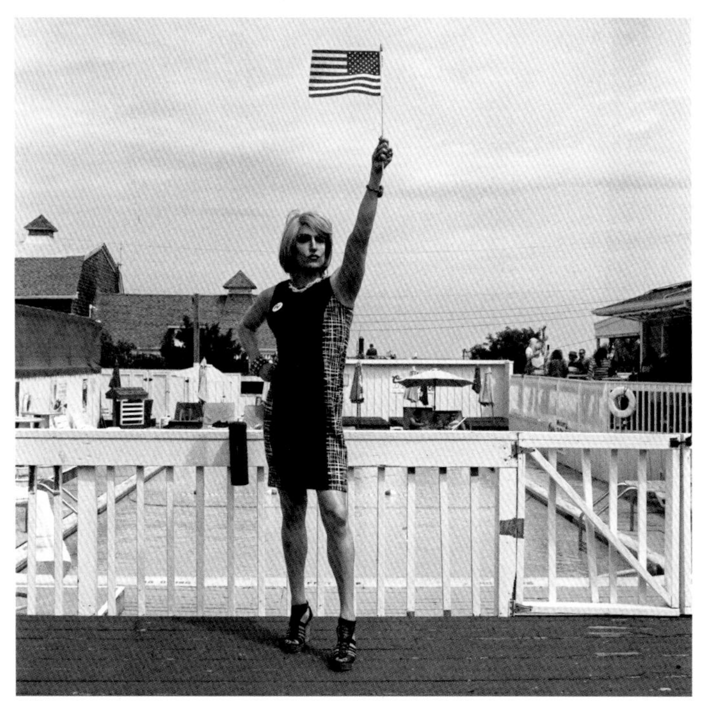
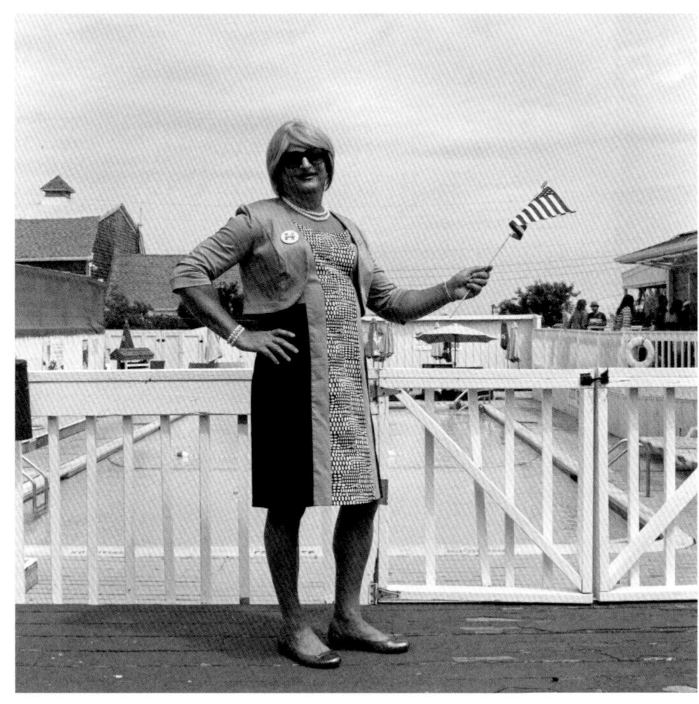
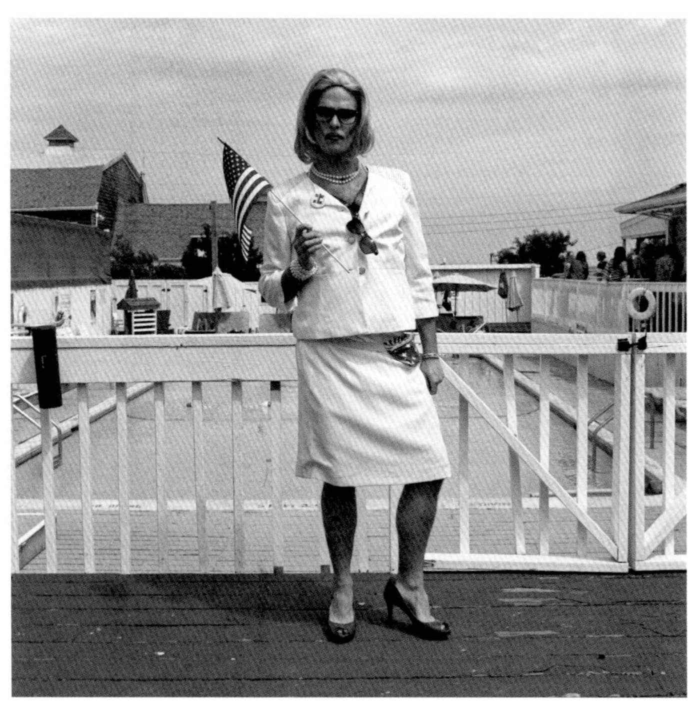
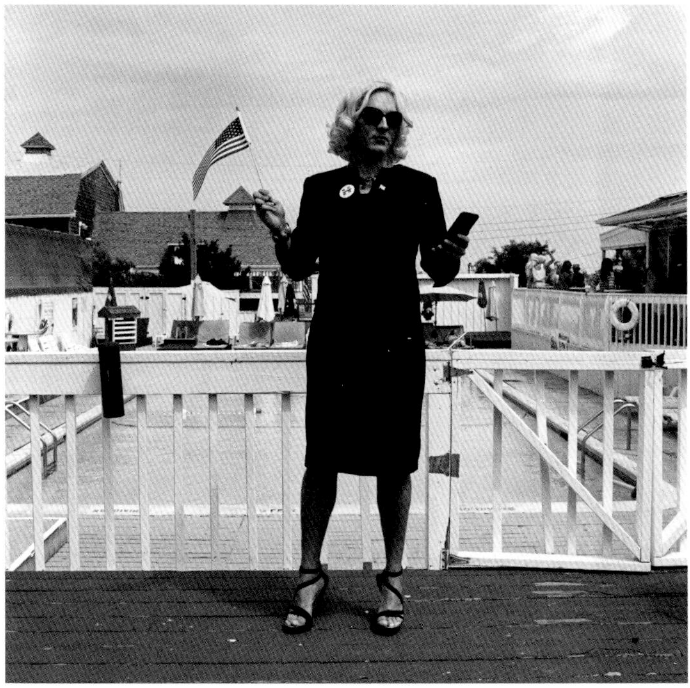

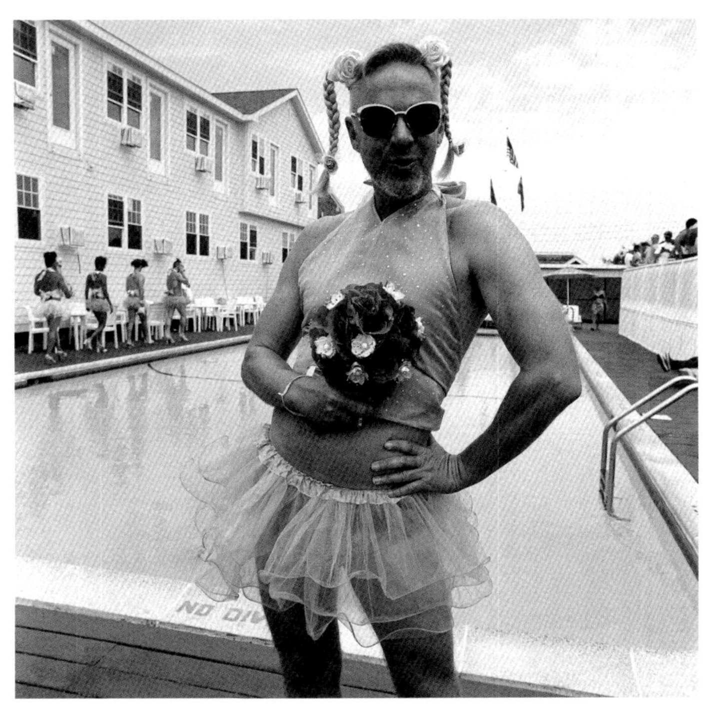

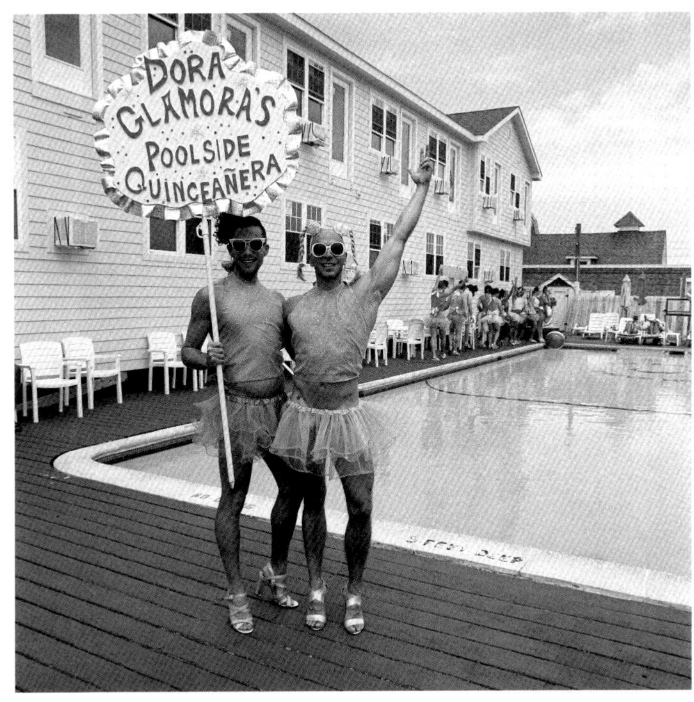
DORA GLAMORA'S
POOLSIDE
QUINCEAÑERA

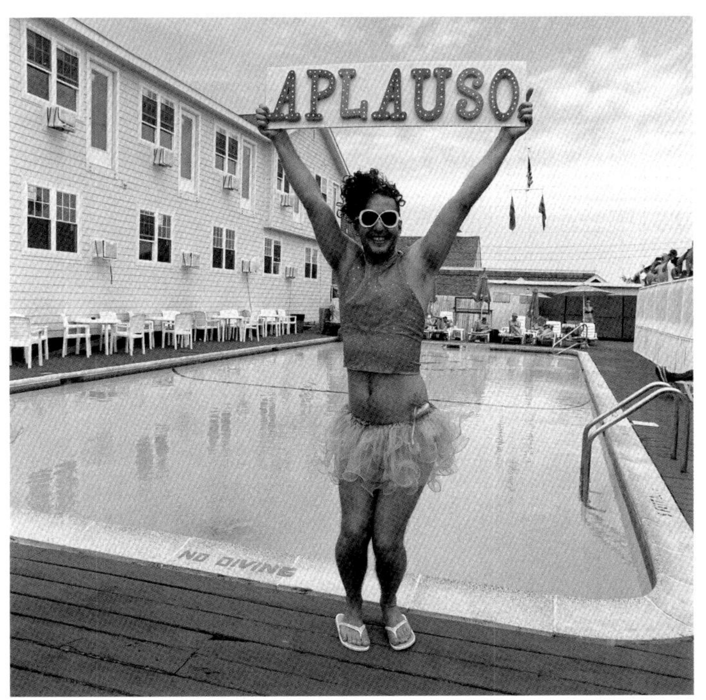
APLAUSO

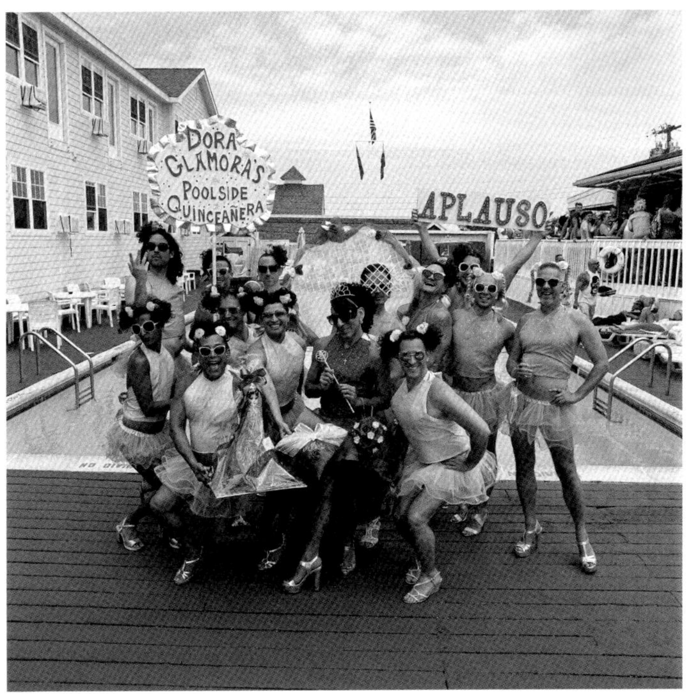
DORA GLAMORA'S
POOLSIDE
QUINCEAÑERA
APLAUSO

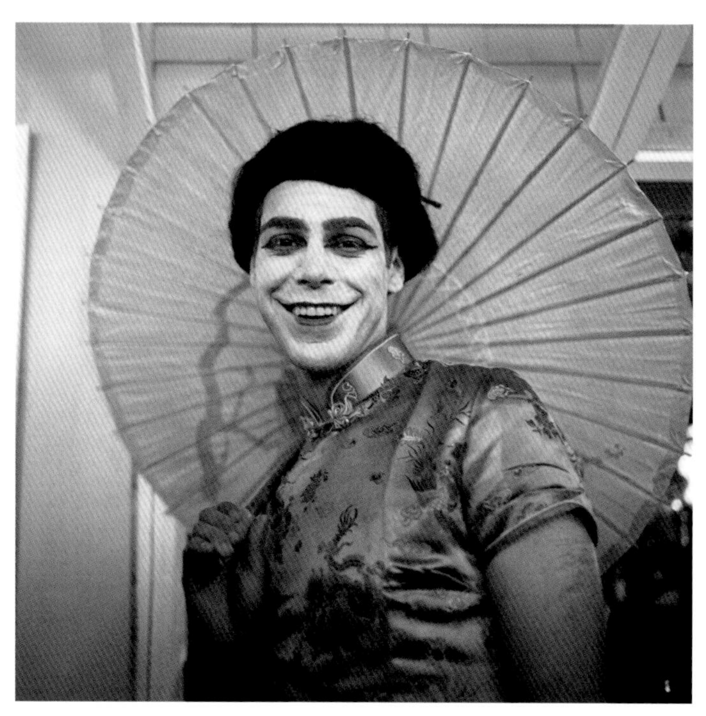

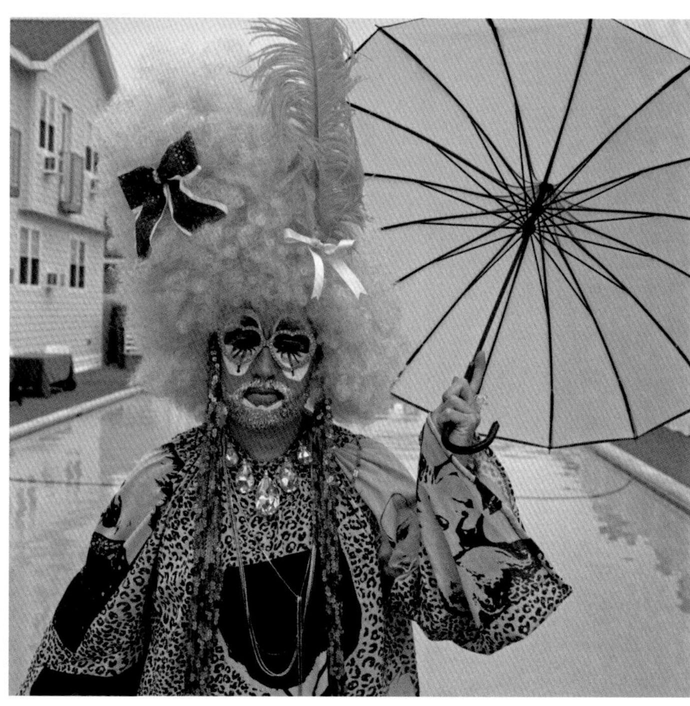

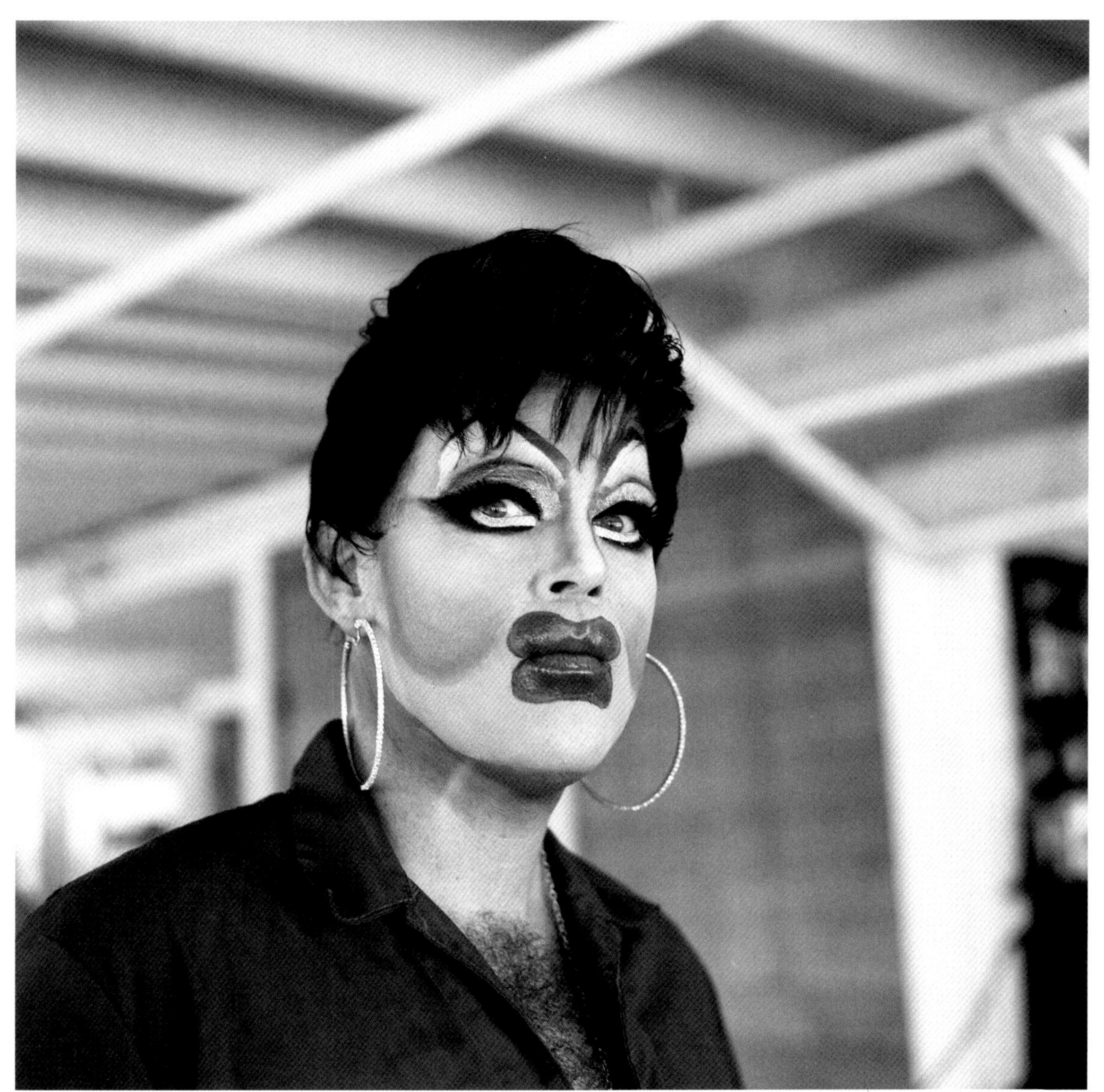

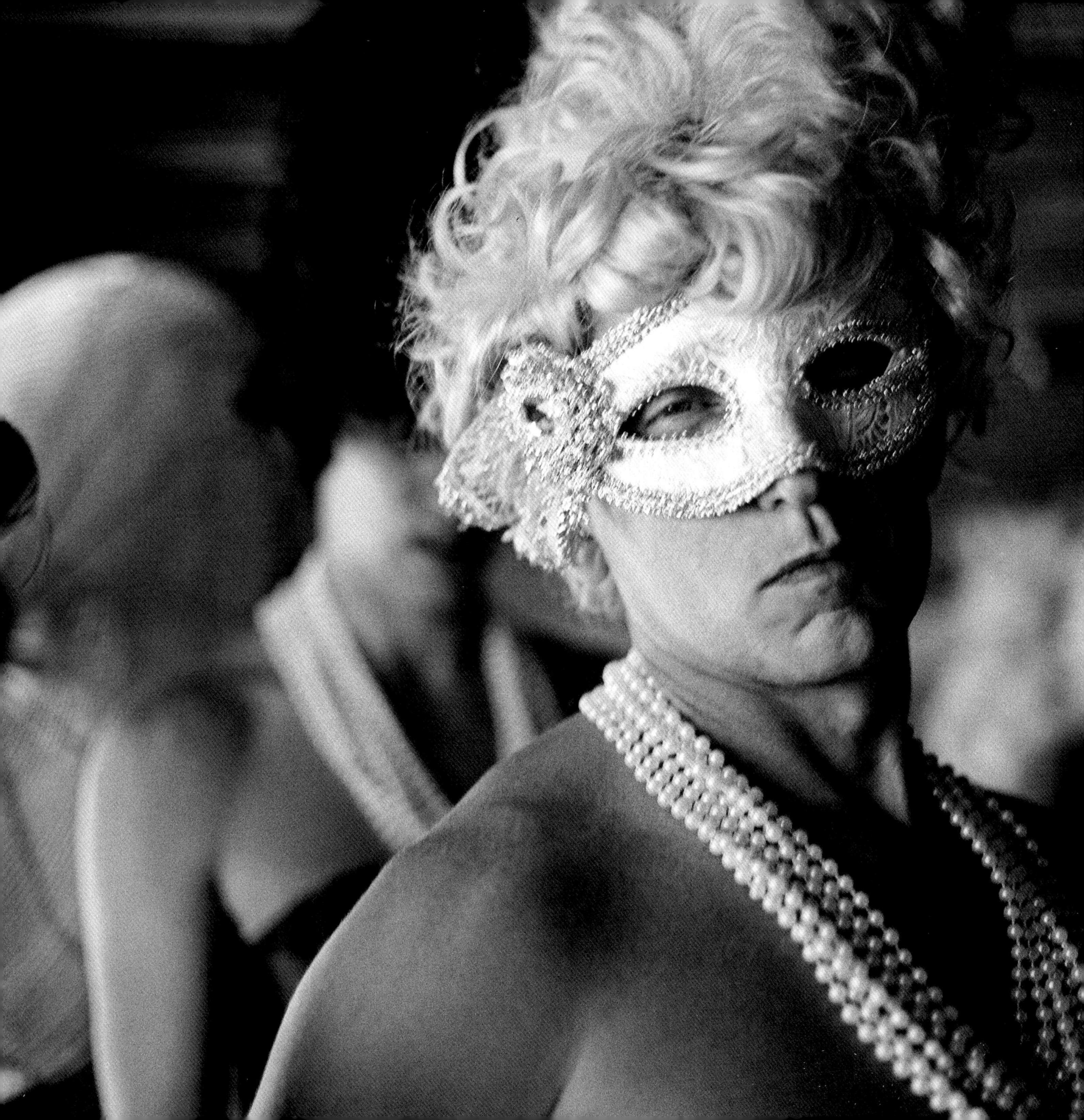

"The Invasion means unity, equality, LOVE! It's a day that brings everyone together no matter what your sexual orientation is."

Dennis J Noboa

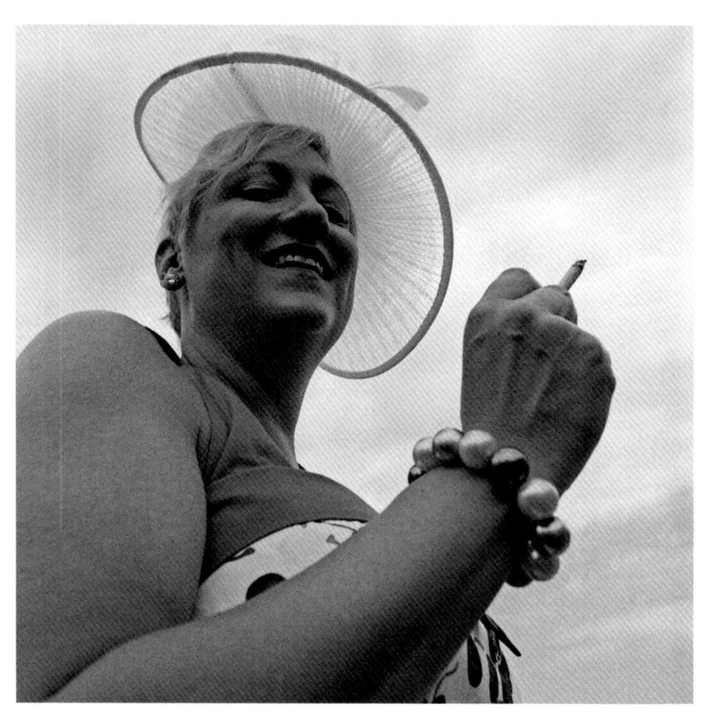

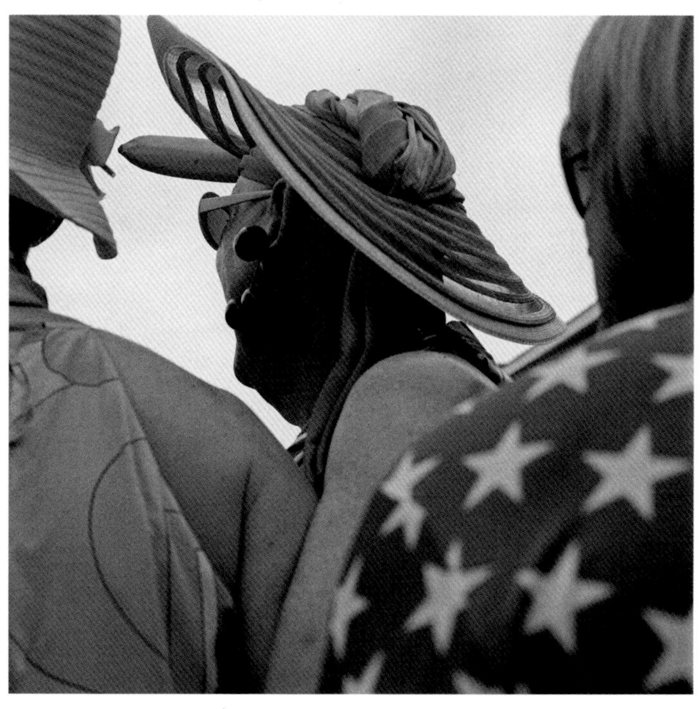

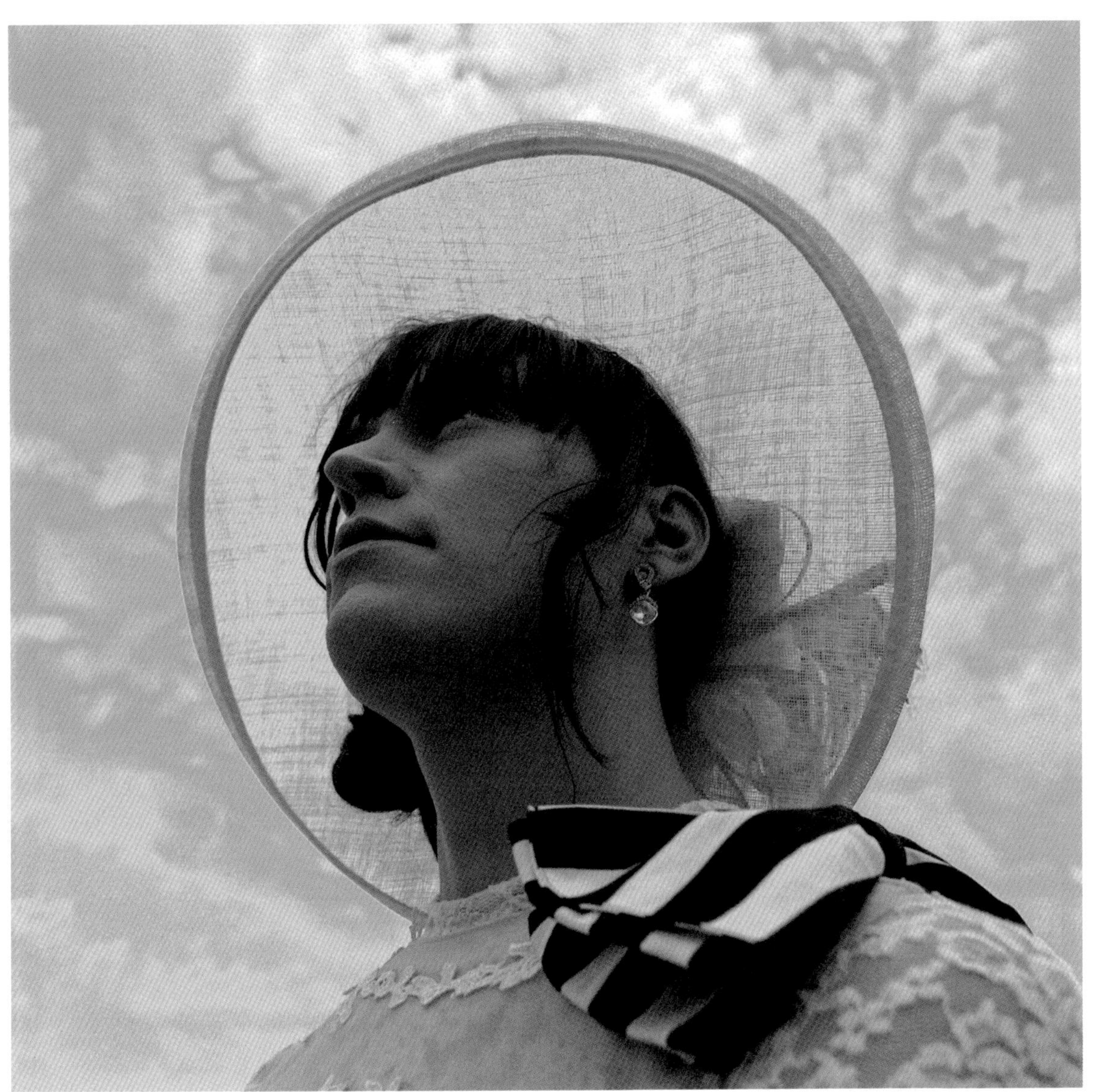

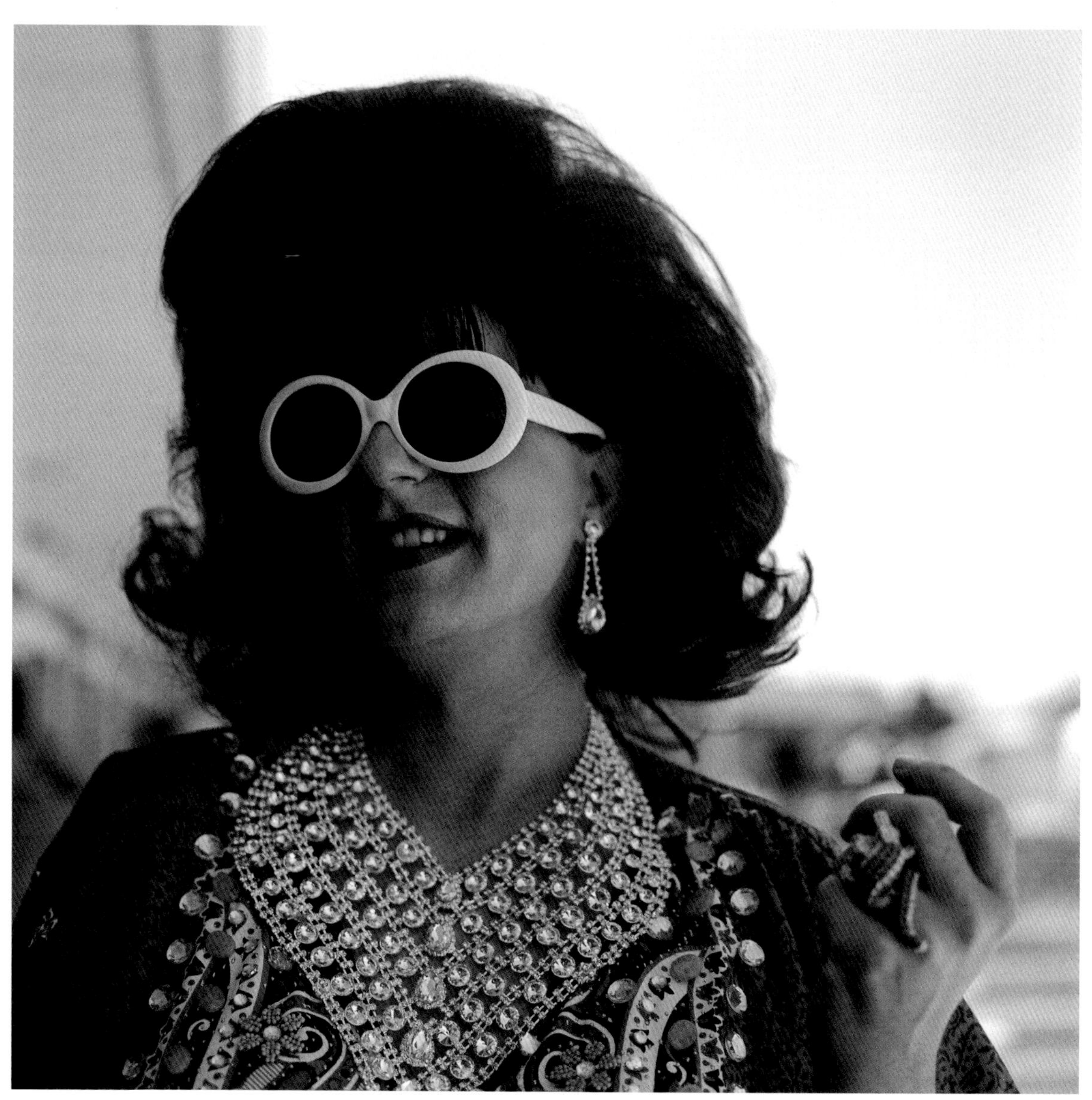

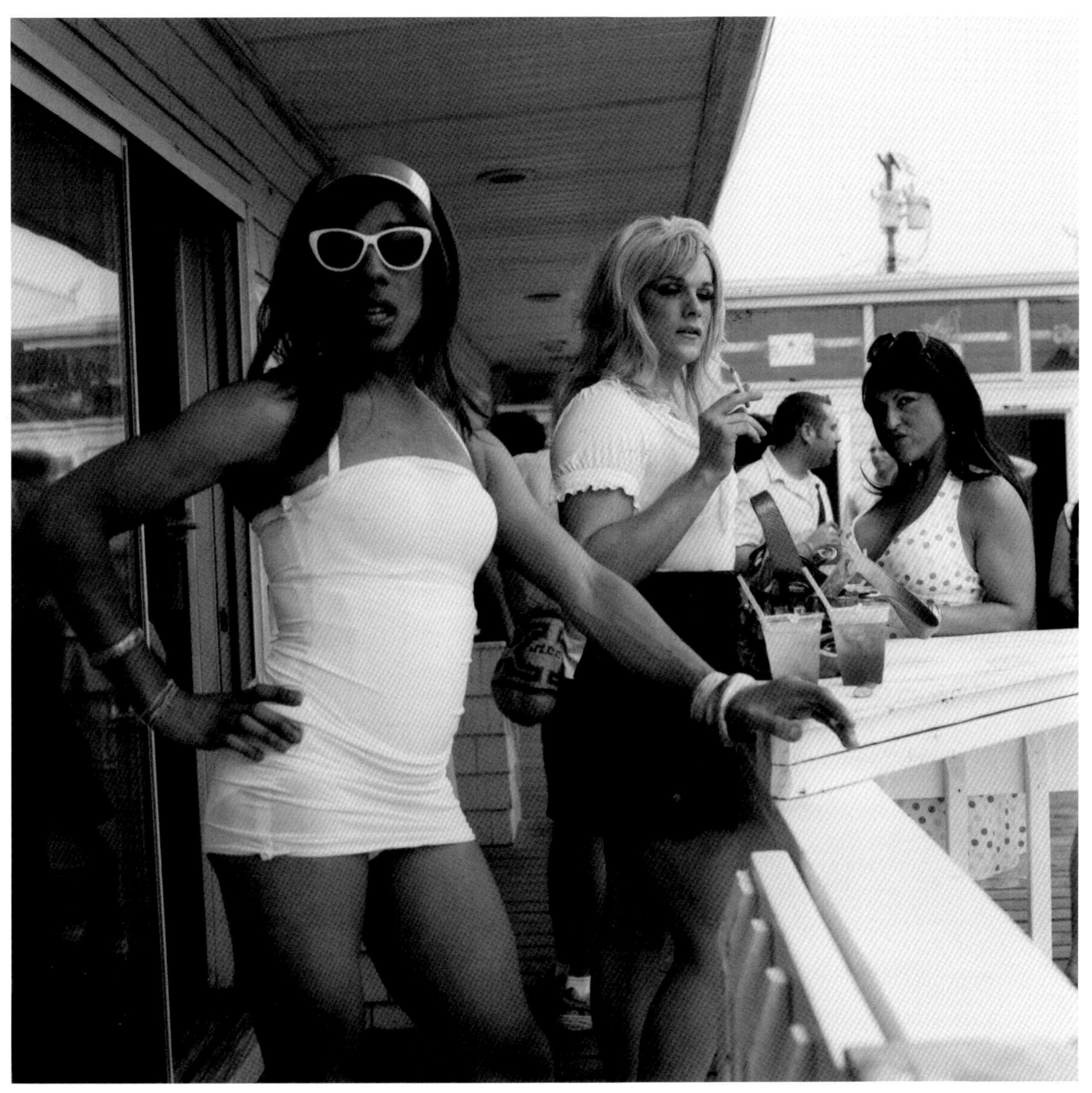

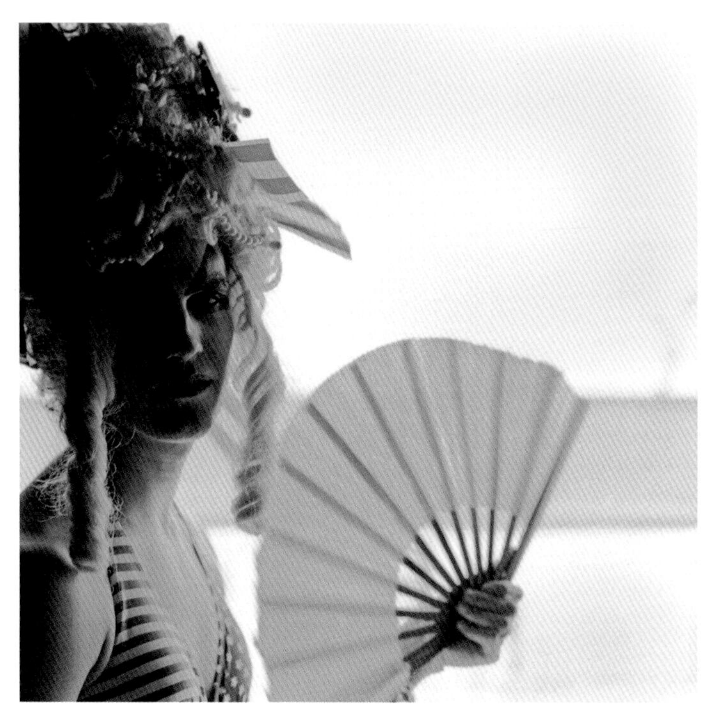

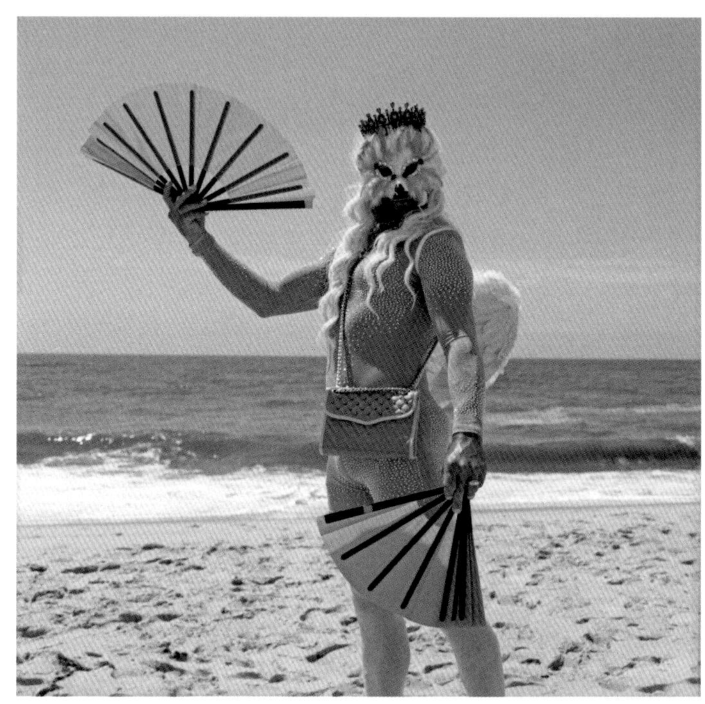

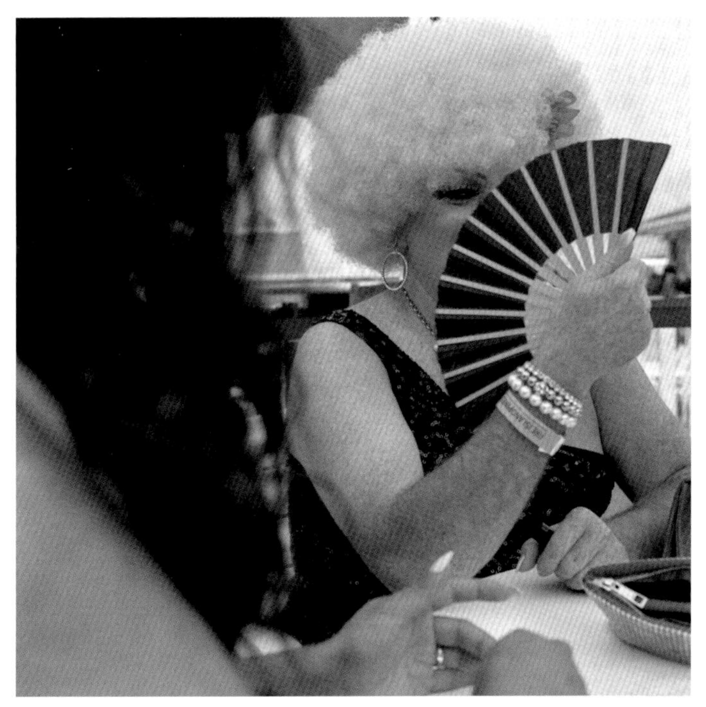

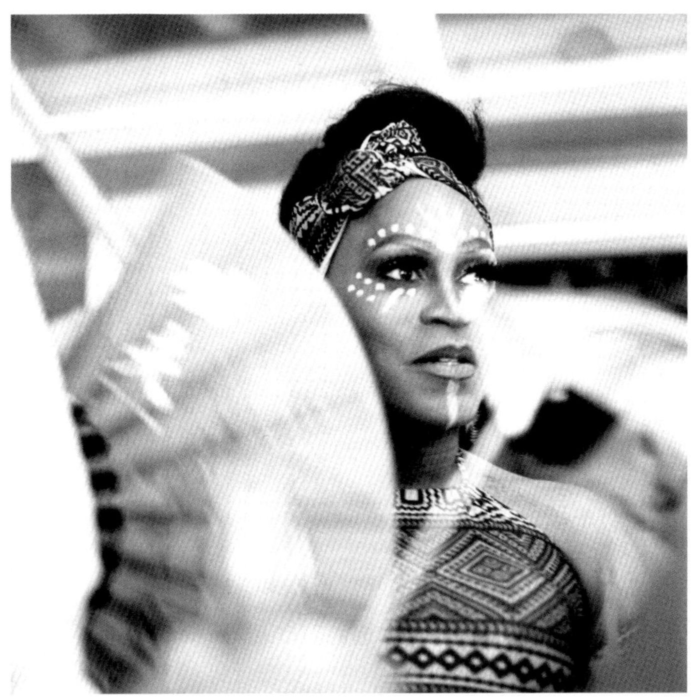

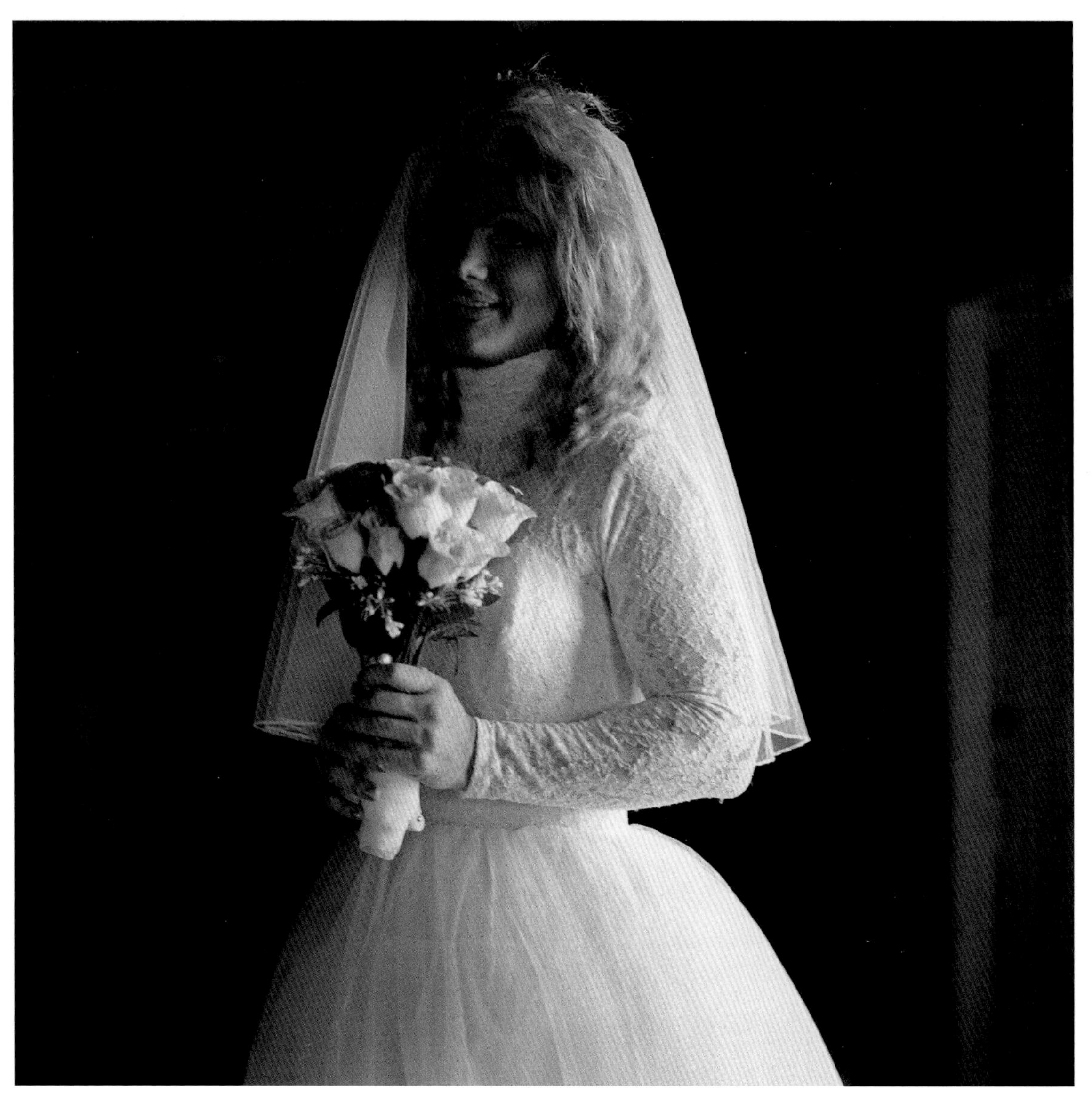

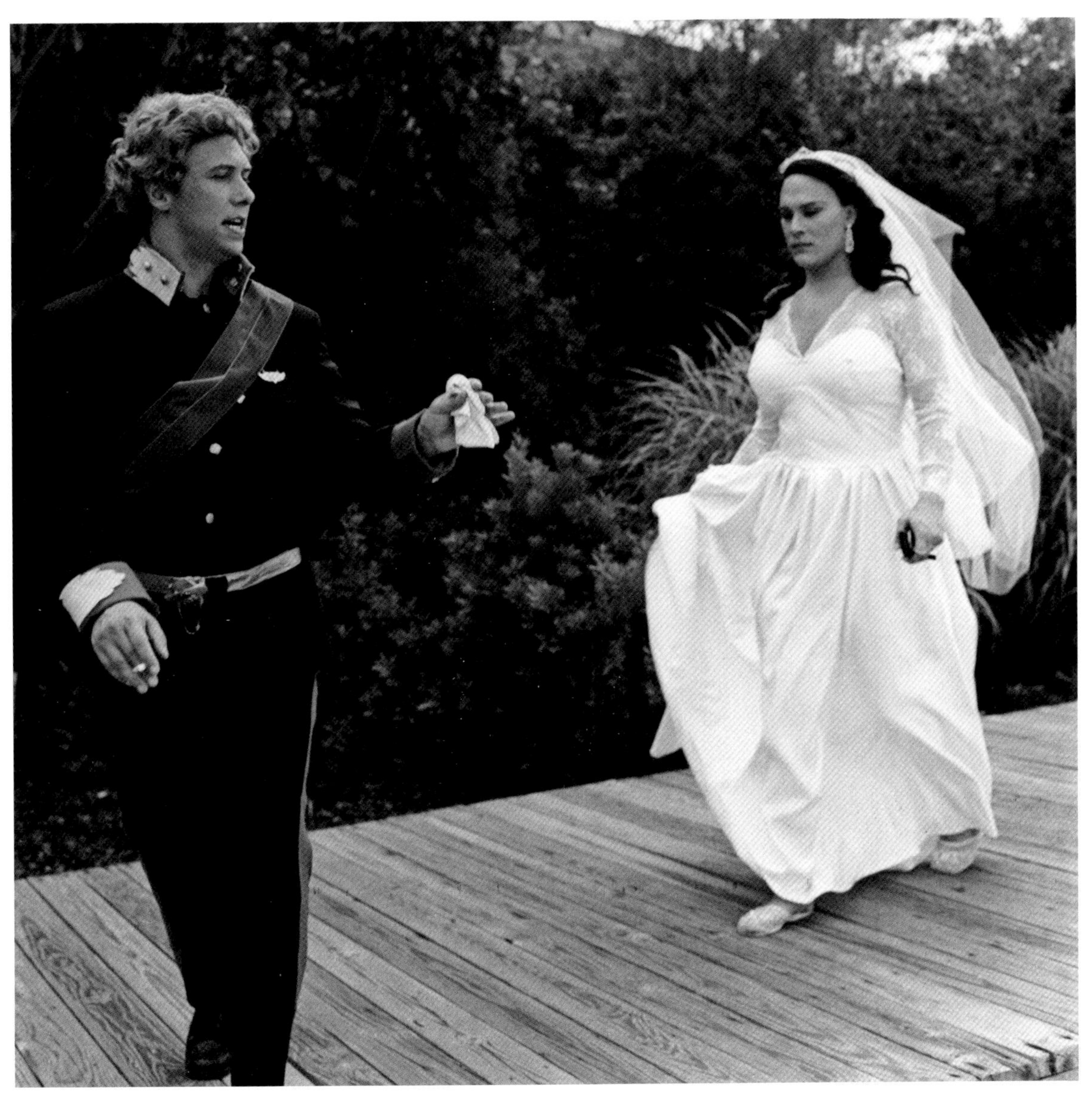

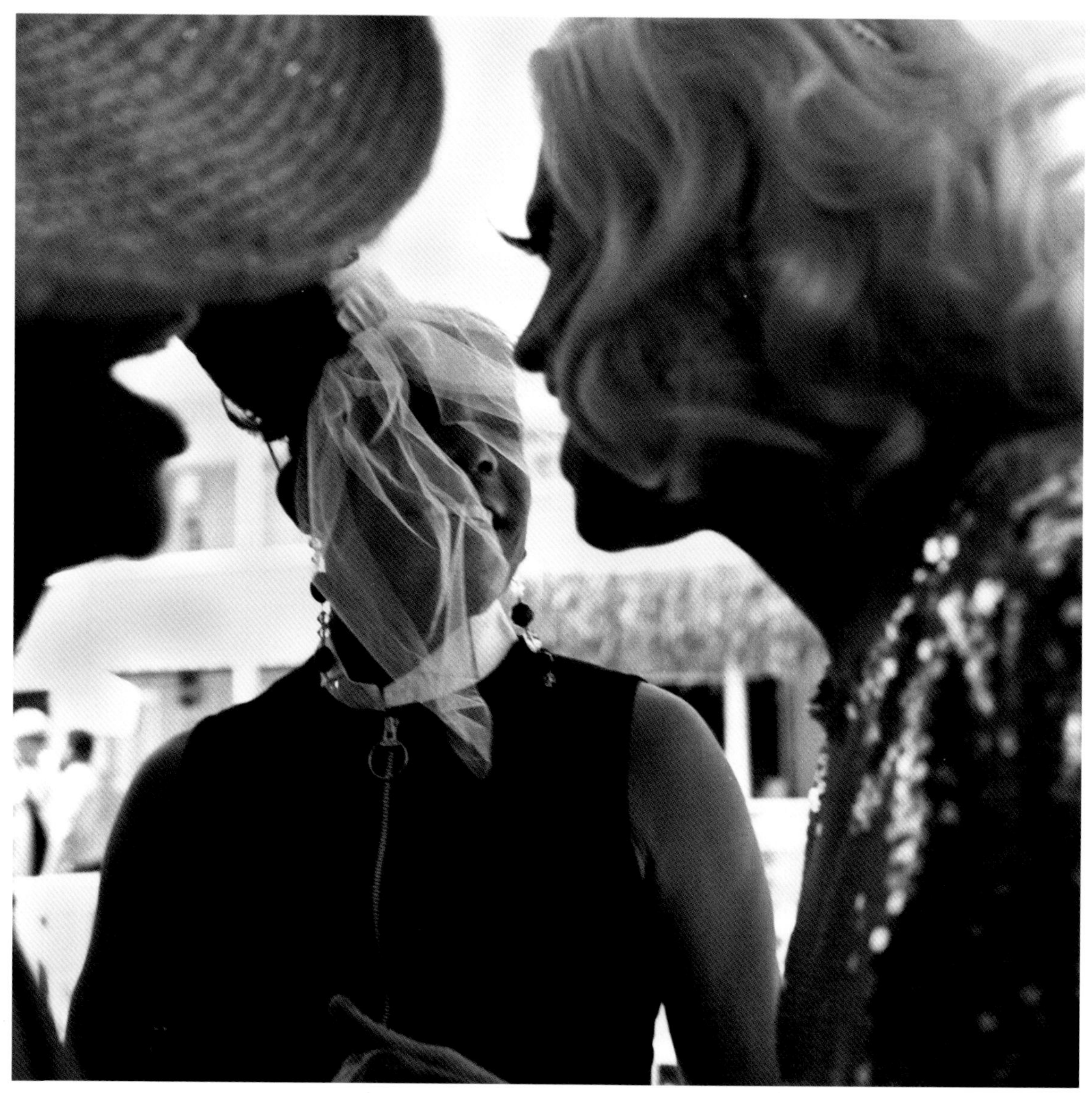

INVASION

The dock in Cherry Grove bustles with the energy of departure, and Captain Ken Stein steers the ferry, laden with hundreds of queens. Their spirited renditions of "God Bless America" and "The Star-Spangled Banner" reverberate across the bay and herald their approach. Thousands gather at the dock in The Pines to await their arrival. As Mr. Klein signals with a honk, the ferry arrives, queens waving jubilantly to the crowded harbor, docked boats, and onlookers filling every window and balcony.

Fireworks and confetti explode overhead, music blares, and joyful shouts fill the air. The sounds amplify the already electrifying atmosphere. As the boat docks, Panzi grabs the microphone, igniting The Invasion, a spectacular fusion of Drag Ball, protest, rebellion, liberation, and unapologetic glamour.

Like a grand theater production, the boat's side door swings open, revealing queens descending one by one, or in small groups, down a crimson carpet. They always dazzle with improvised or choreographed performances. The dances, songs, and stunts are all guided by Panzi's irreverent humor, captivating the audience and drawing them into the spectacle.

Beyond the glitter and glamour, the Invasion Ball carries subtle yet profound political messages. Each queen, continuing a tradition dating back to the first Invasion, advocates for their beliefs and expressions, now amplified by national and international media coverage.

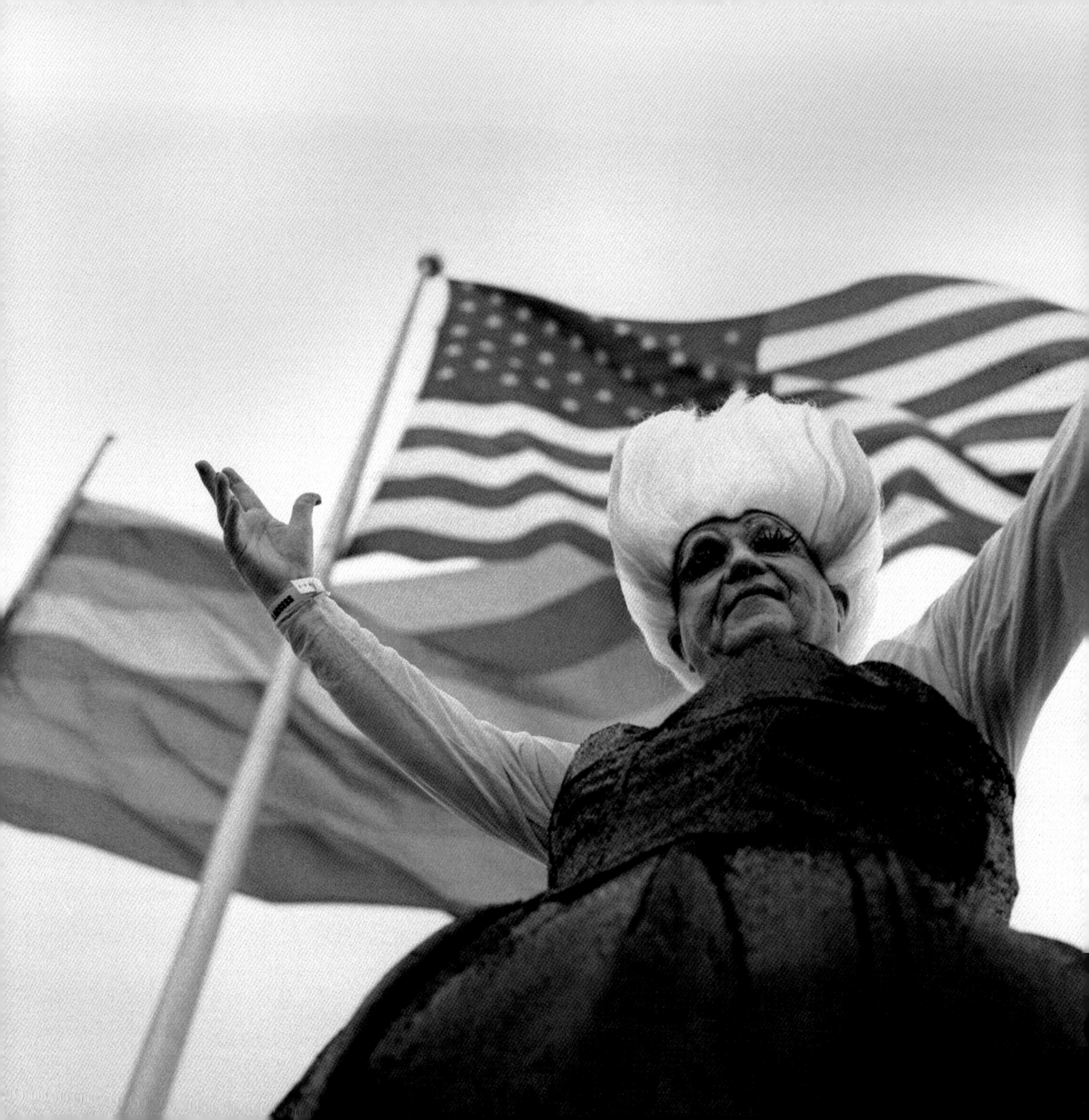

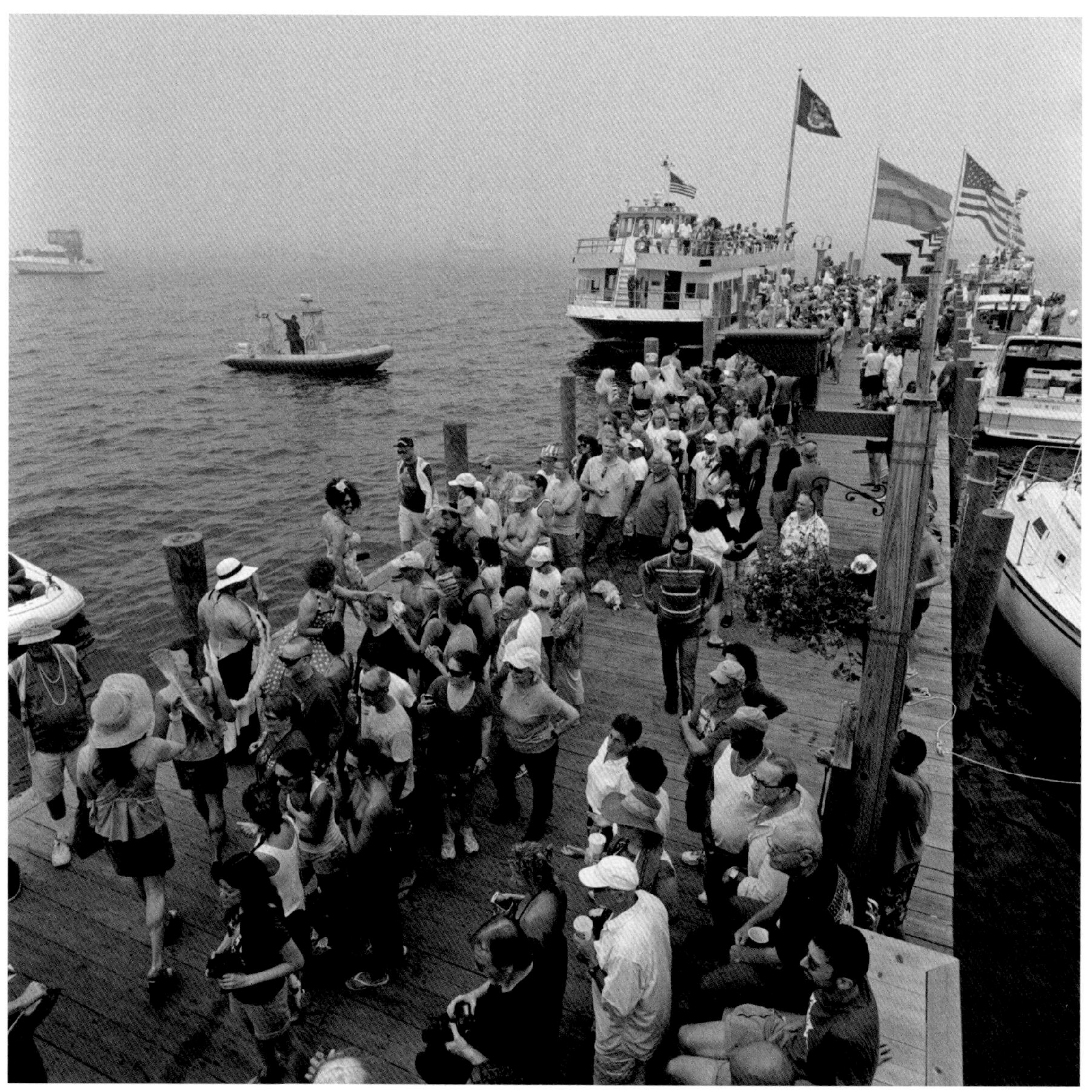

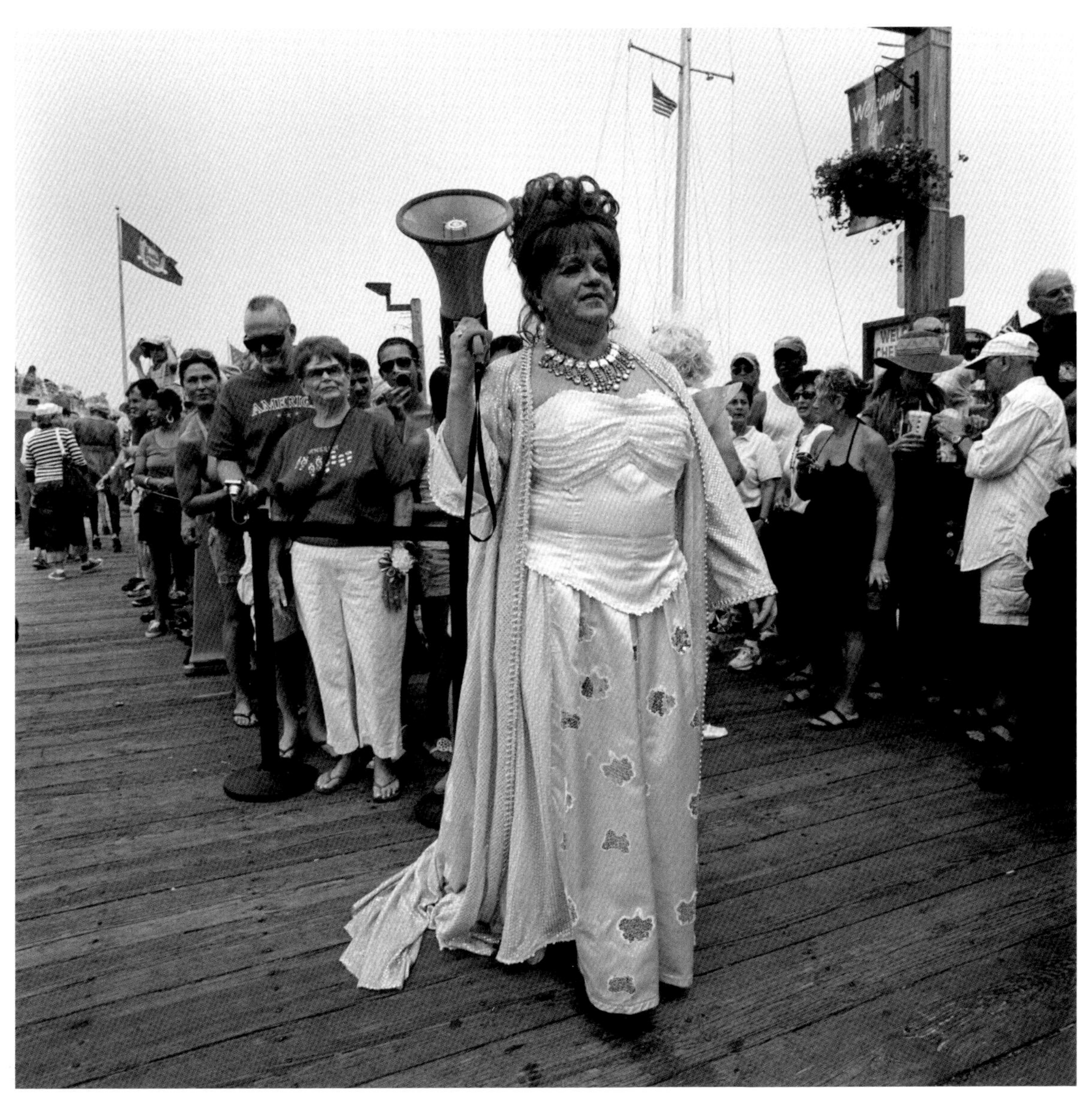
Welcome

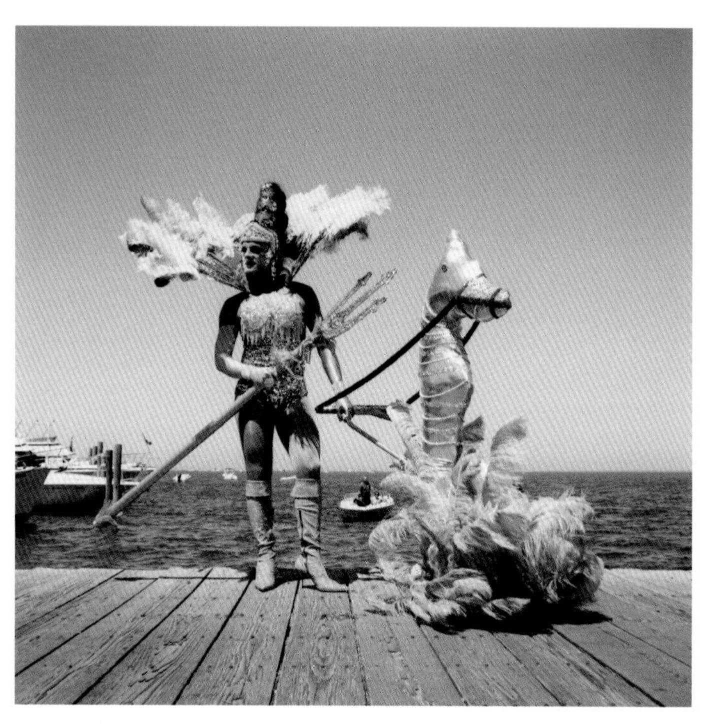

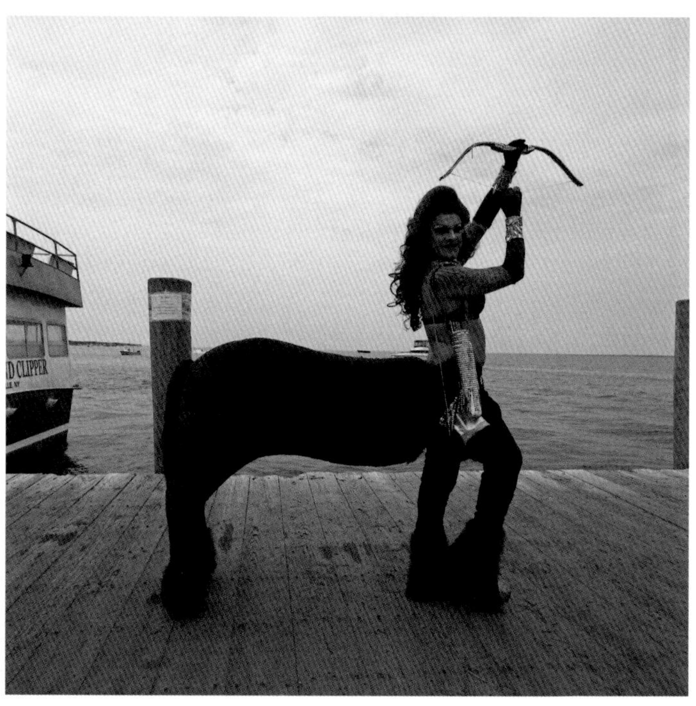
ND CLIPPER
LLE NY

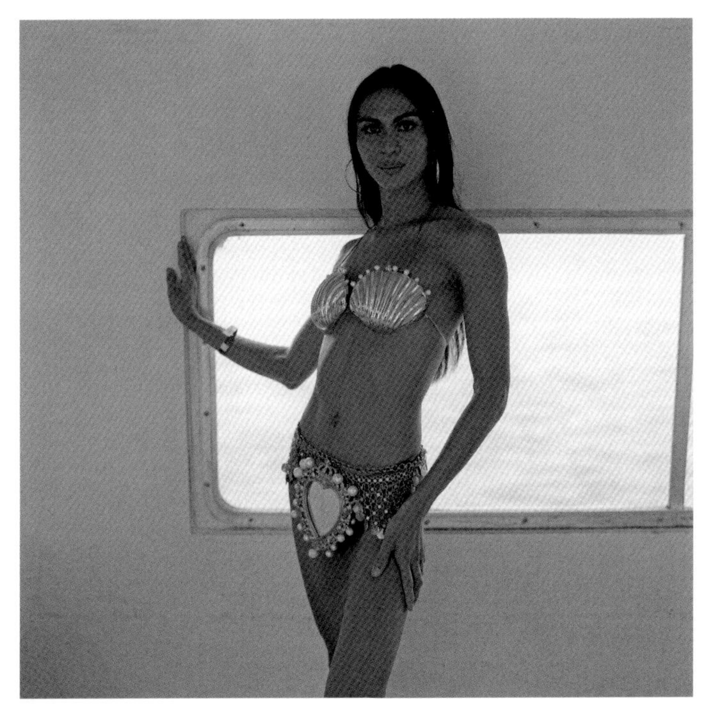

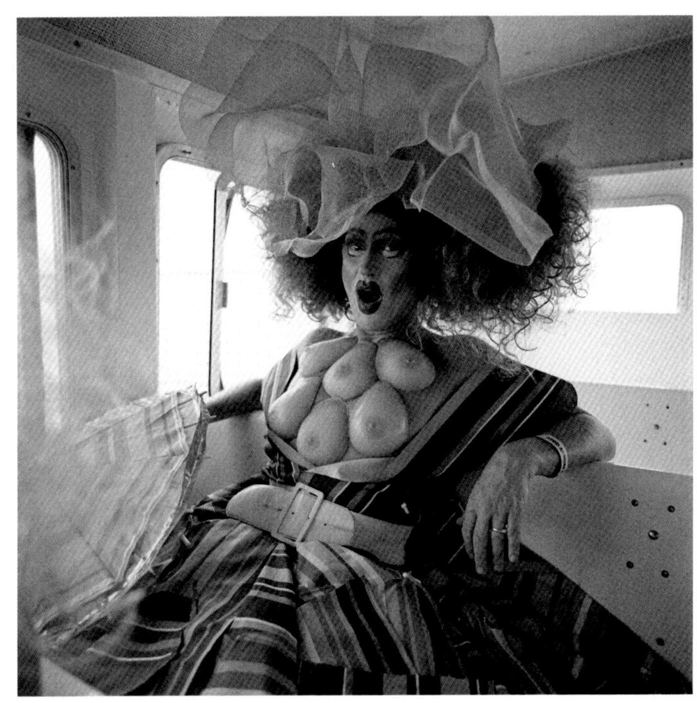

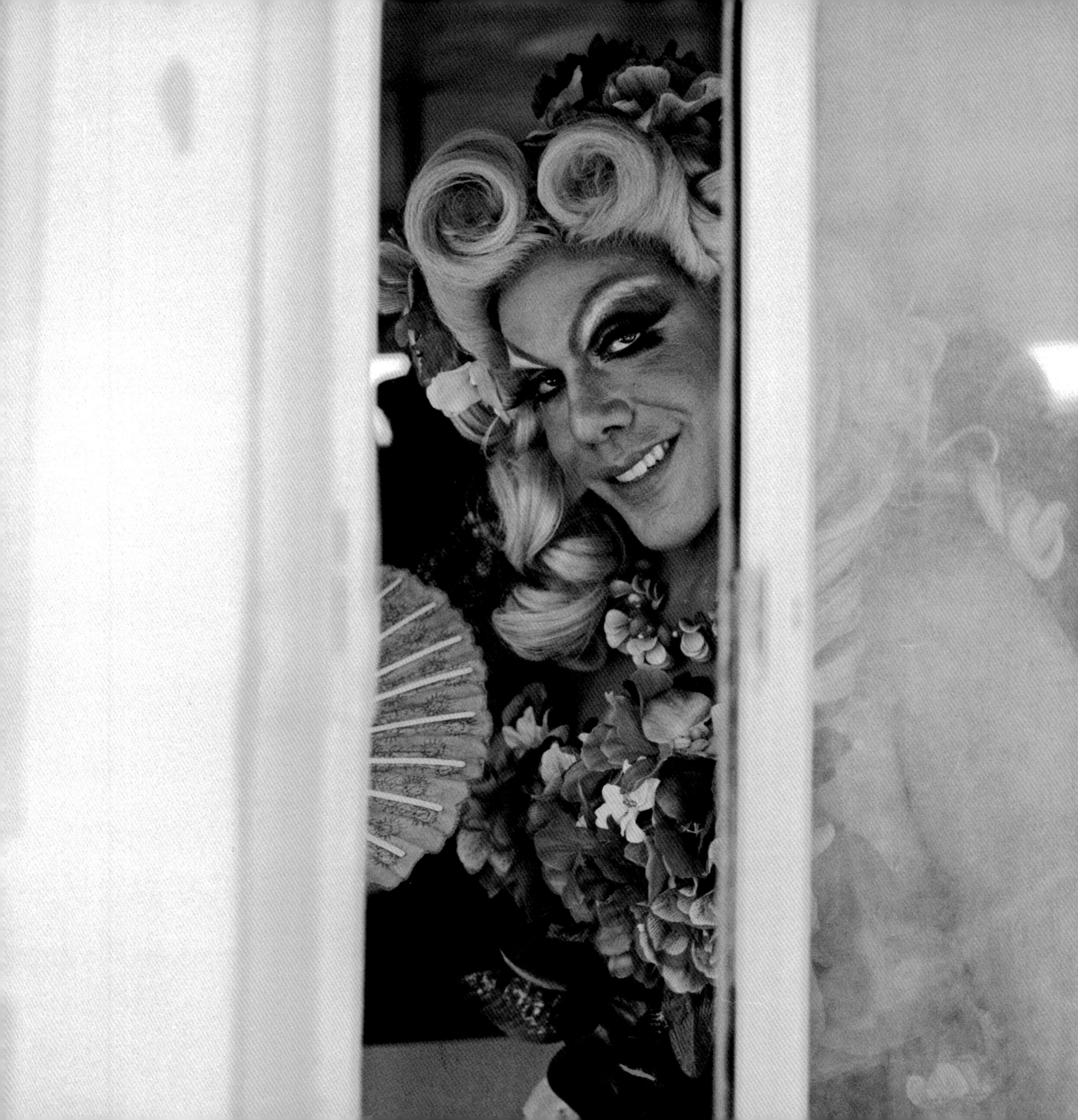

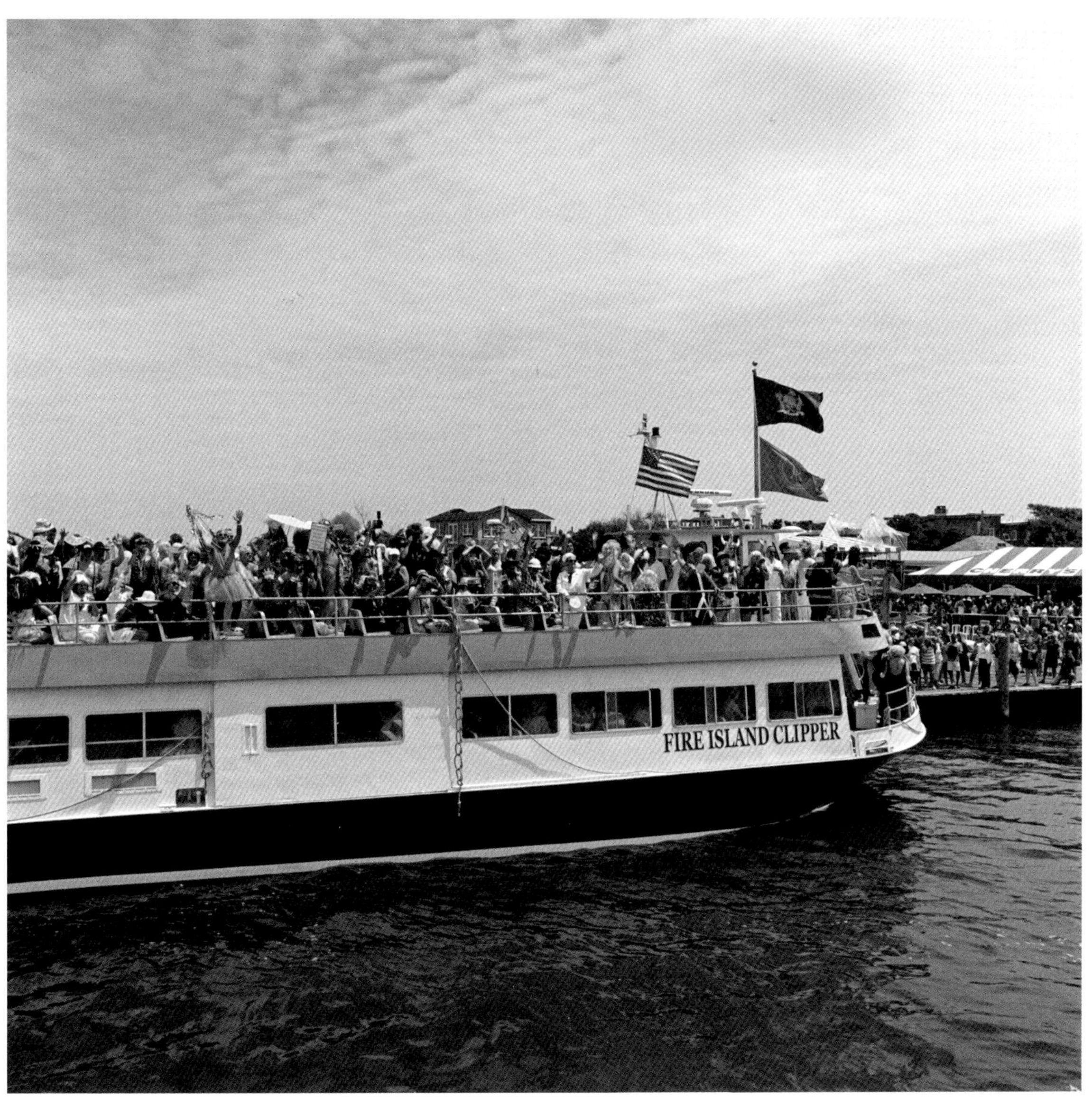
FIRE ISLAND CLIPPER

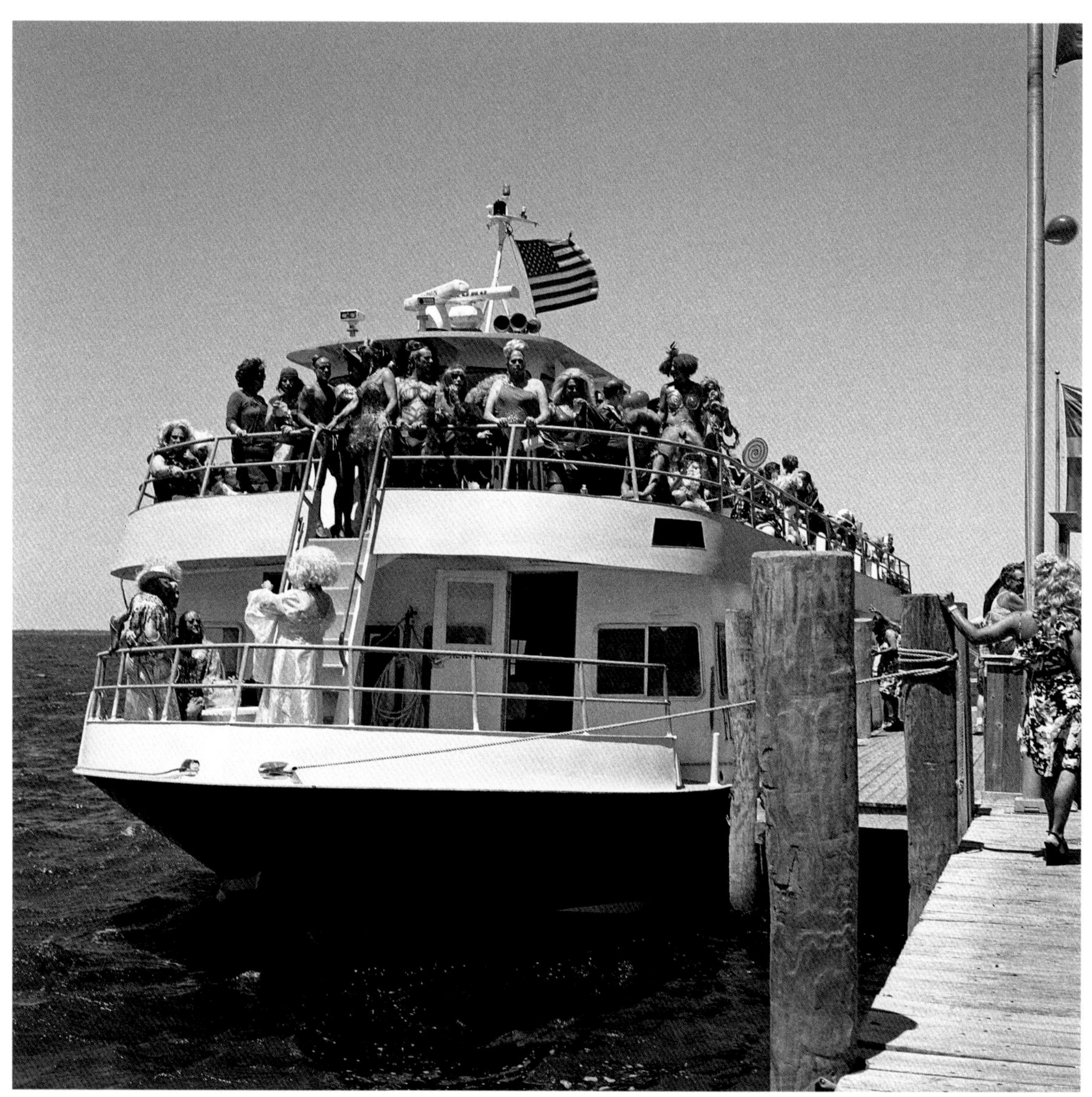

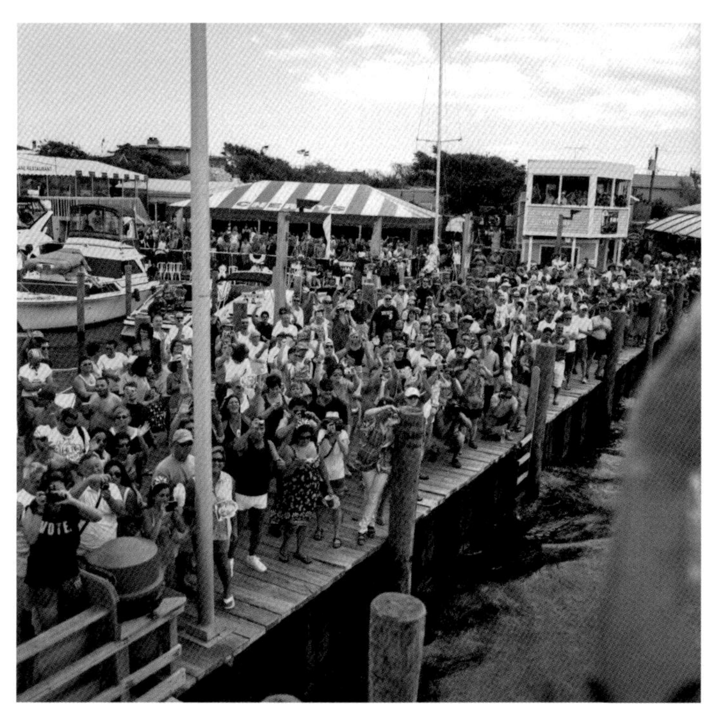
VOTE

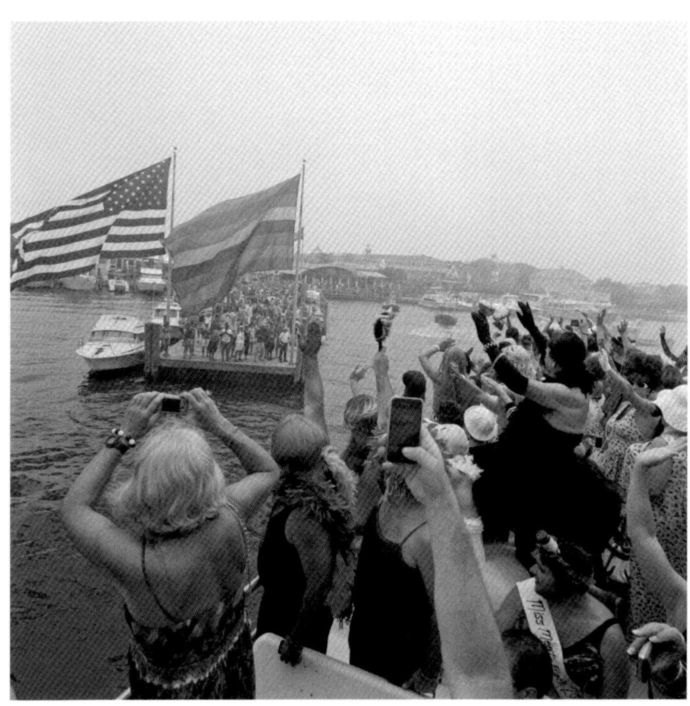

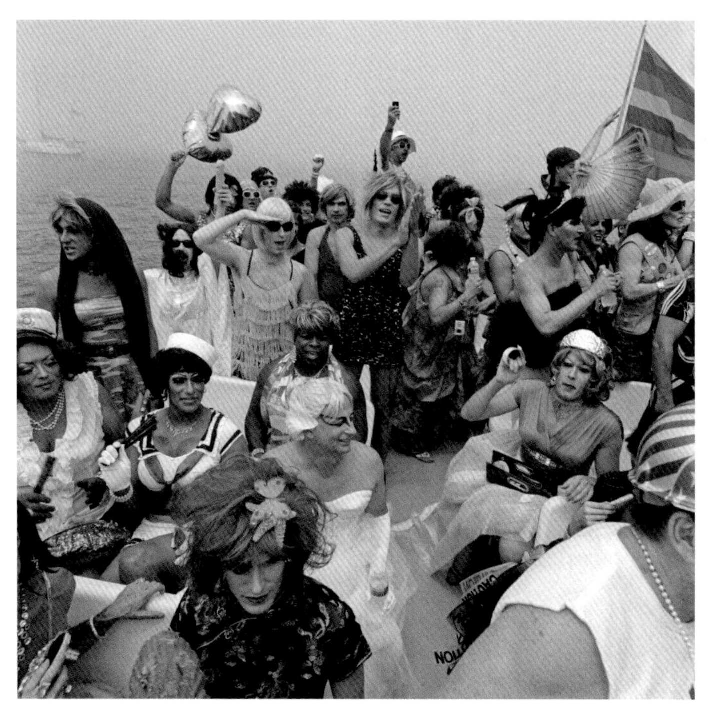

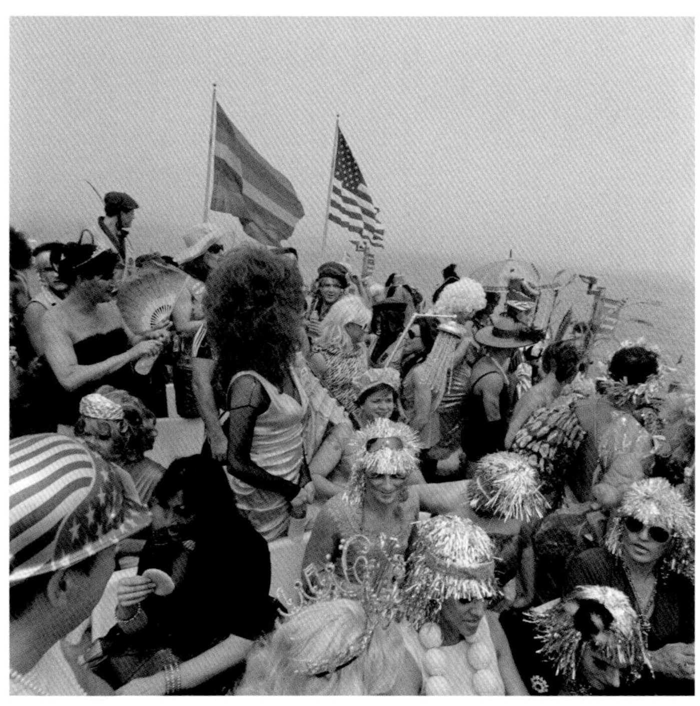

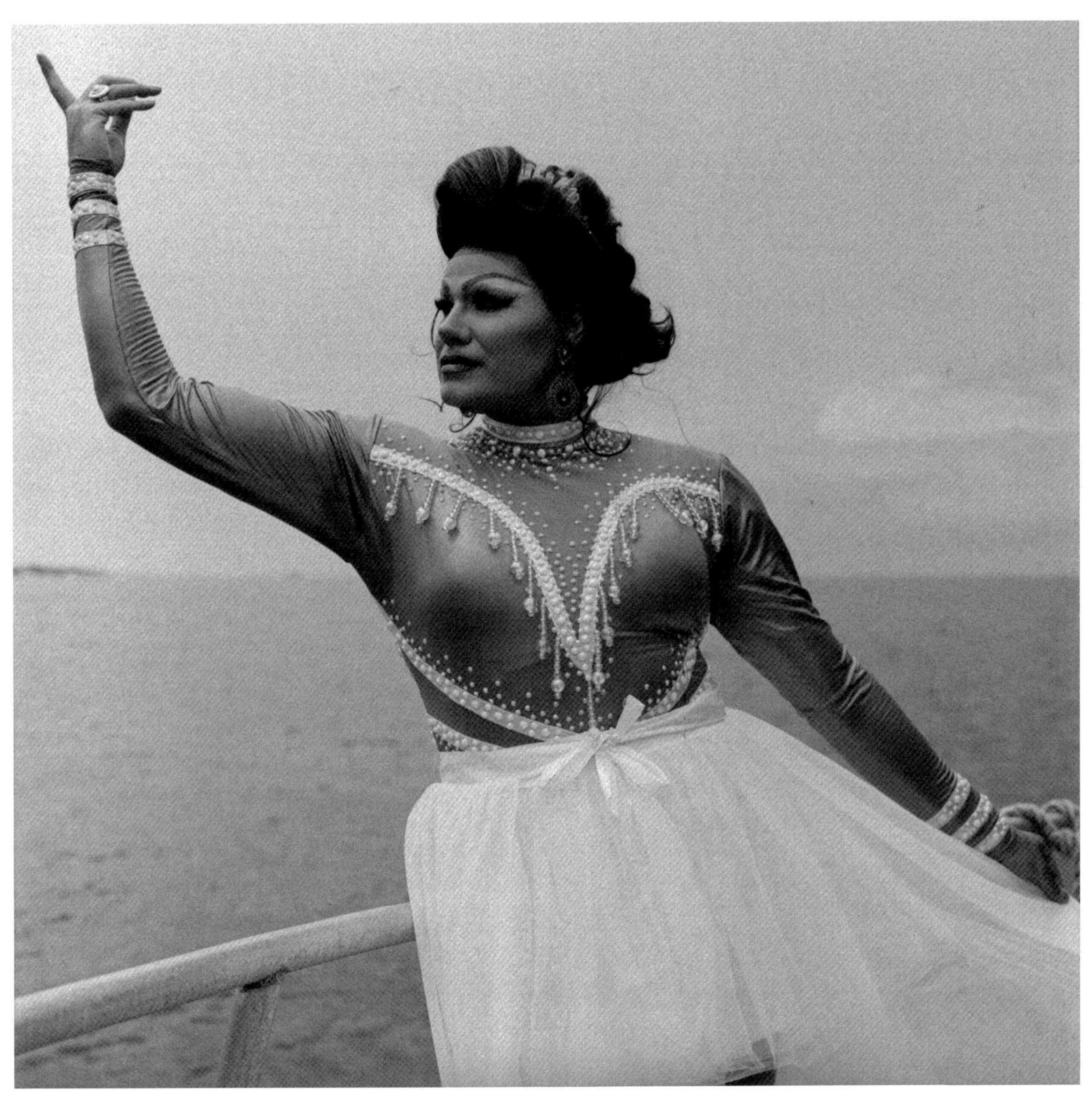

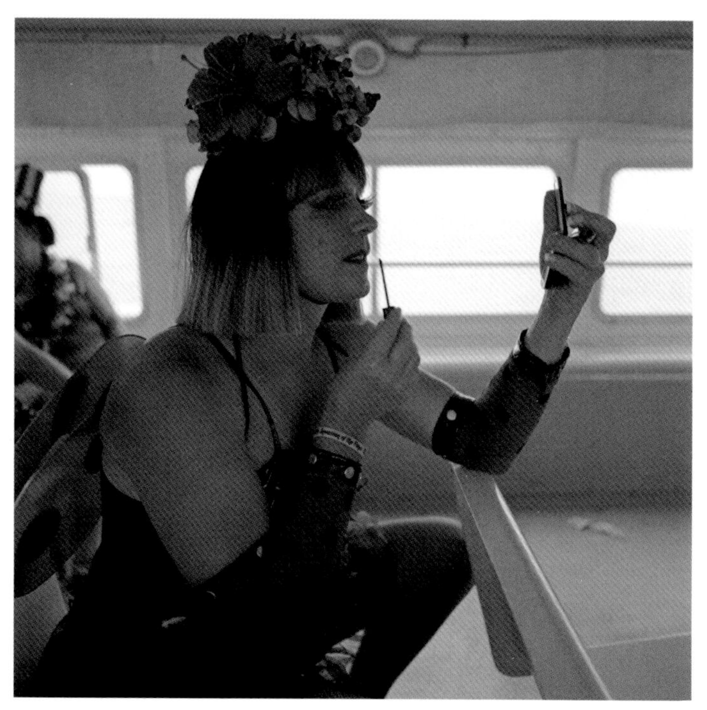

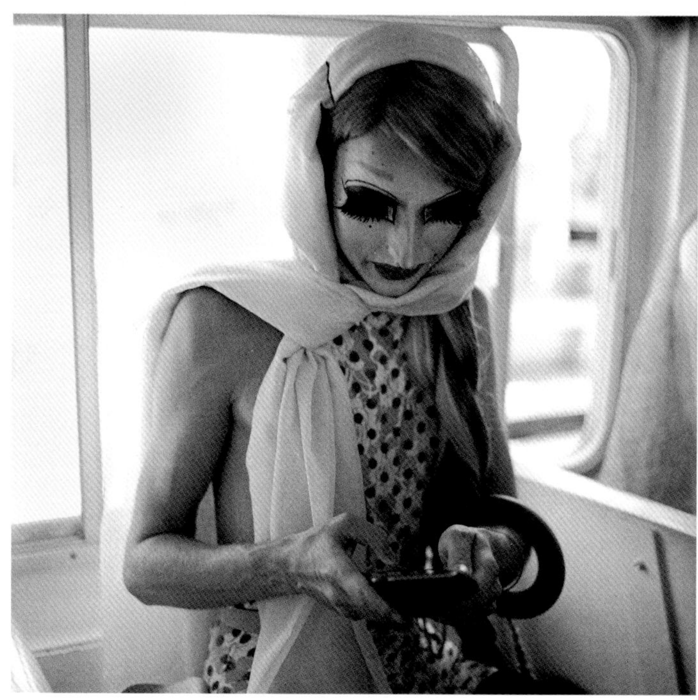

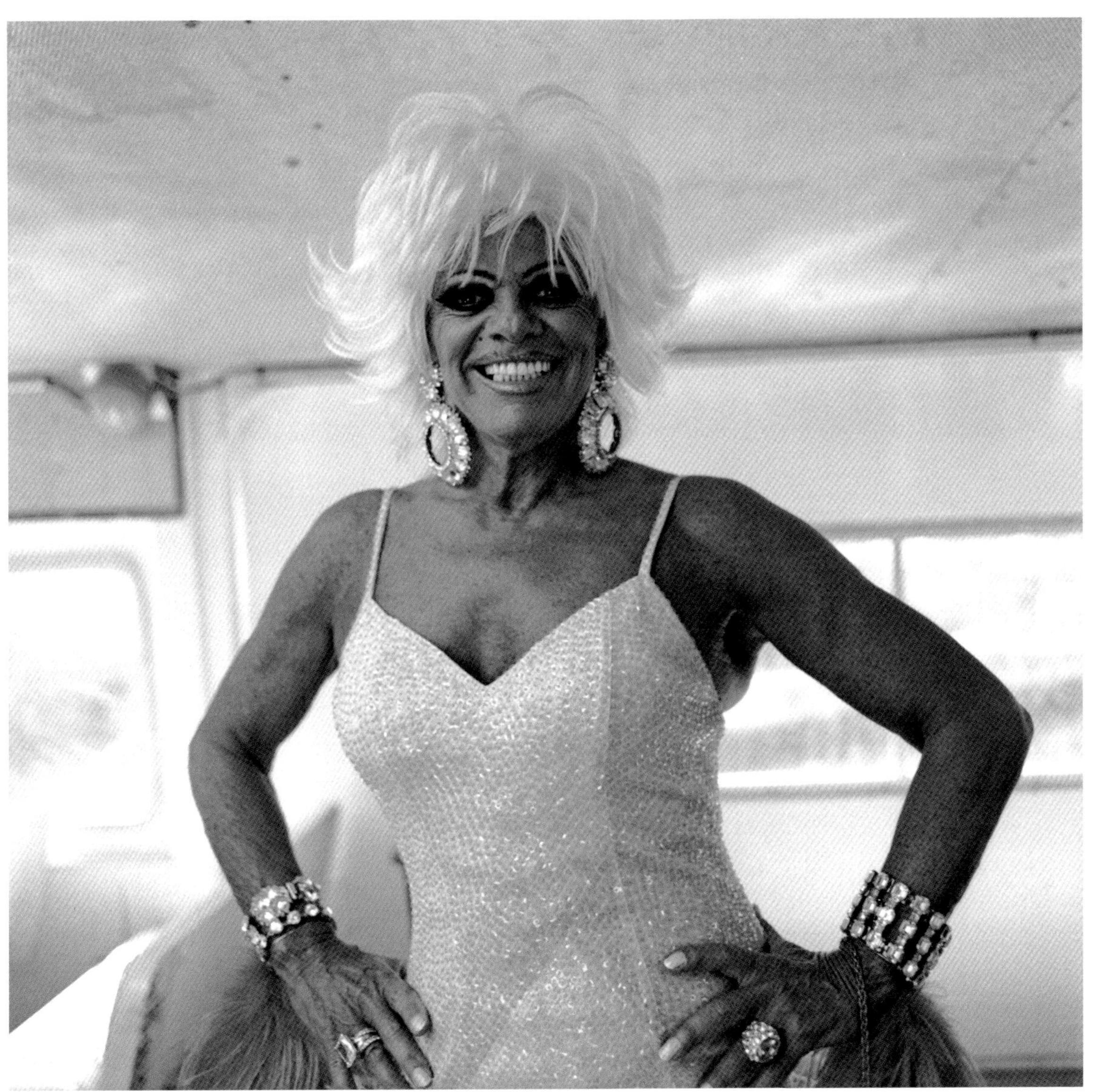

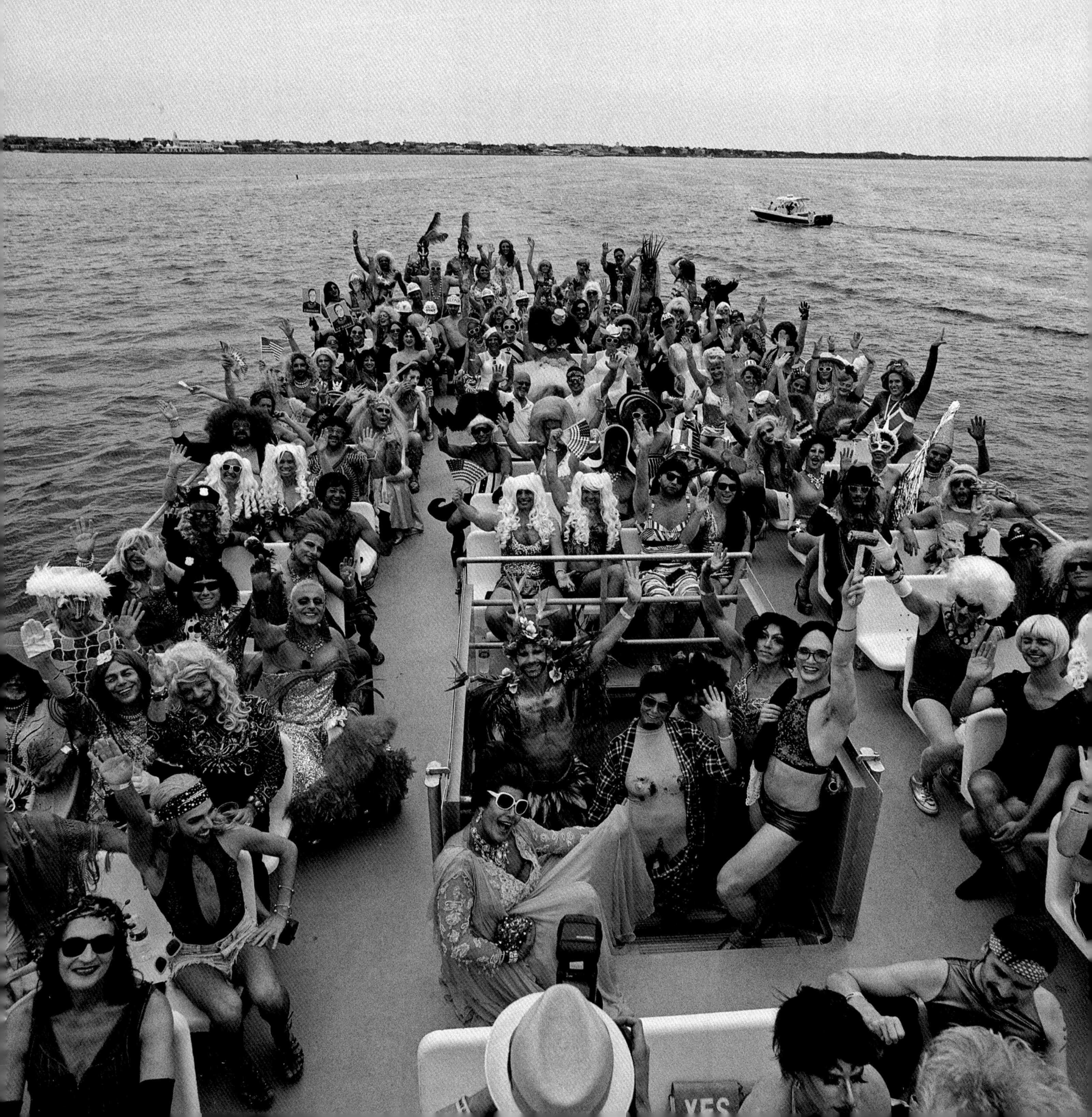
YES

"What I love most about The Invasion is the camaraderie of the participants, particularly during the private interlude between the departure crowds of the Grove and the arrival throngs in the Pines, on the Queens' flotilla, alone on the Great South Bay."

Hal Hayes

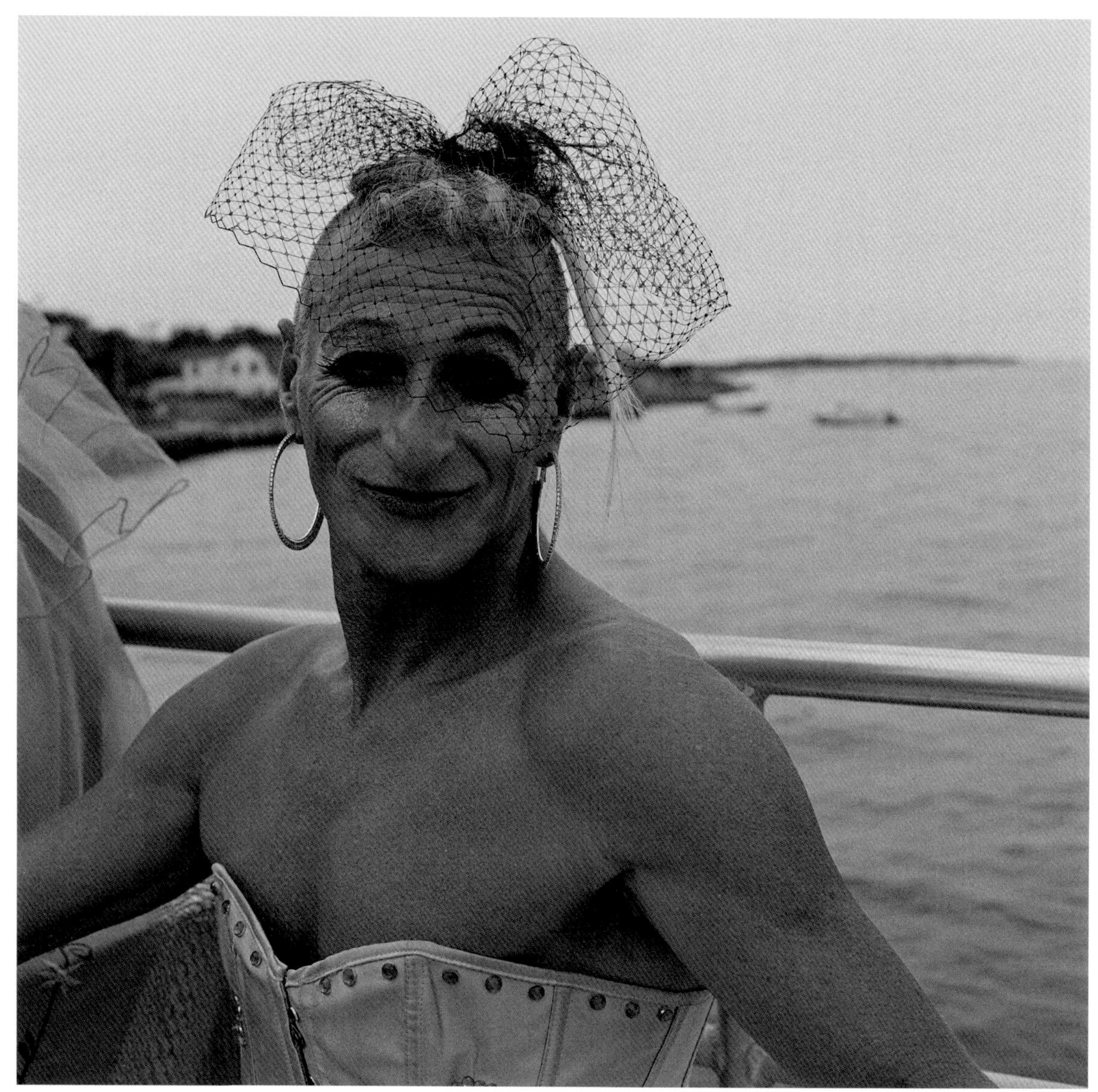

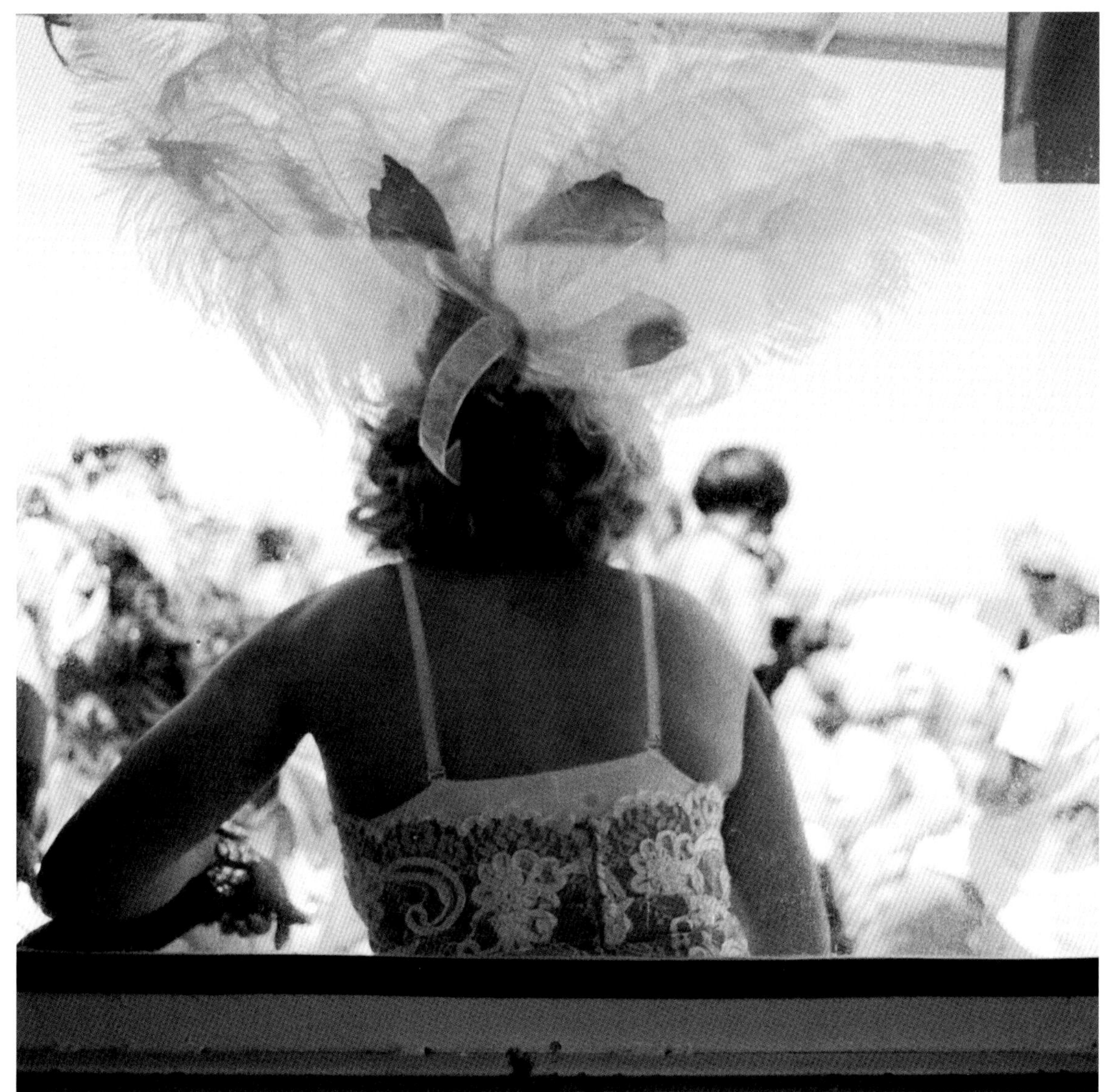

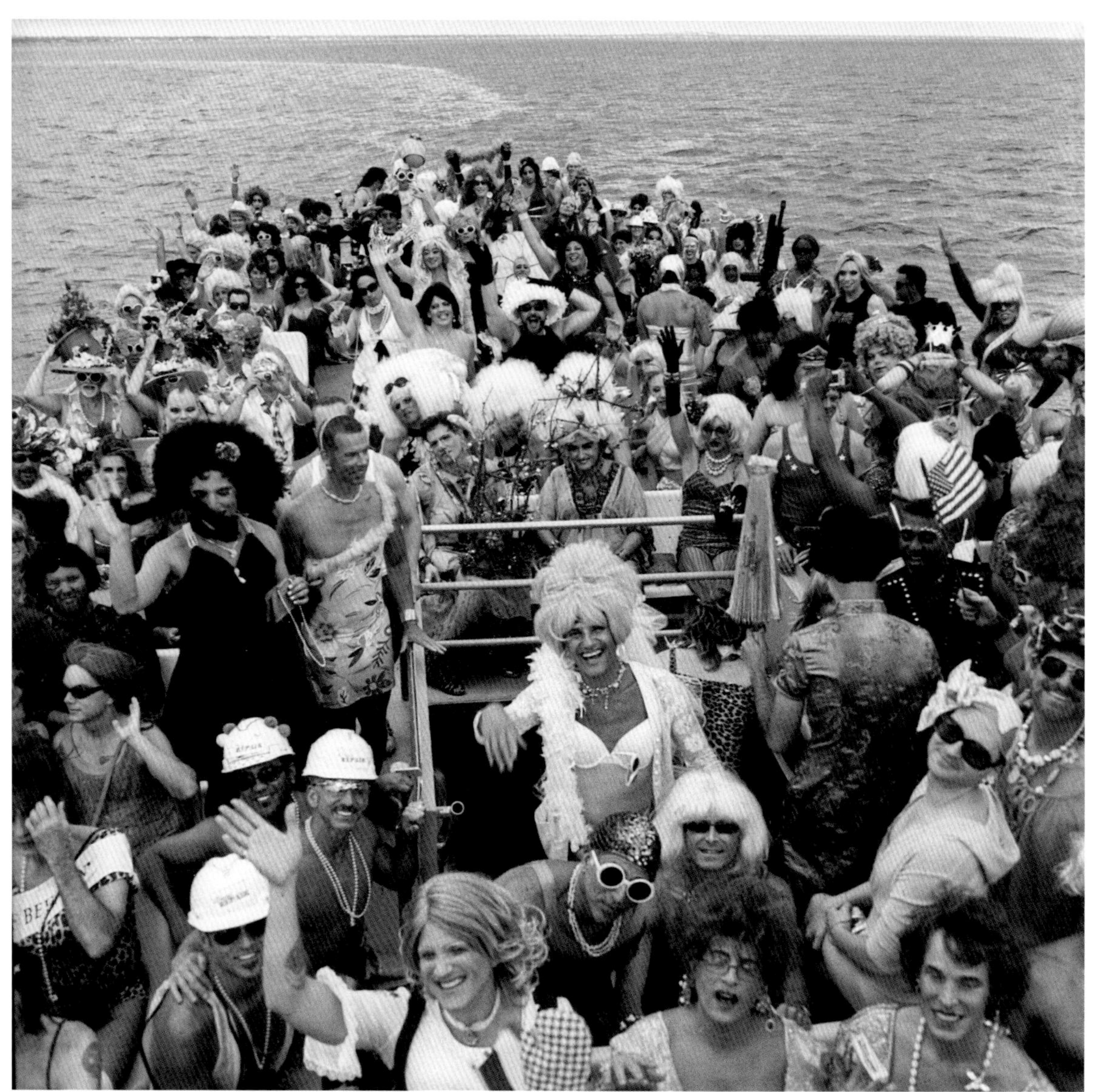

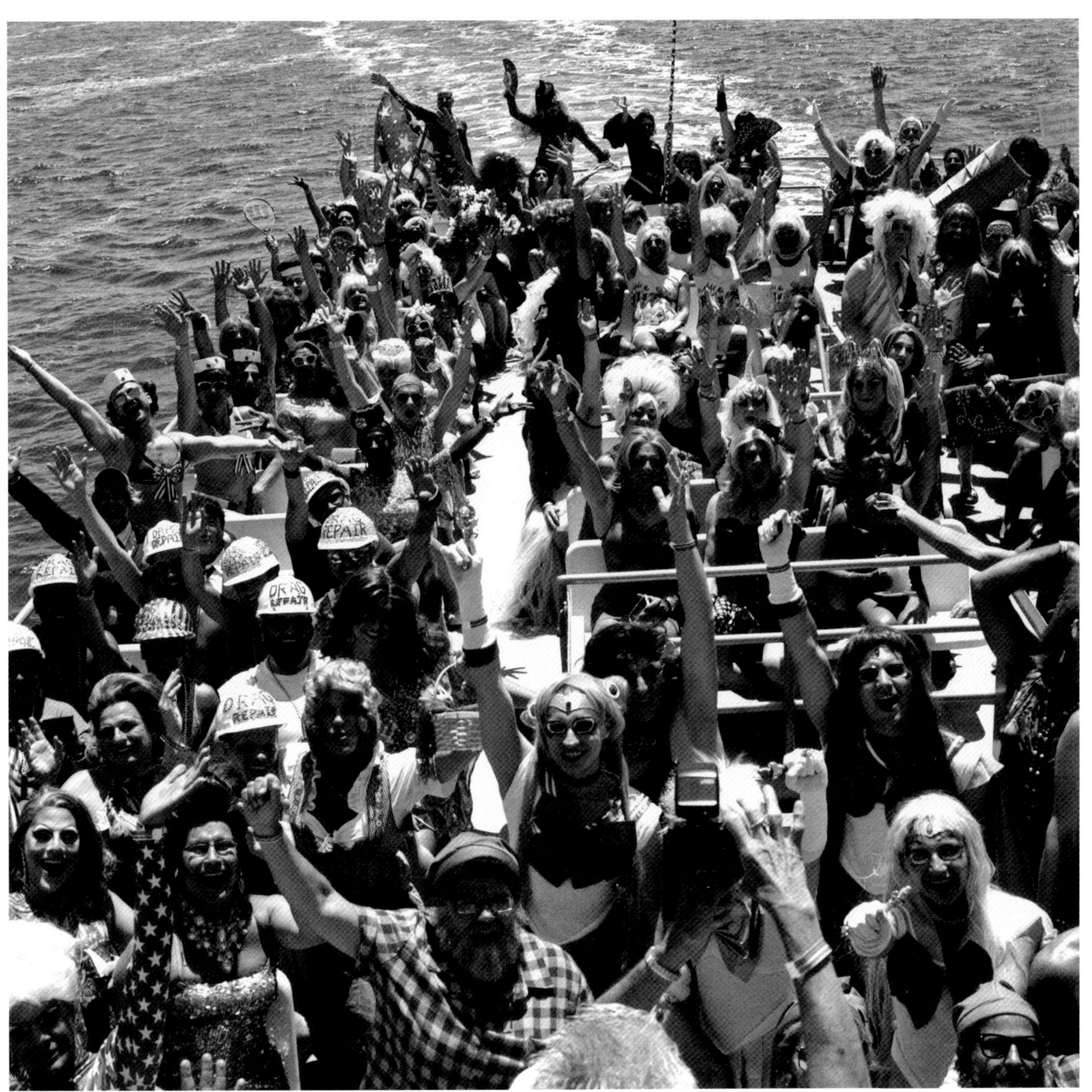
DRAG REPAIR

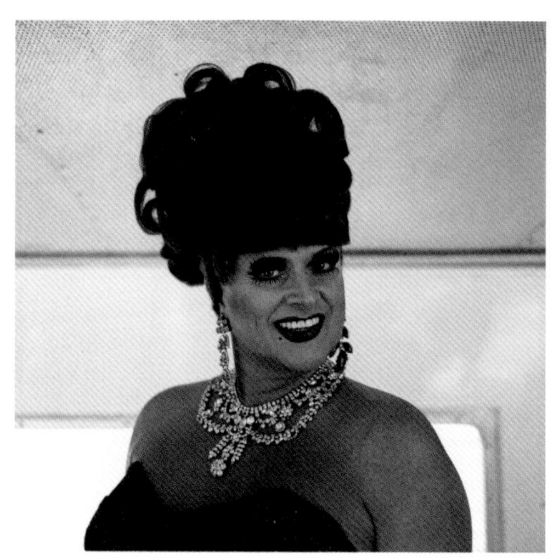

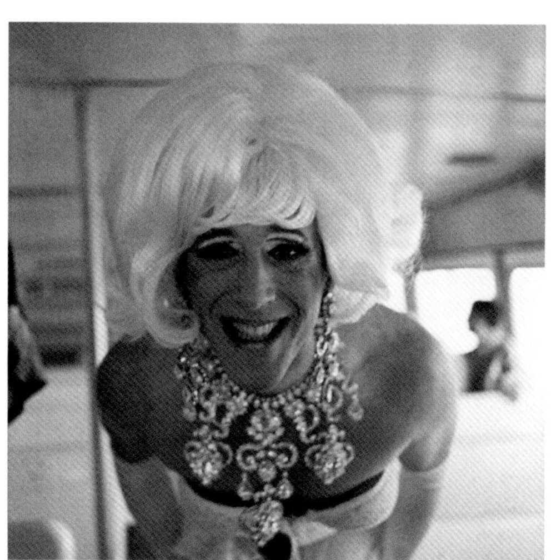

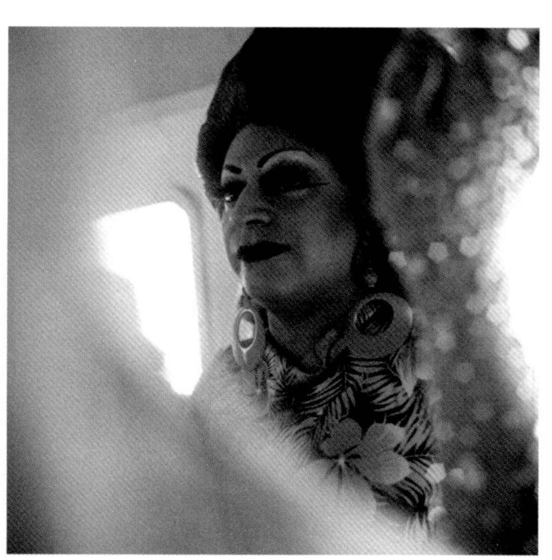

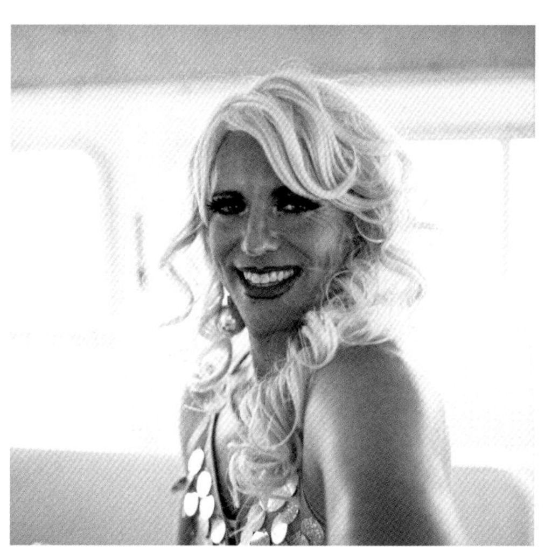

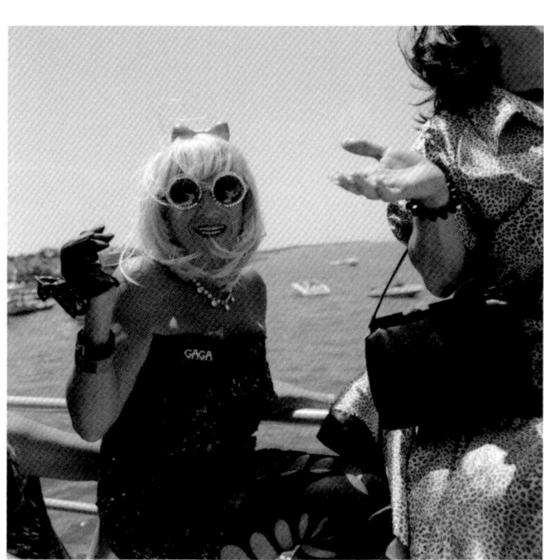
GAGA

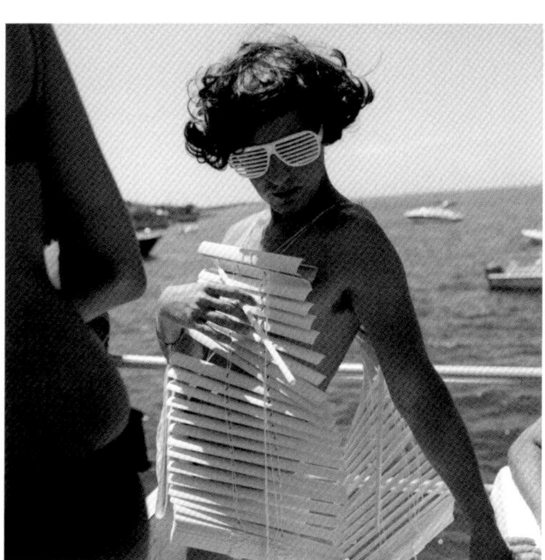

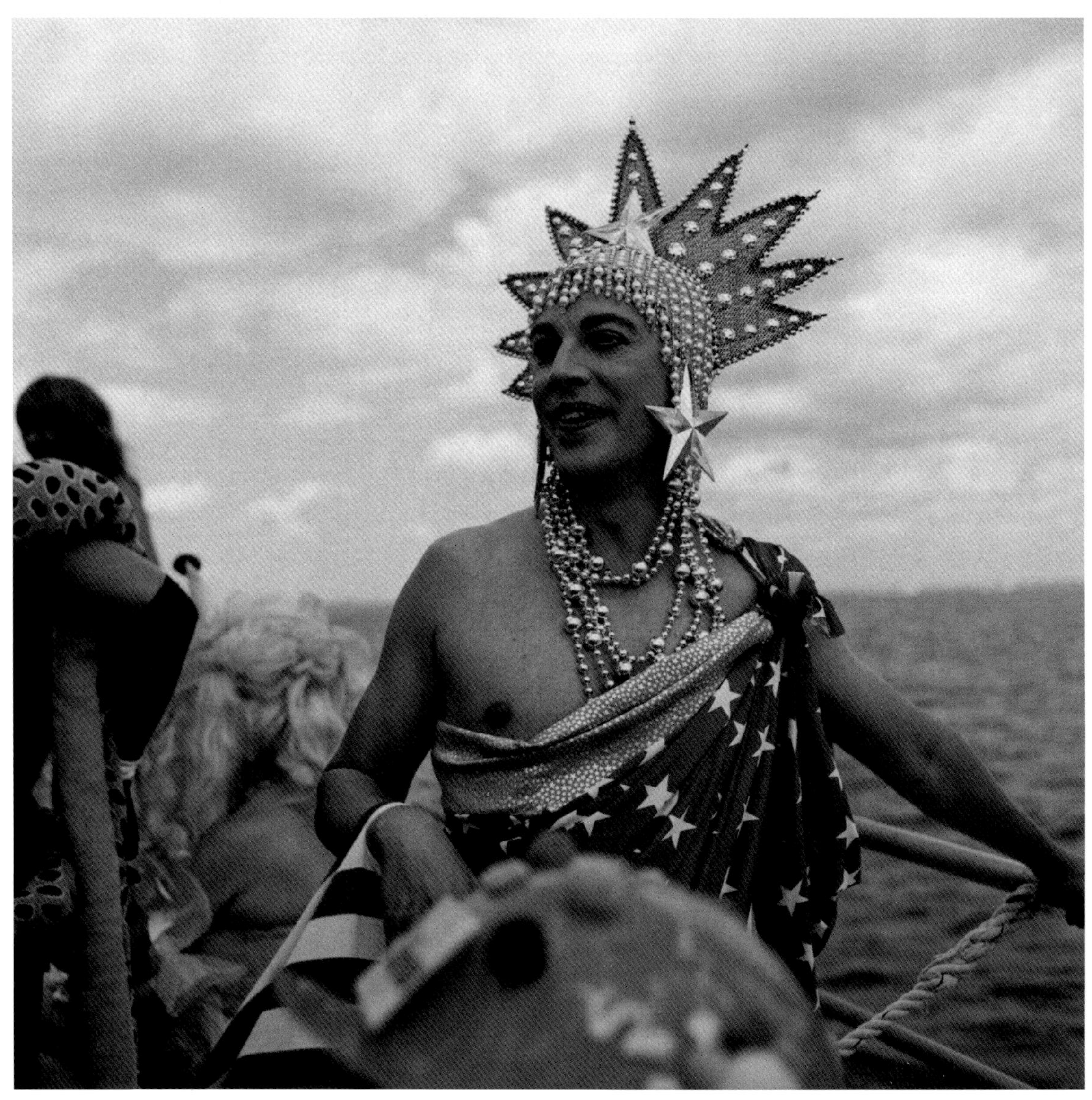

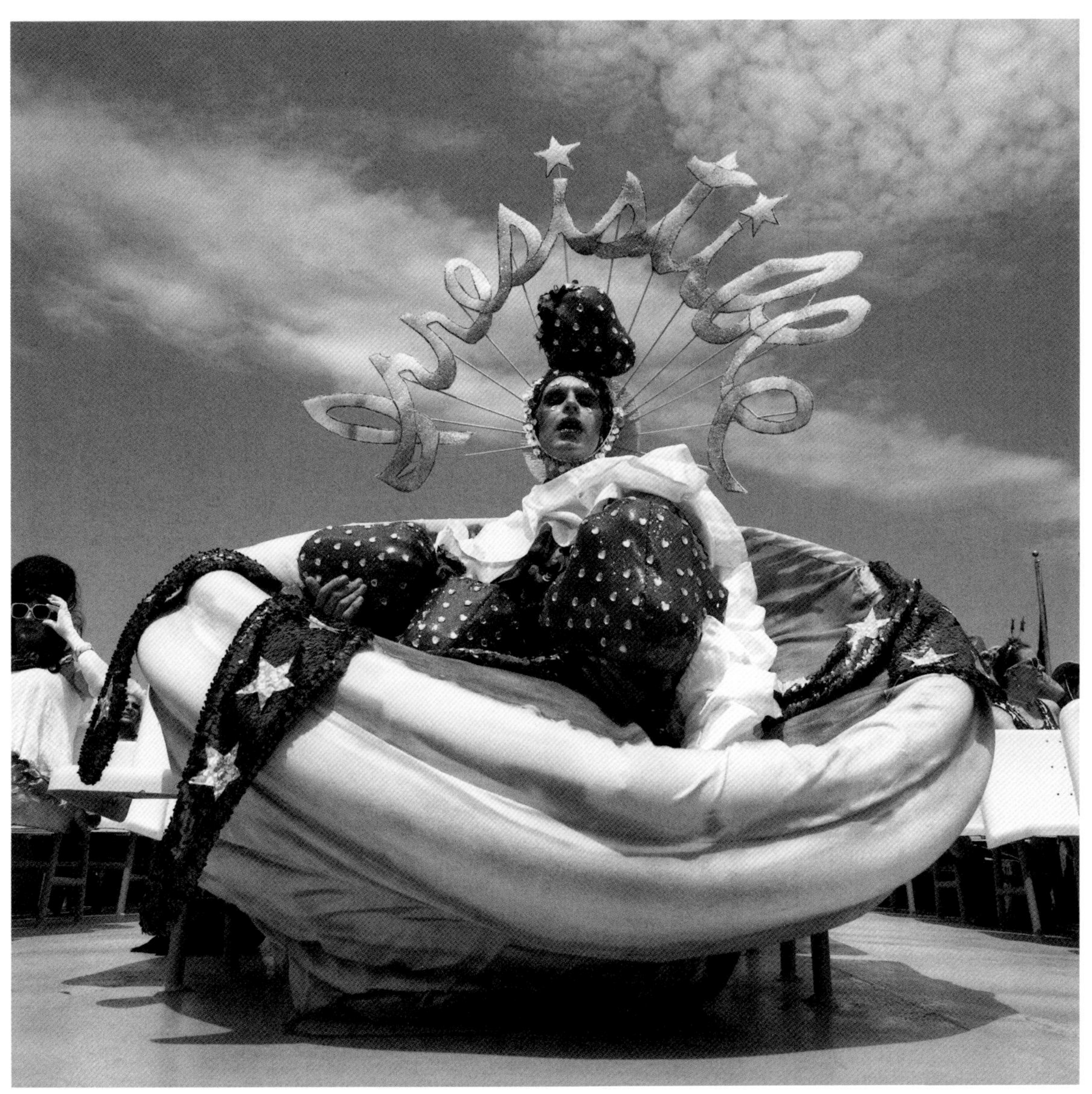

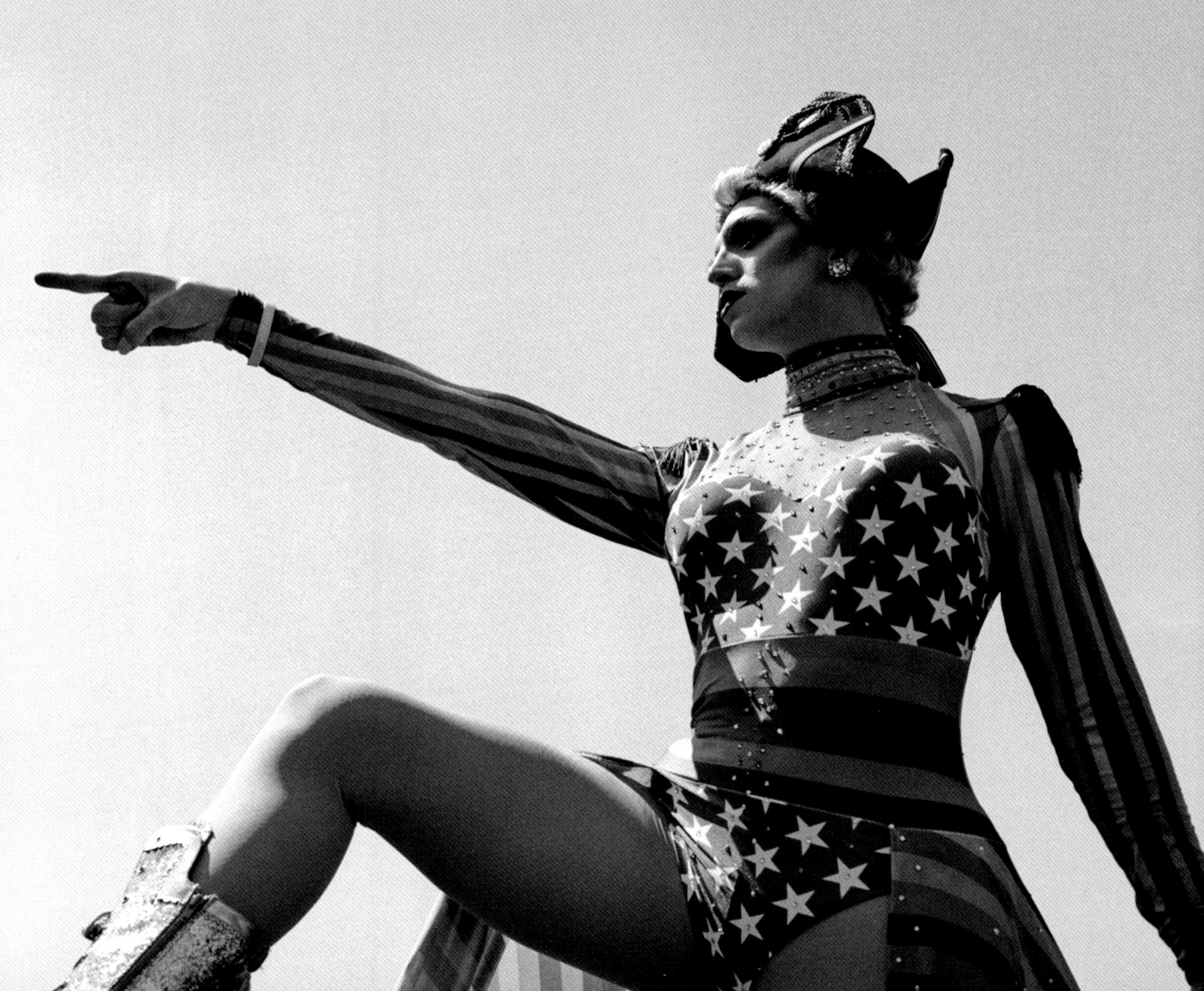

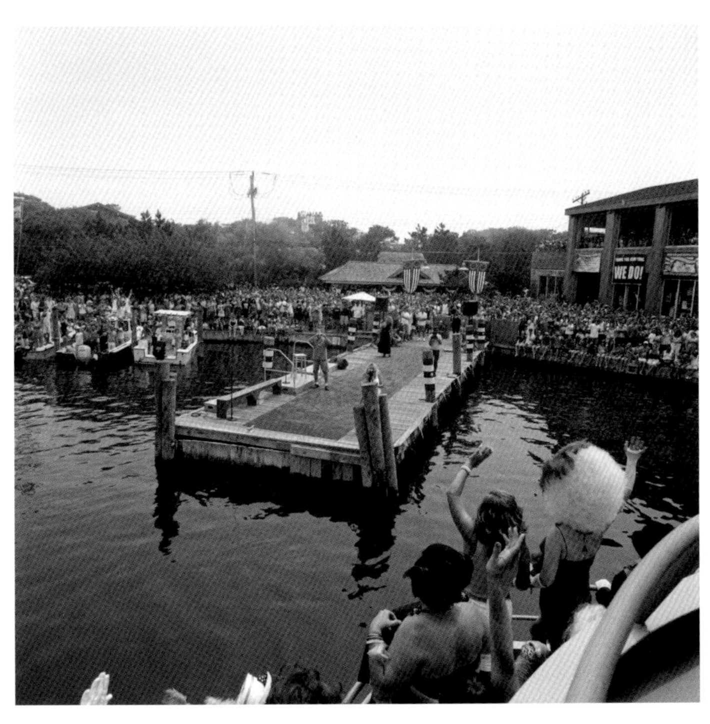
WE DO!

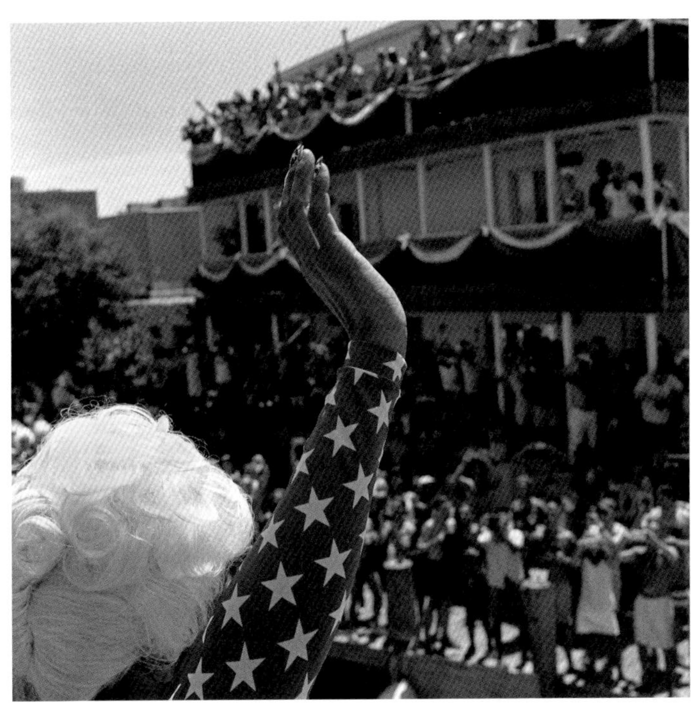

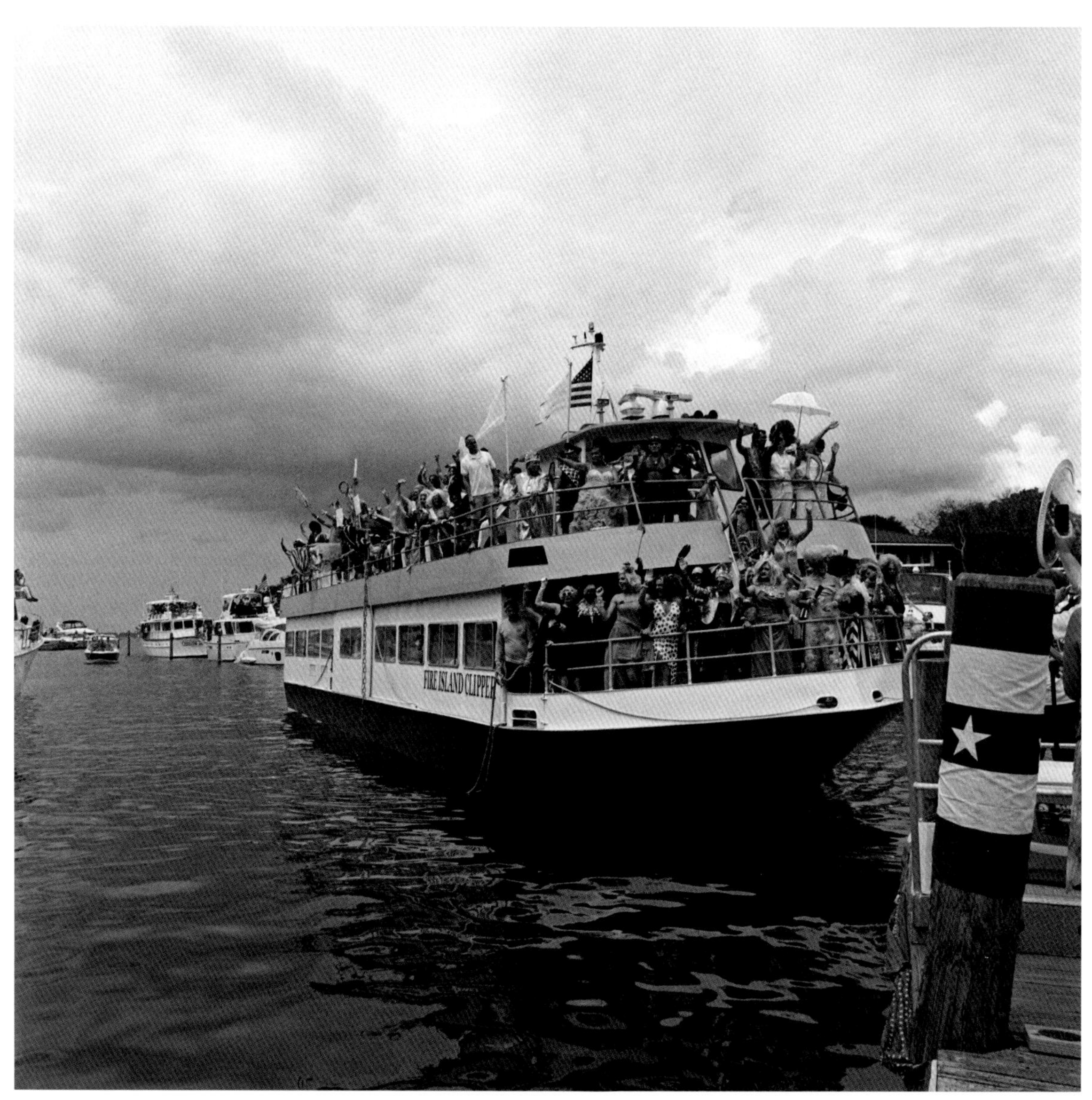
FIRE ISLAND CLIPPER

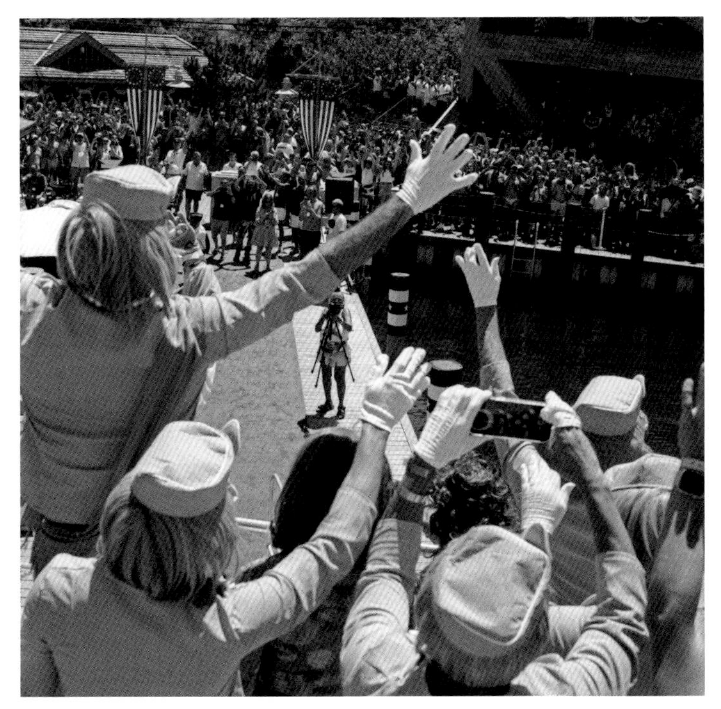

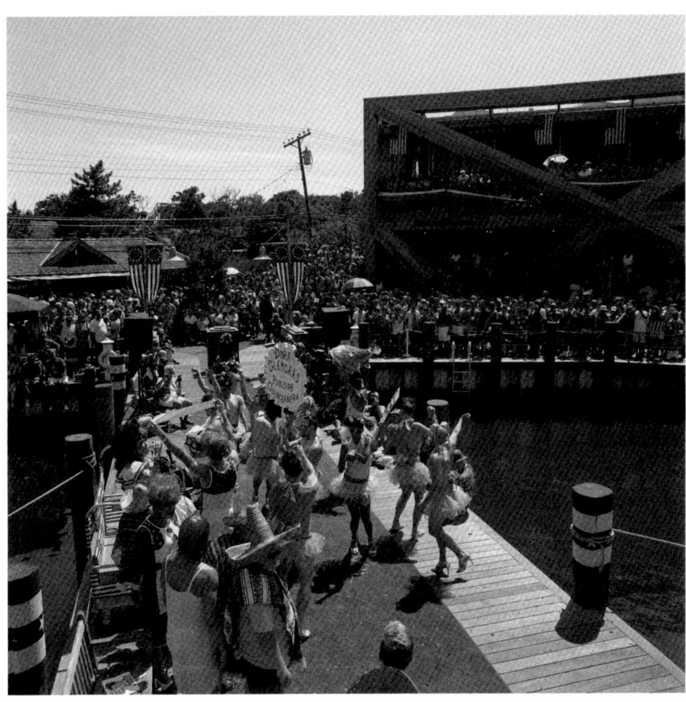

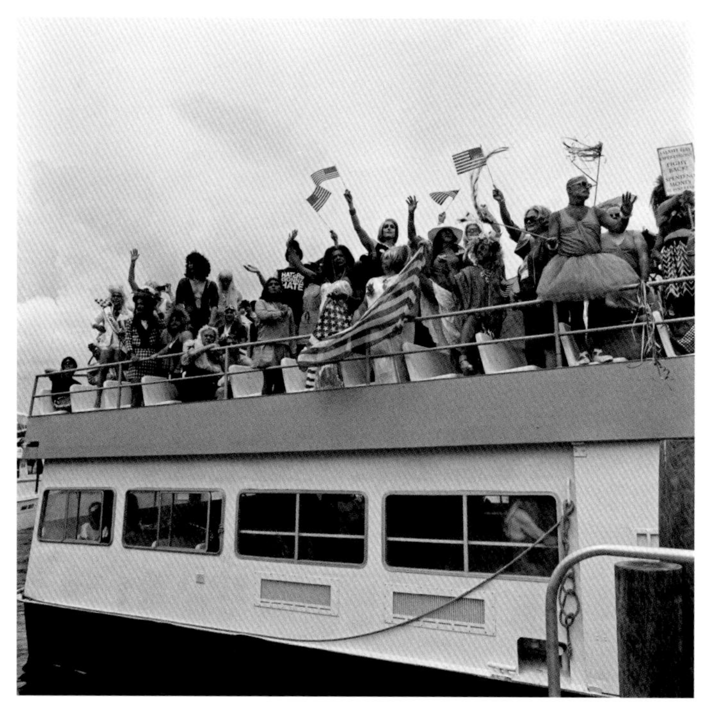

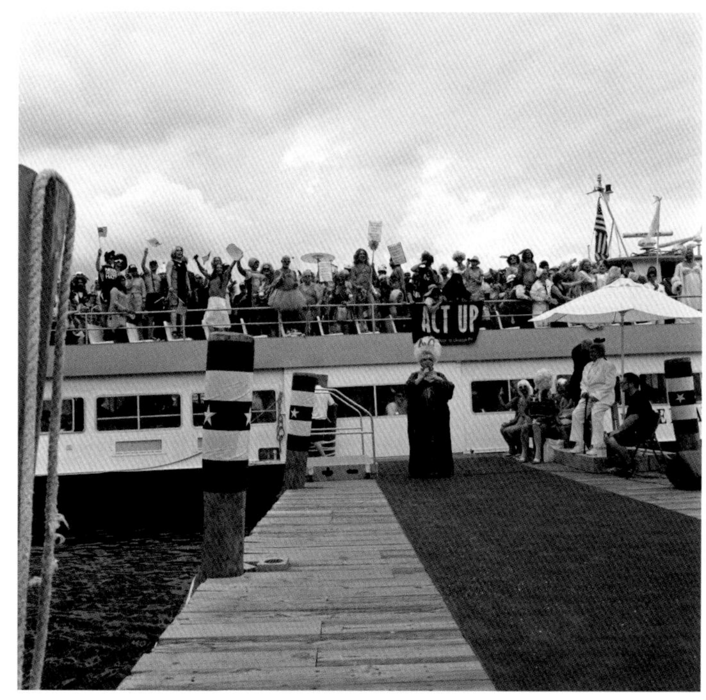
ACT UP

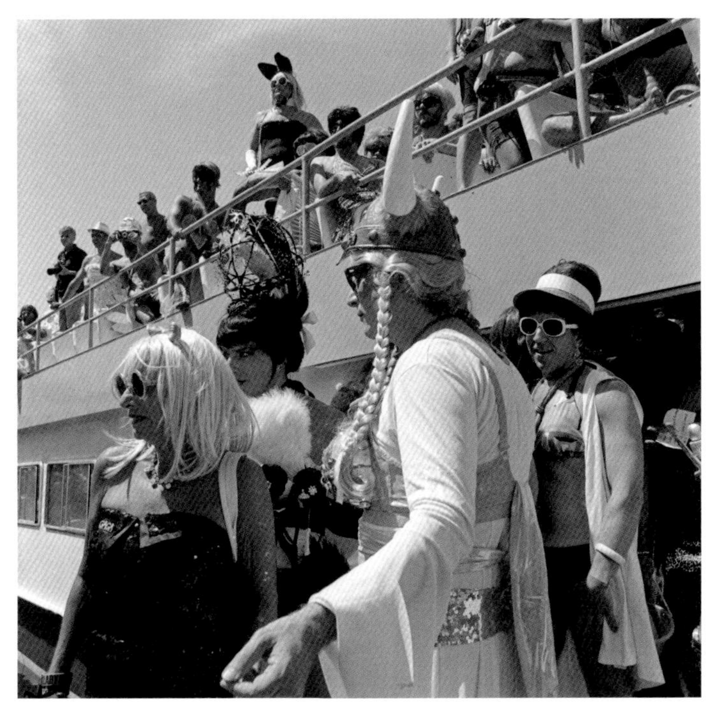

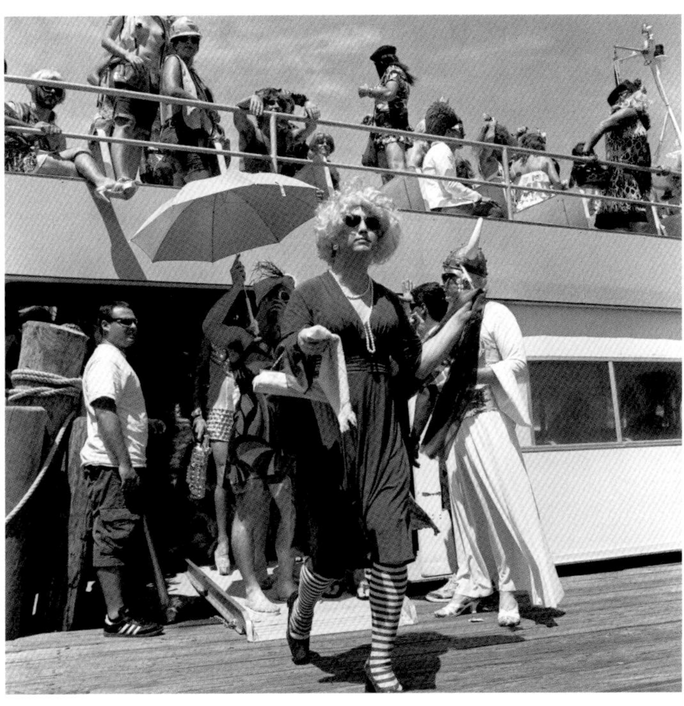

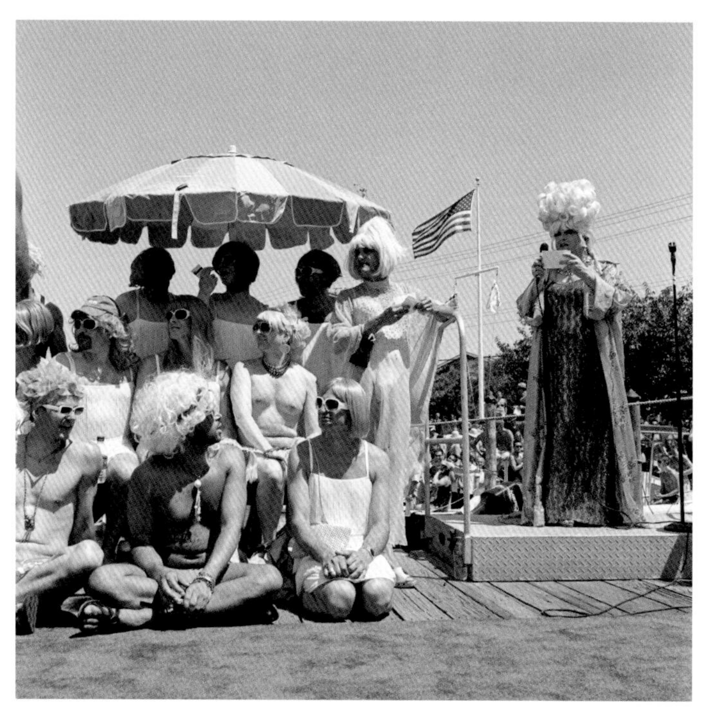

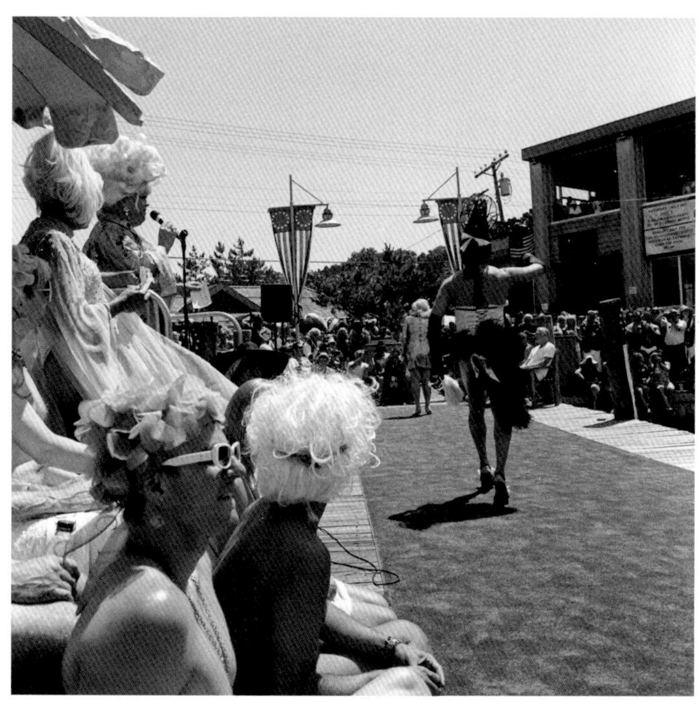

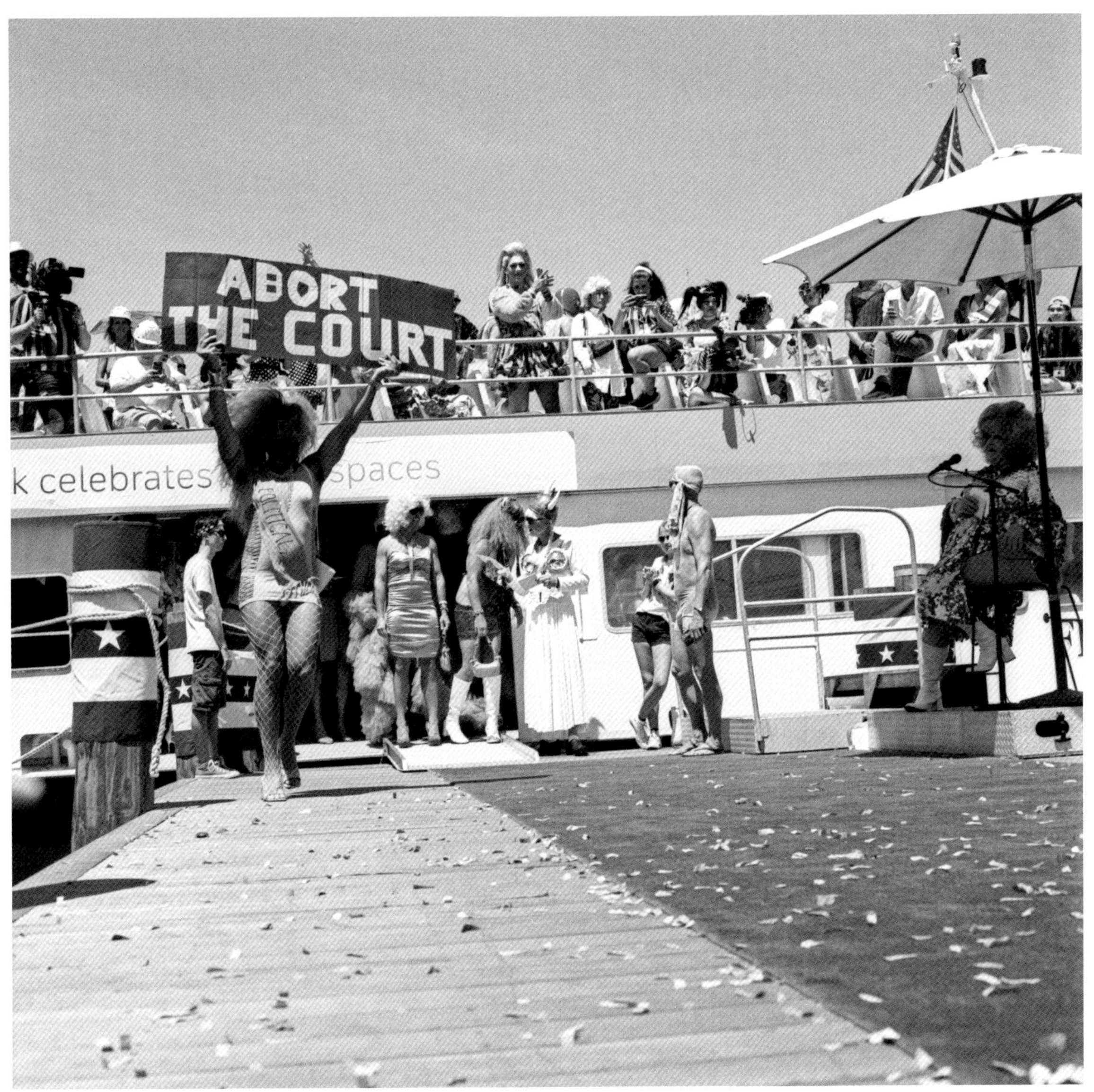
ABORT
THE COURT
k celebrates
spaces

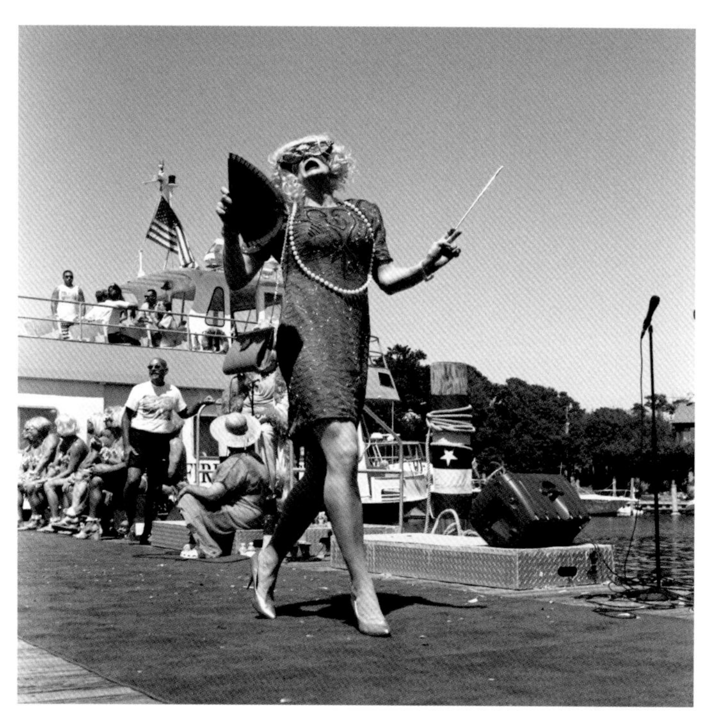

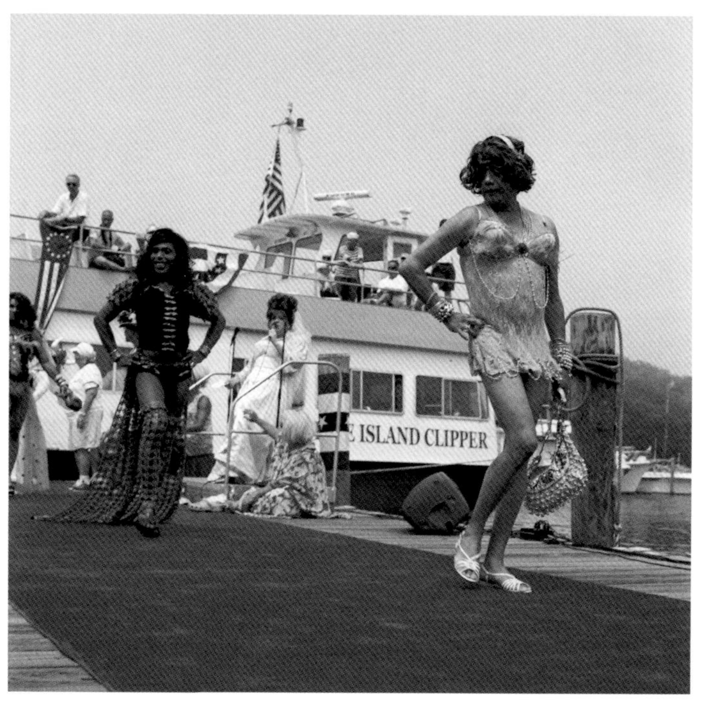
ISLAND CLIPPER

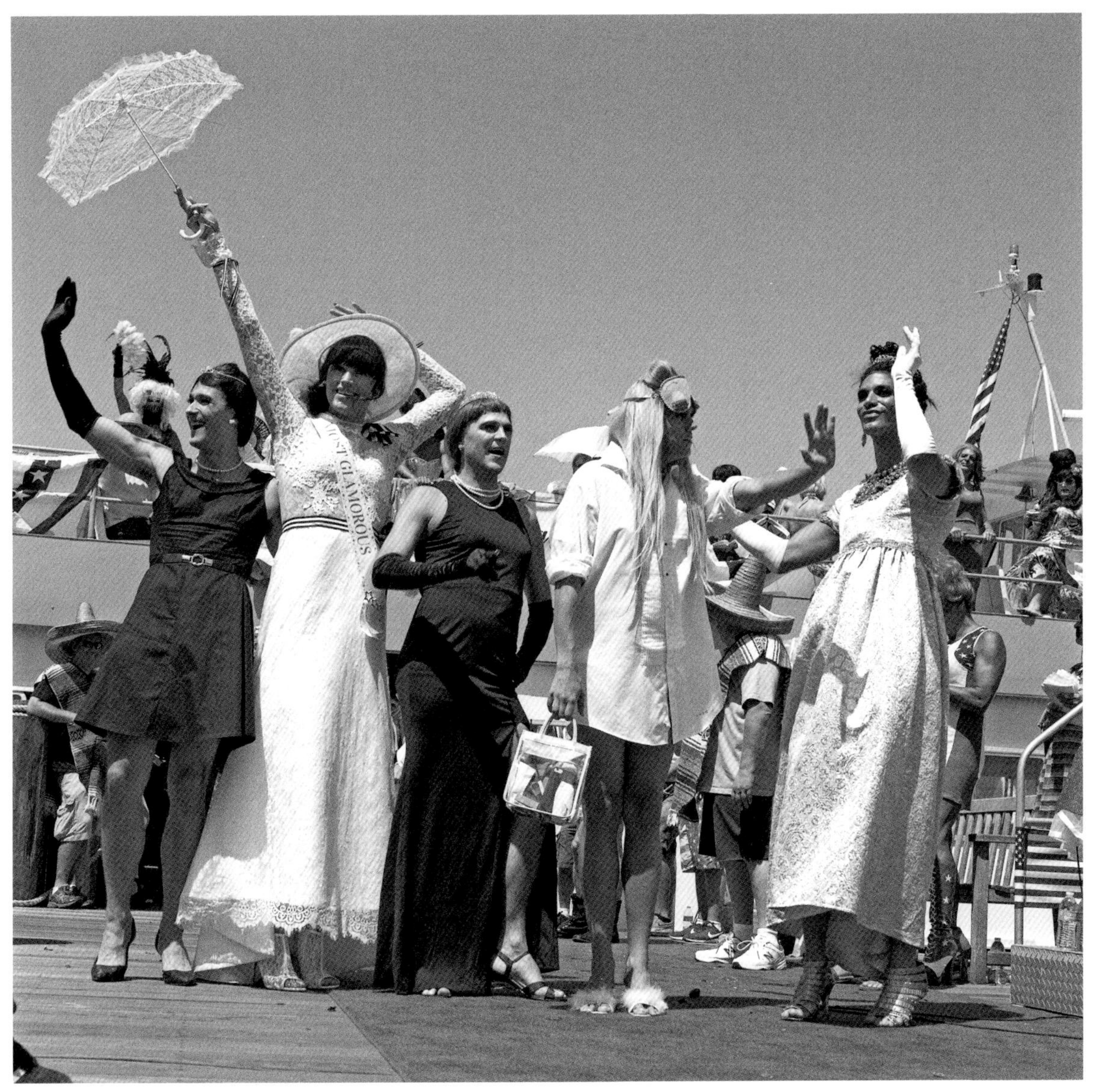
GLAMOROUS

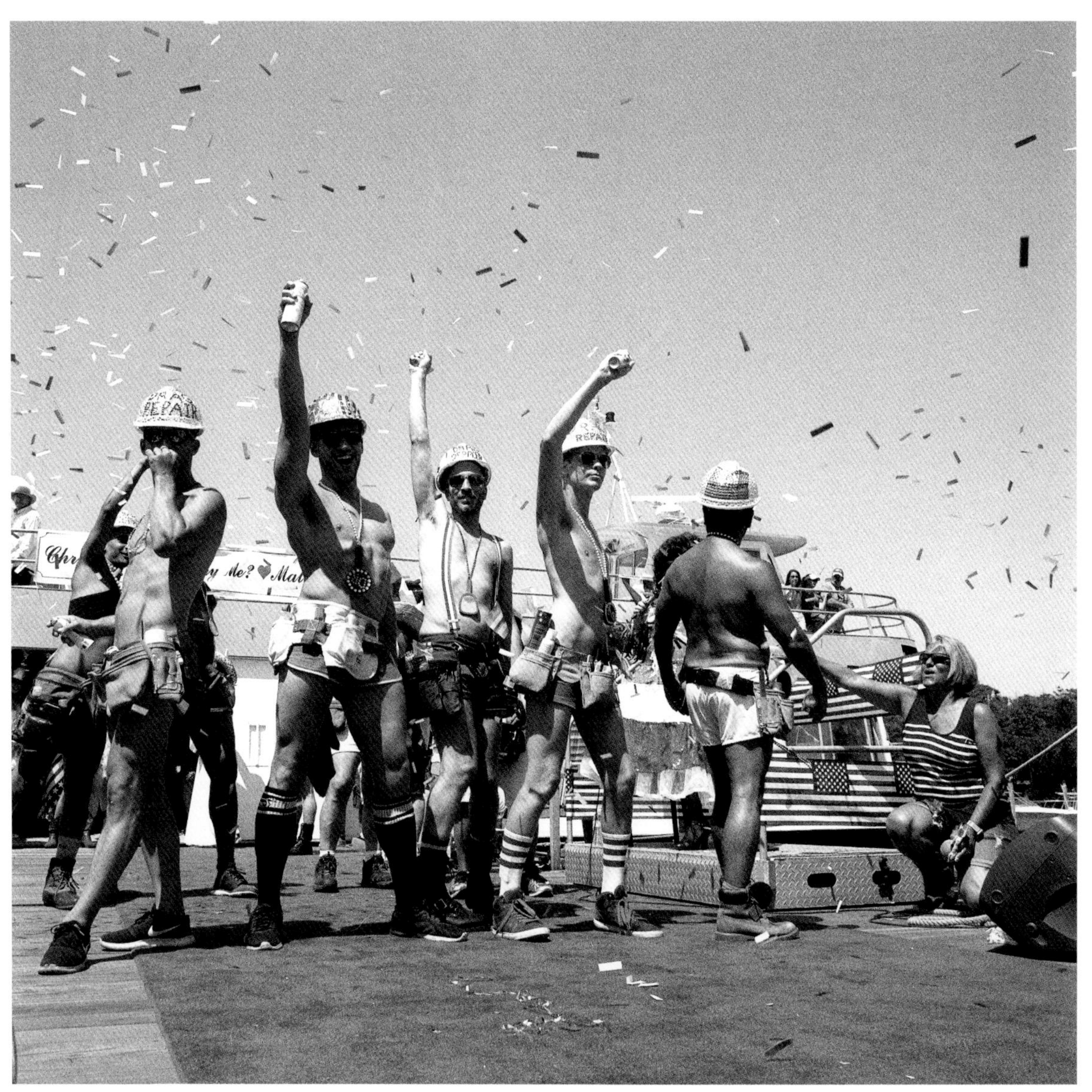
REPAIR
REPAIR

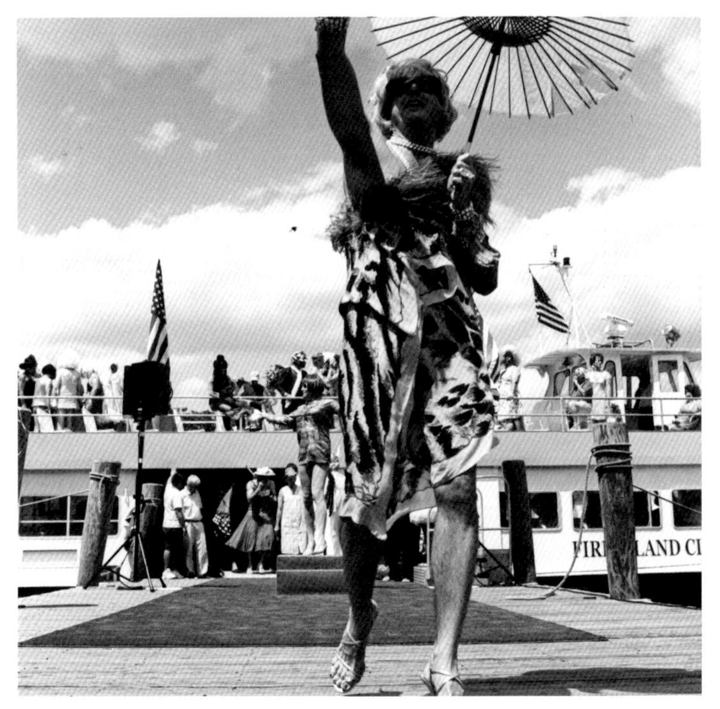

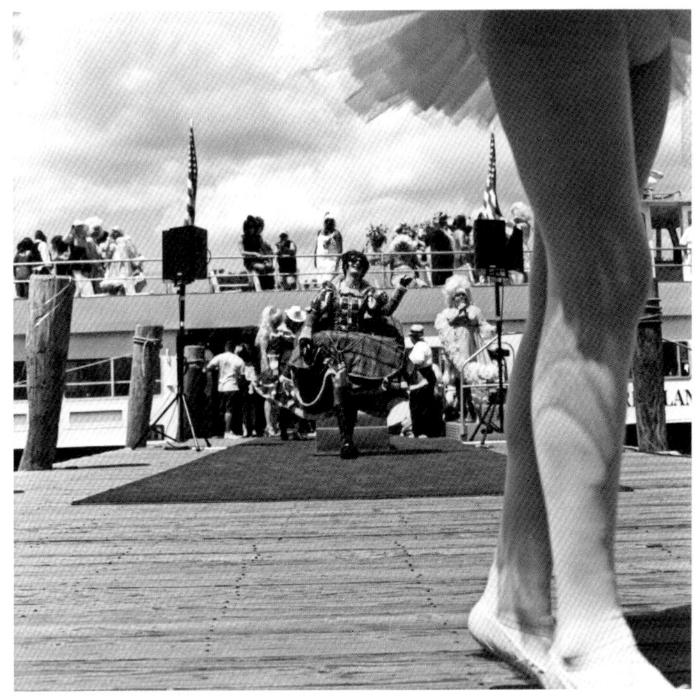

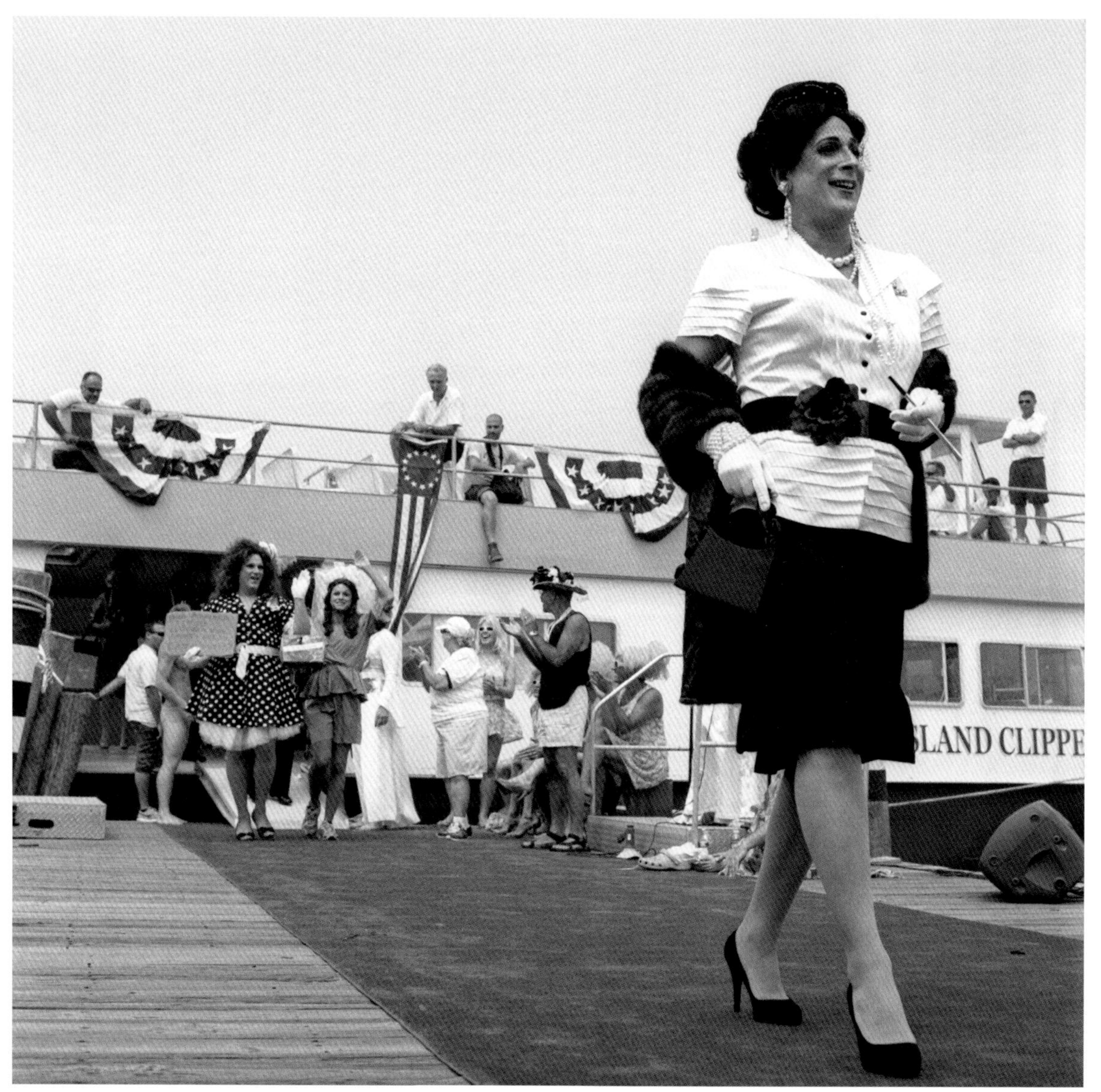
SLAND CLIPPE

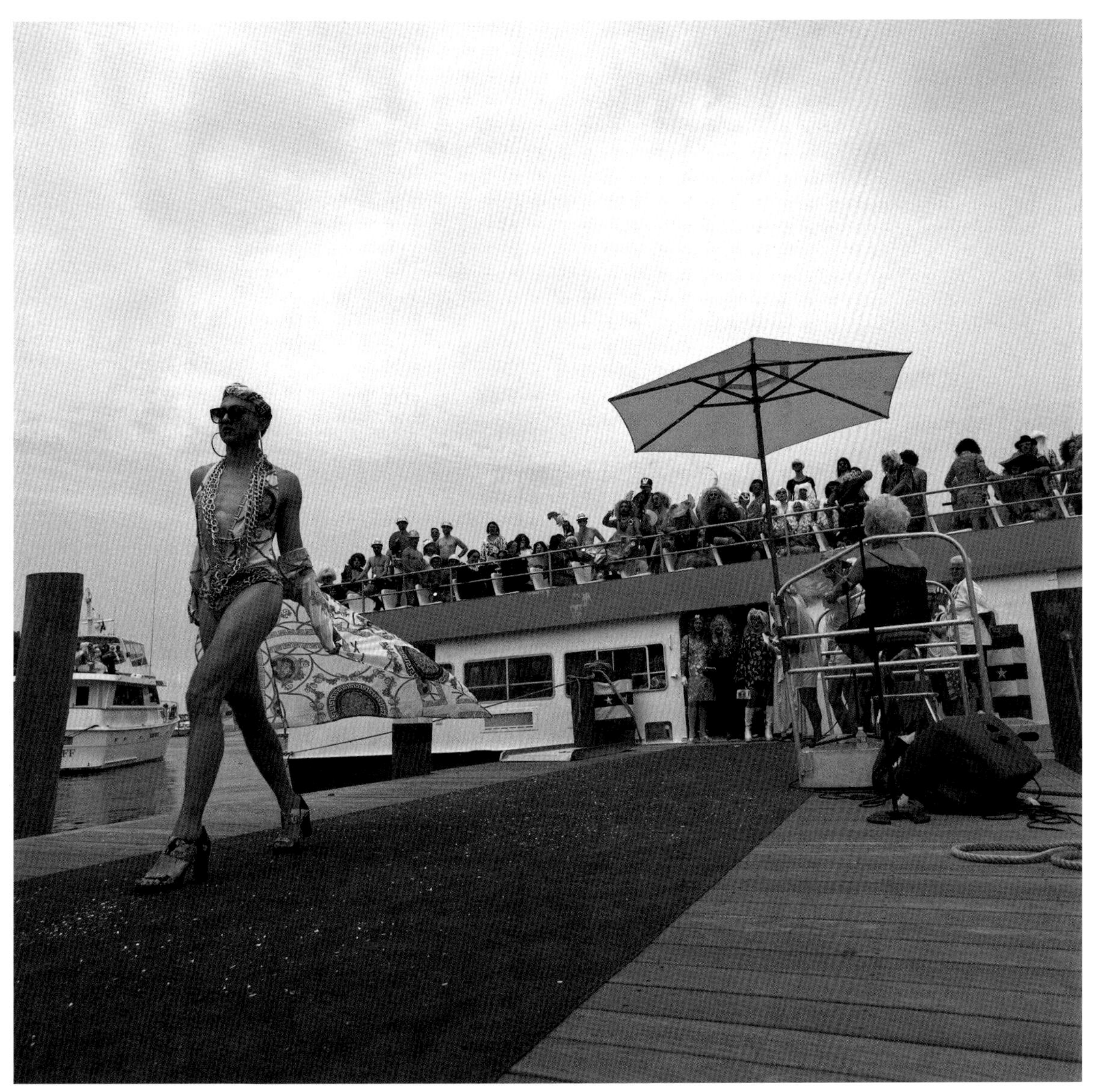

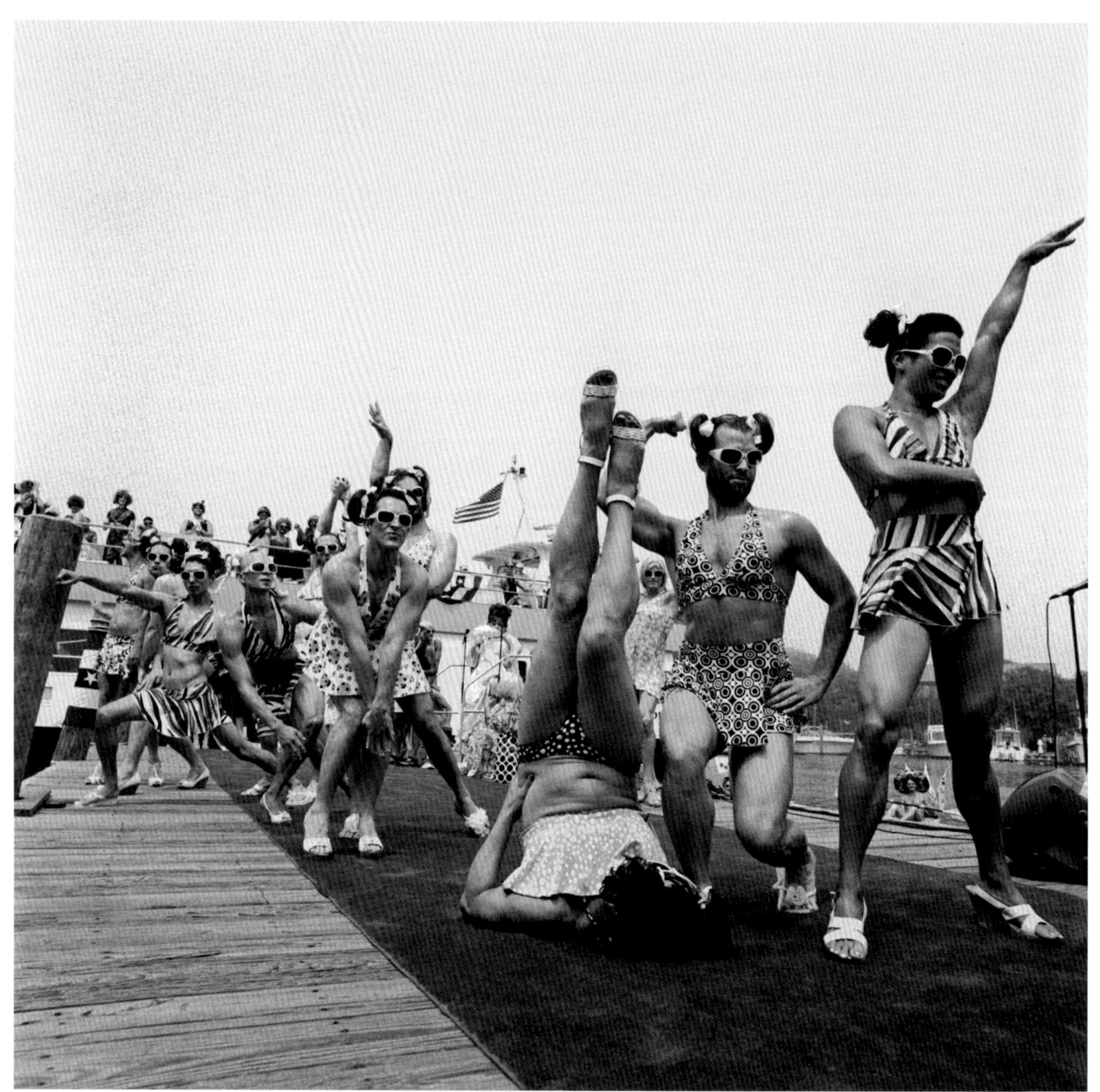

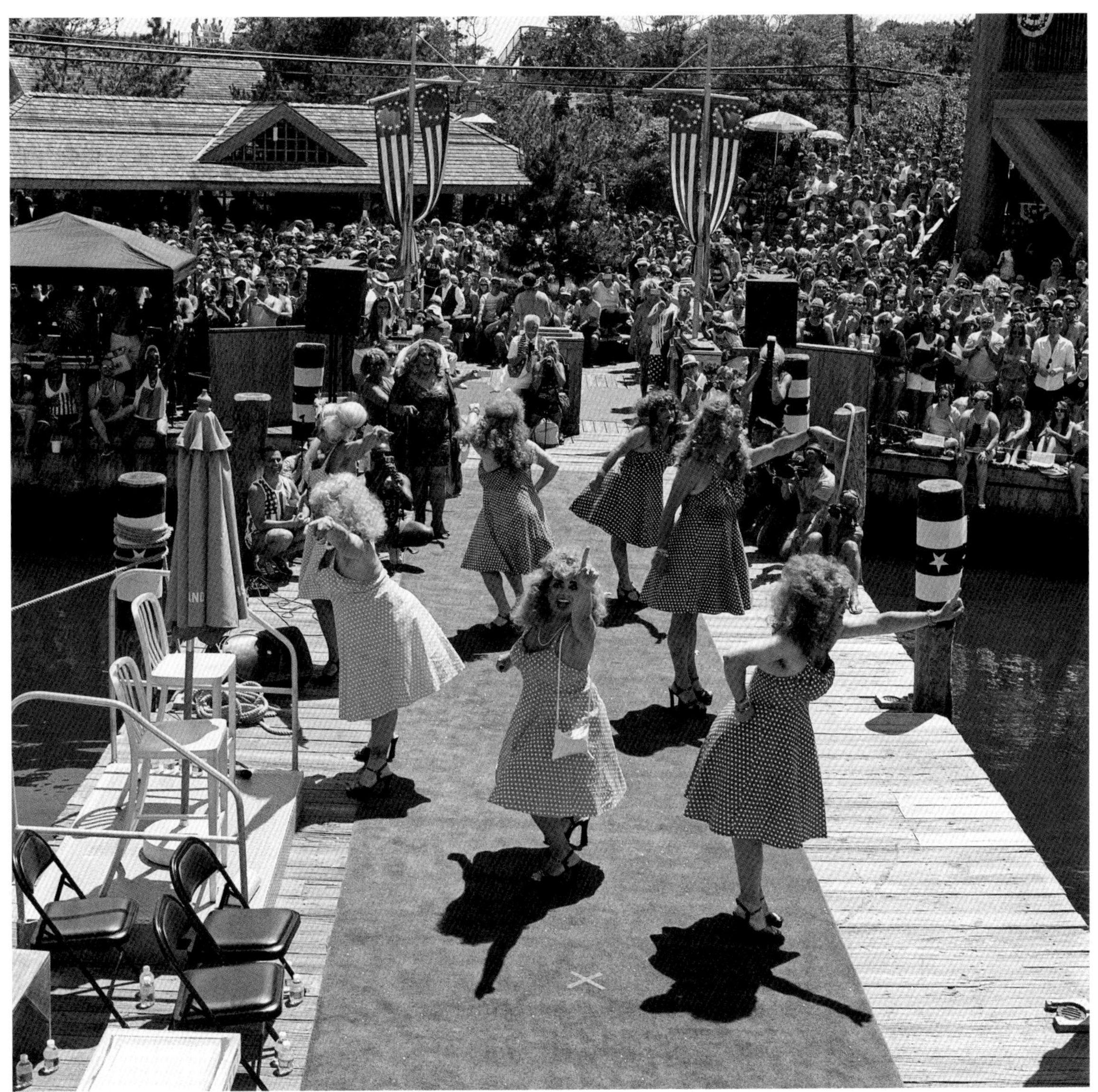

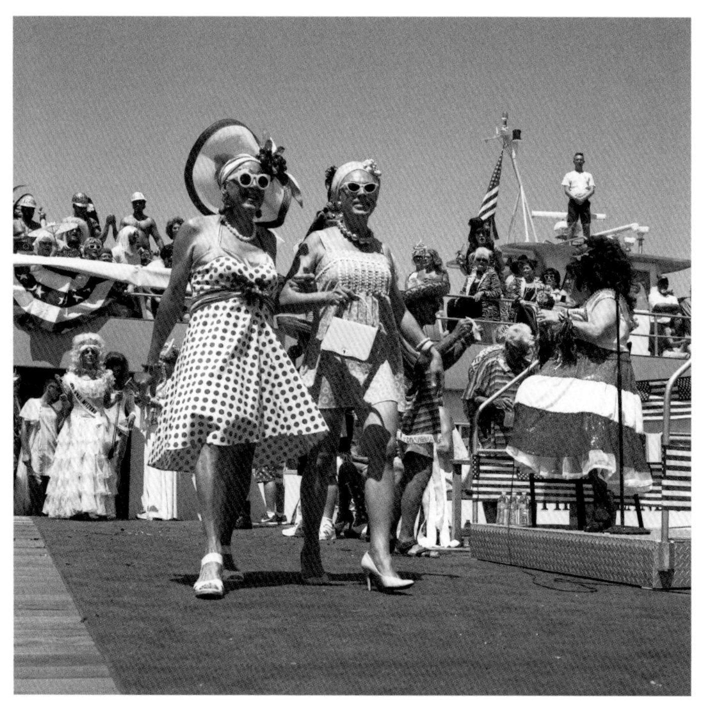

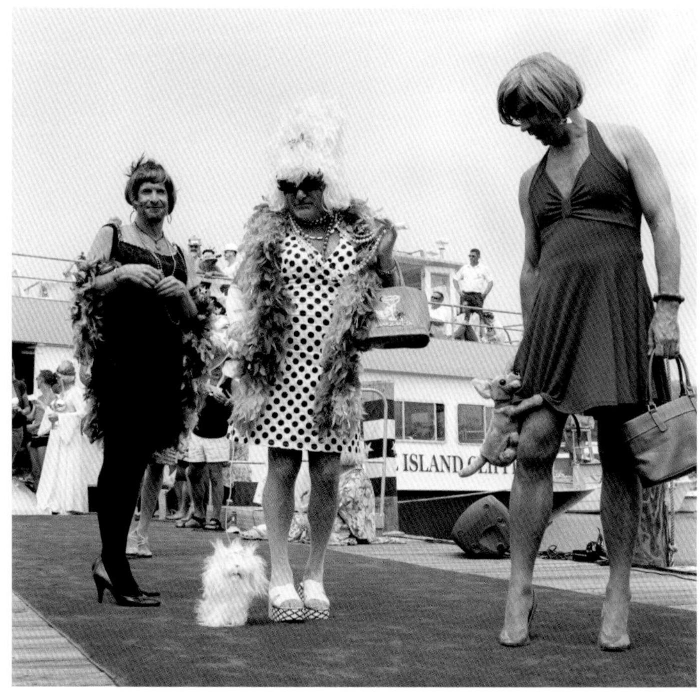

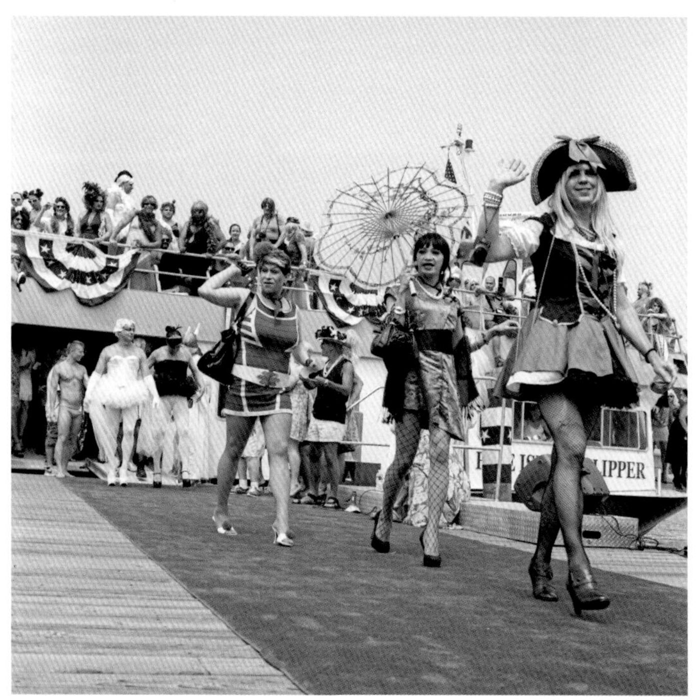

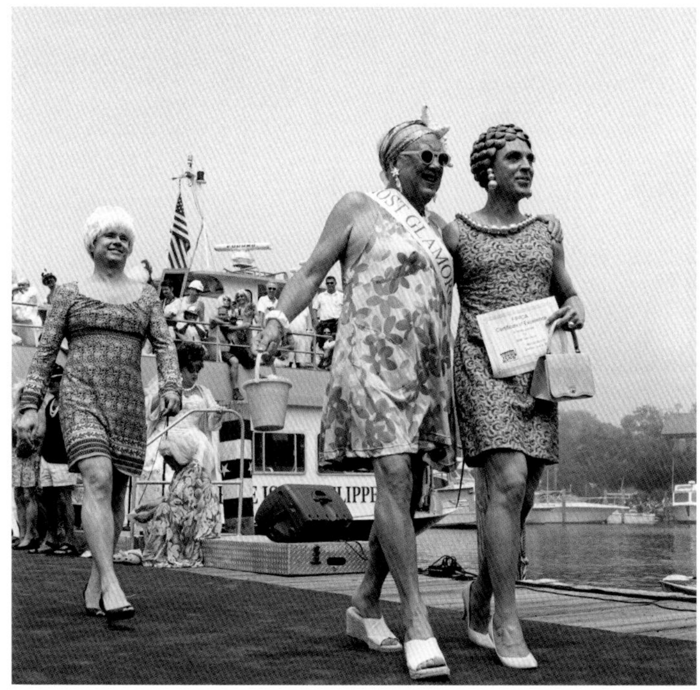

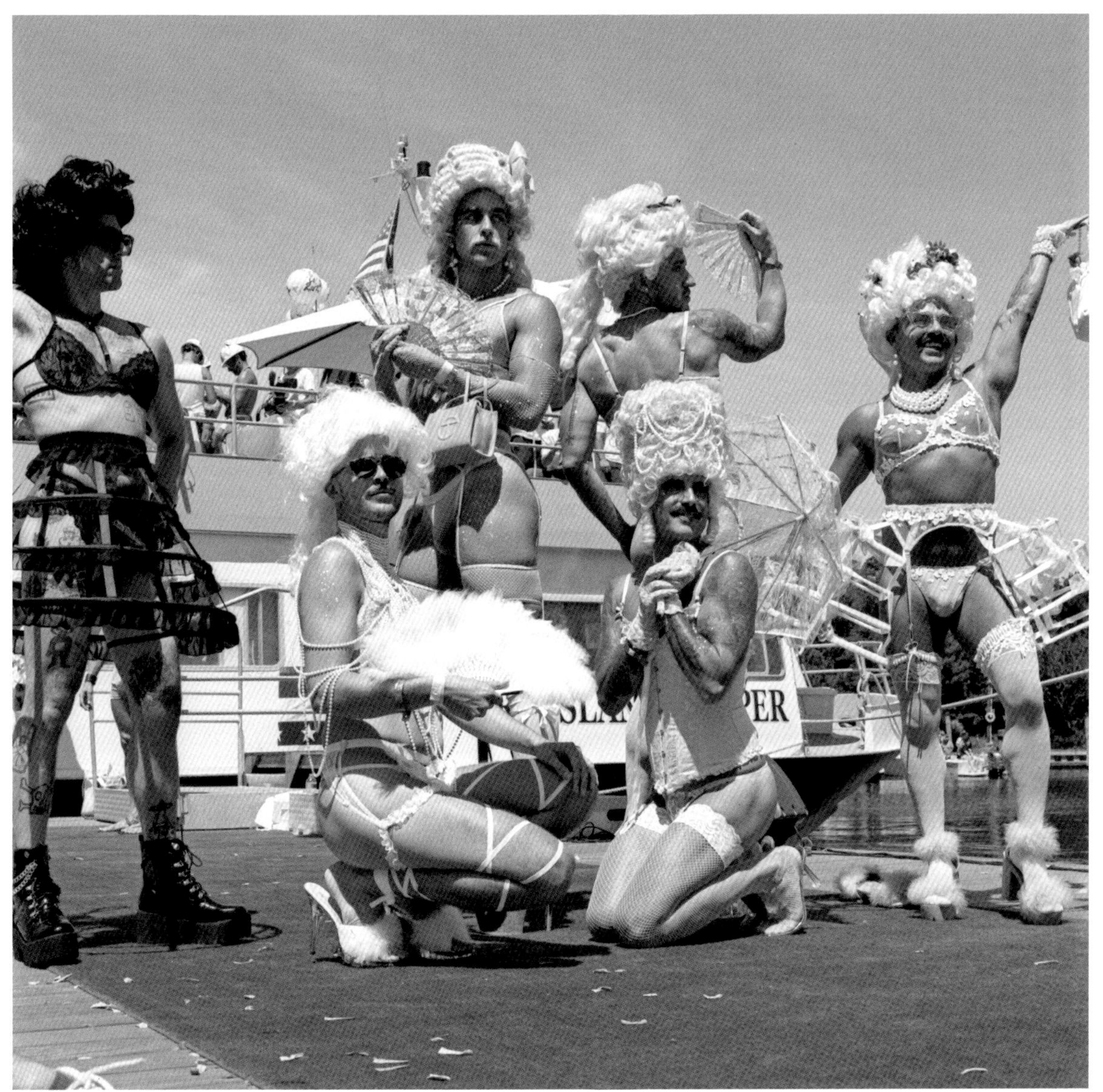

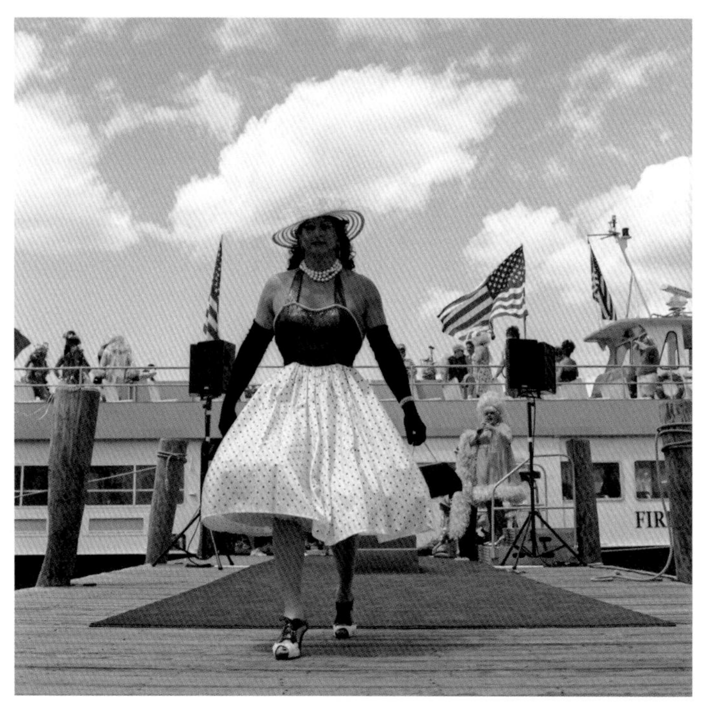
FIR

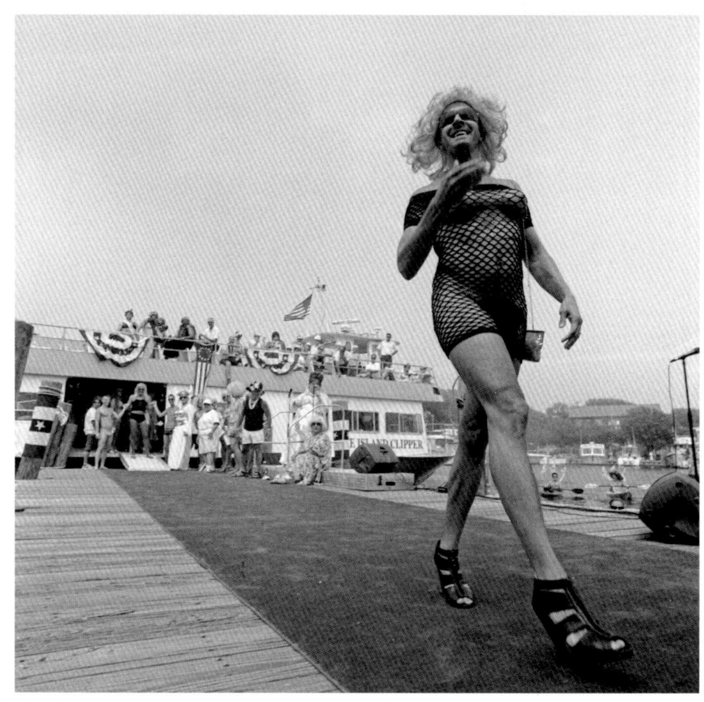
E ISLAND CLIPPER

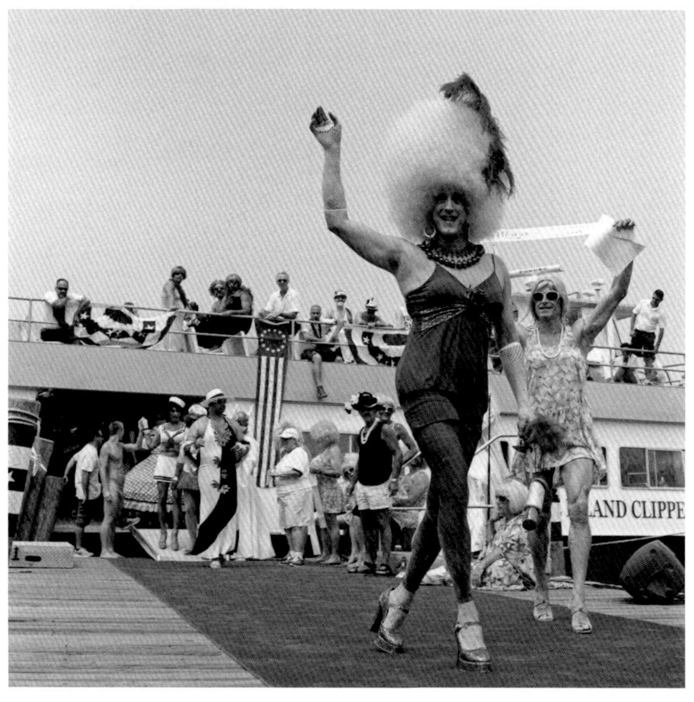
LAND CLIPPE

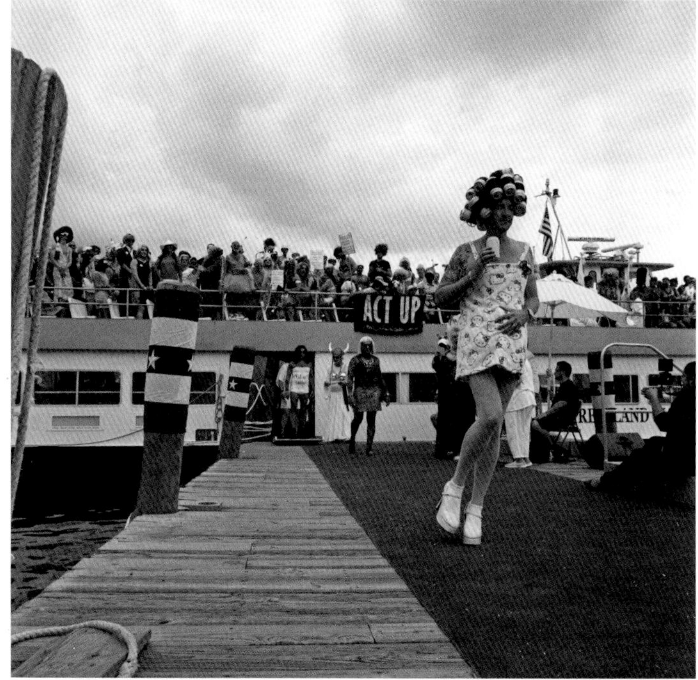
ACT UP

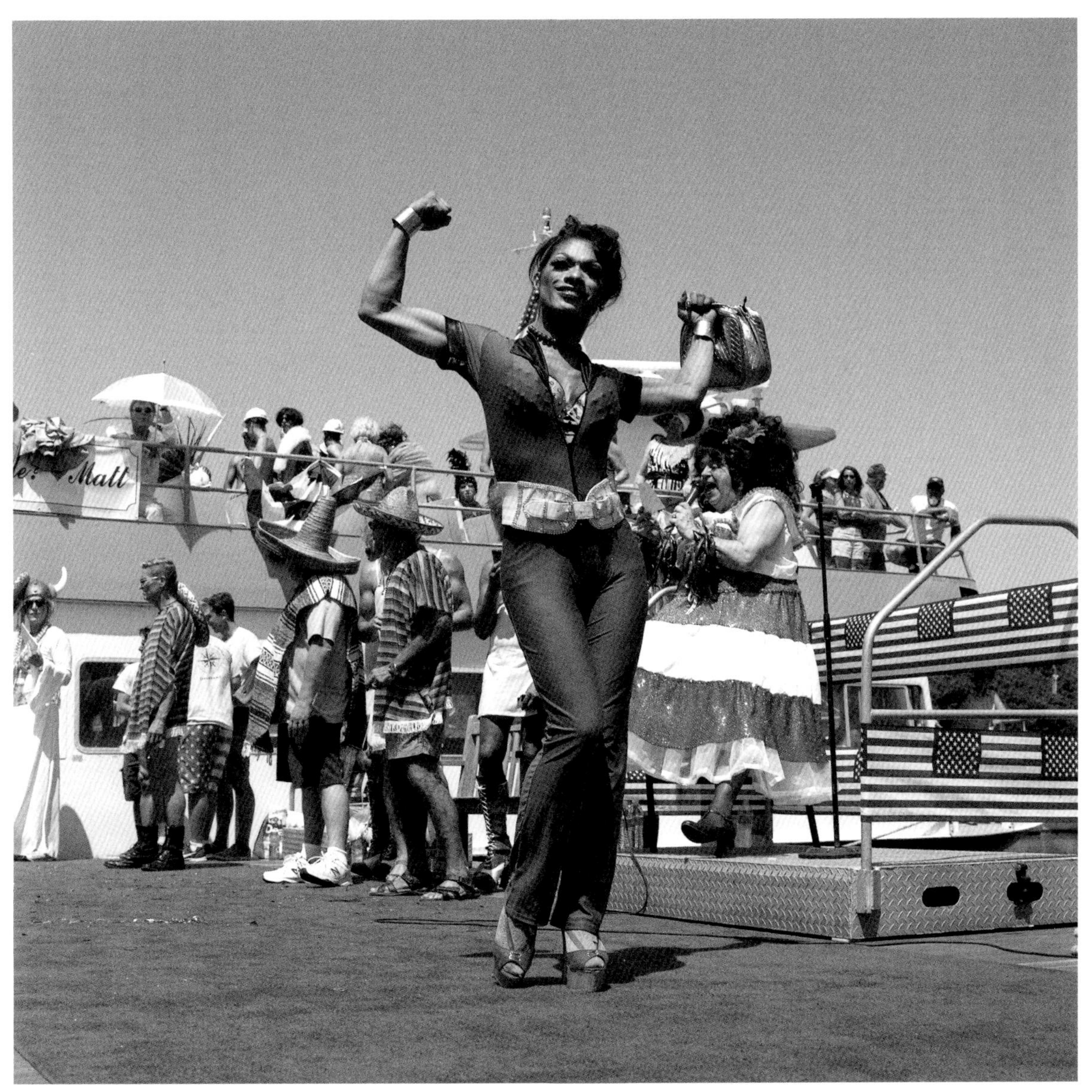
Matt

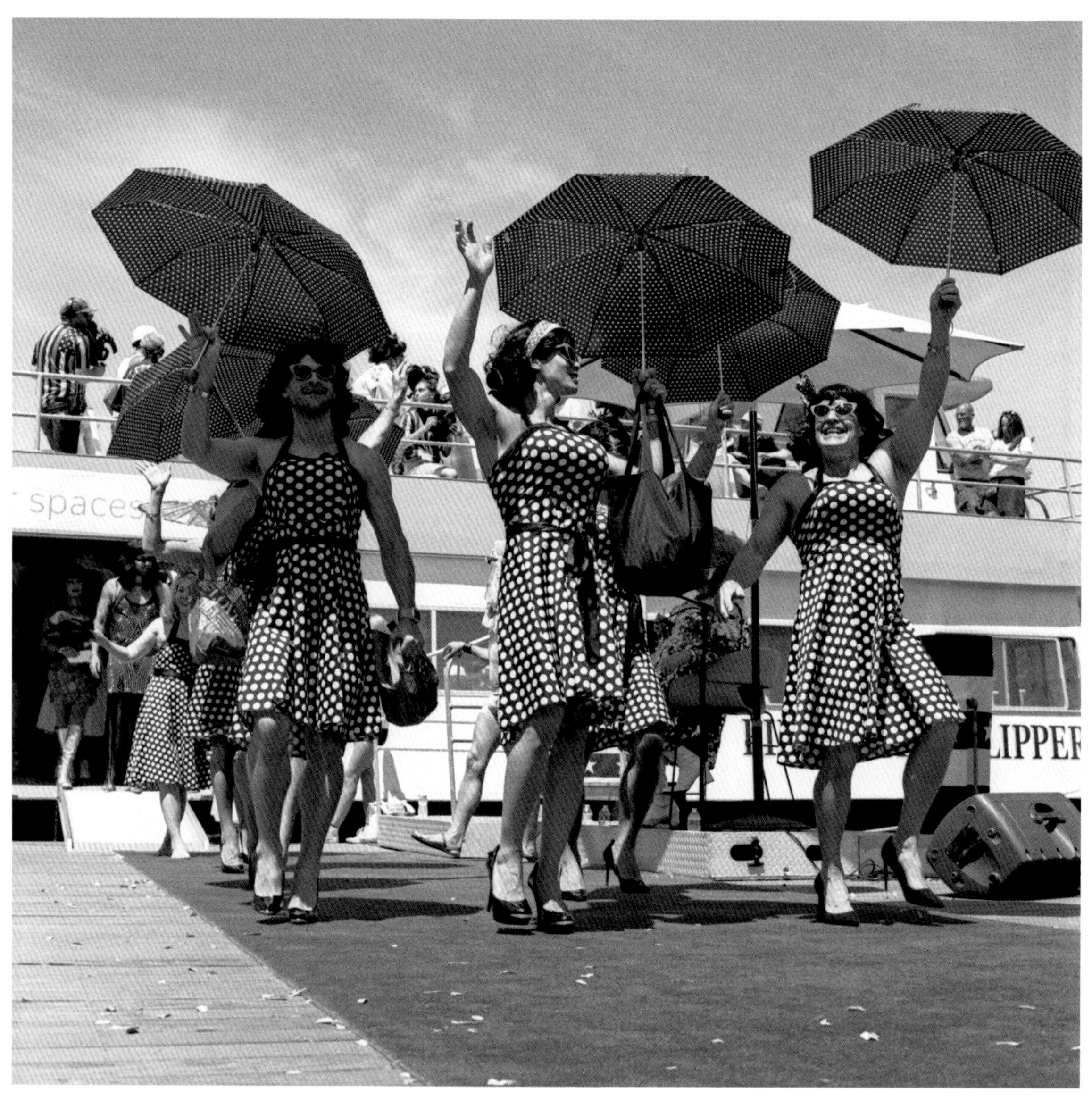
spaces
LIPPER

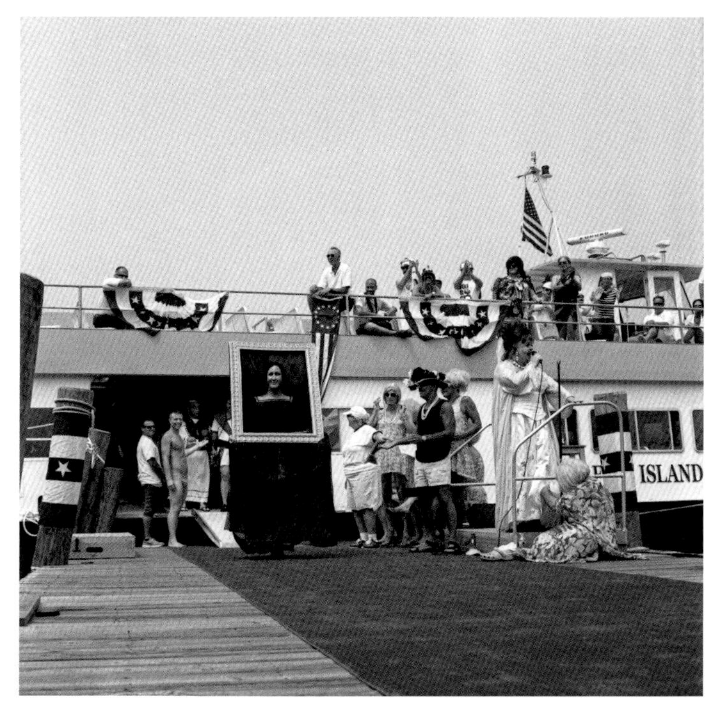
ISLAND

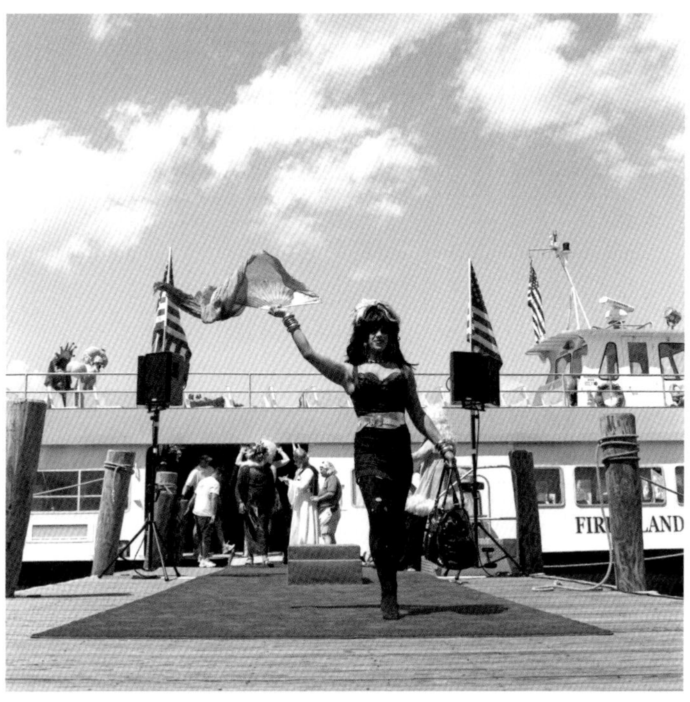

POOL PARTY

As the last queen steps off the boat, Panzi closes The Invasion ceremony. With a heartfelt message, she reminds everyone of its deep-rooted purpose: a celebration of defiance, freedom, and unity. Now that the formalities are behind them, the queens make their way to the iconic bars at The Pines and keep alive the long-standing tradition of "high tea". Today, the high tea tradition has evolved into something even grander. Donated by local bars, drinks flow freely, and the queens in elaborate costumes parade down the boardwalk. They pause often to pose for photographers, film–makers, and media crews capturing every glittering detail.

At the heart of the celebration is the pool party, a vibrant scene filled with energy and spontaneity. Some queens take to the poolside stage, dancing and performing for the crowd. Others mingle with onlookers, drawing them into the festivities with every smile and twirl. The air is filled with the clinking of glasses, the pulse of music, and the sound of laughter, as queens, performers, and spectators alike revel in the joy of the moment.

Many take a brief pause from the action, retreating to quiet corners by the pool to rest, adjust their costumes, and ensure their elaborate headpieces remain intact. Yet, there's no time to linger. The hour at The Pines passes quickly, as it always has since the original Invasion. Soon, Mr. Klein's loud horn signals the queens to wrap up the festivities. With hurried smiles and waves, they begin to make their way back to the dock, knowing it's time to return to Cherry Grove. They leave behind the lively pool party but carry with them the memories of yet another triumphant celebration of pride, resilience, and community.

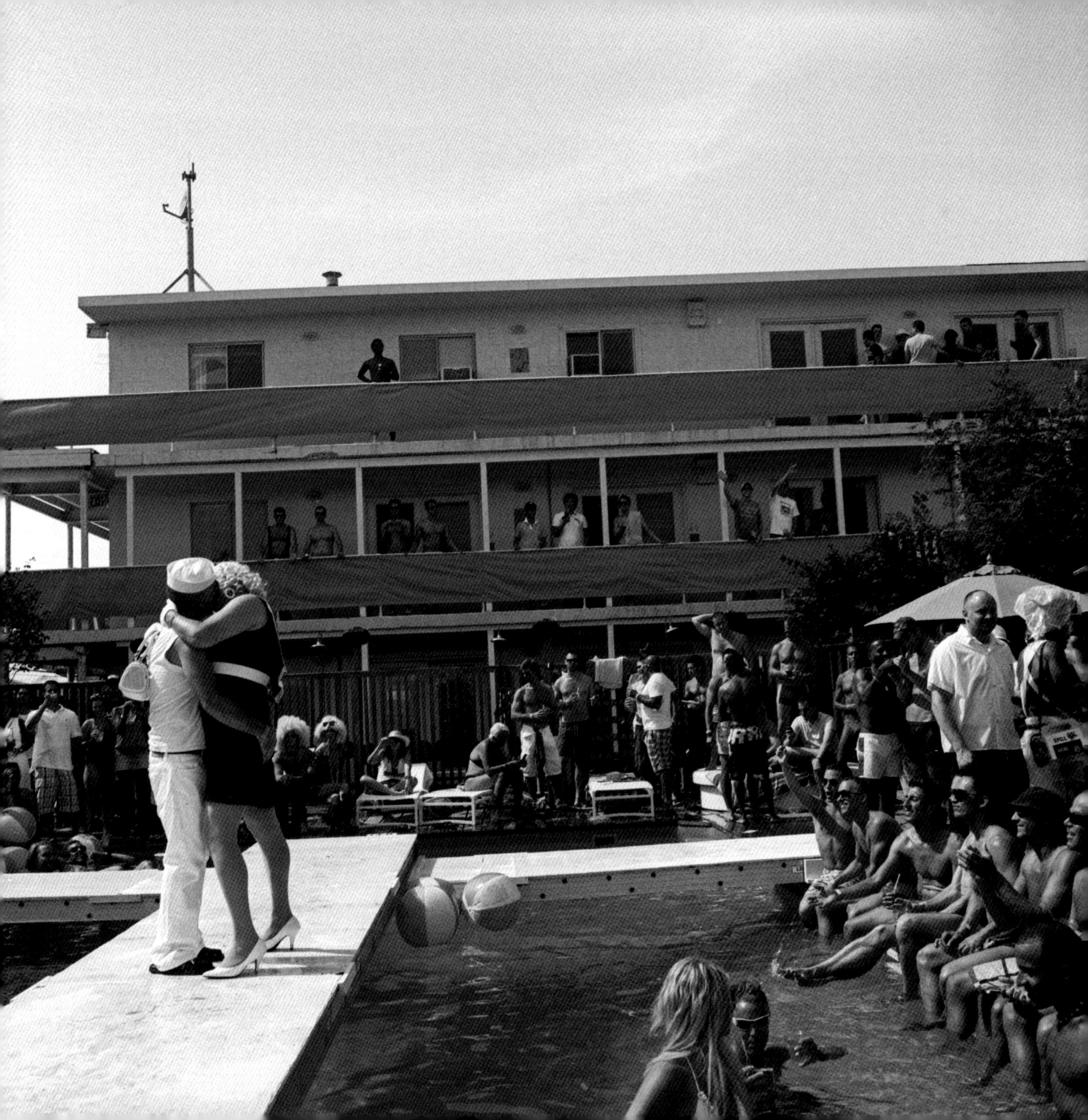

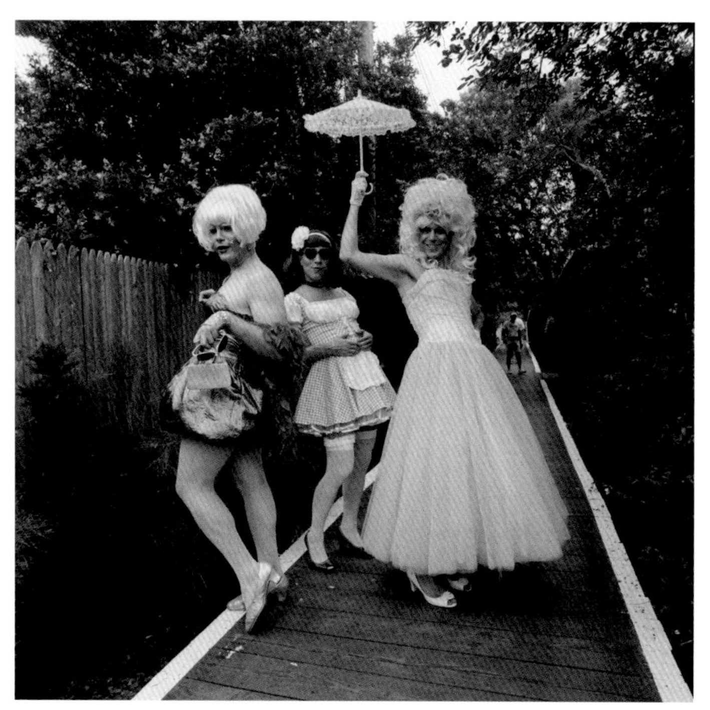

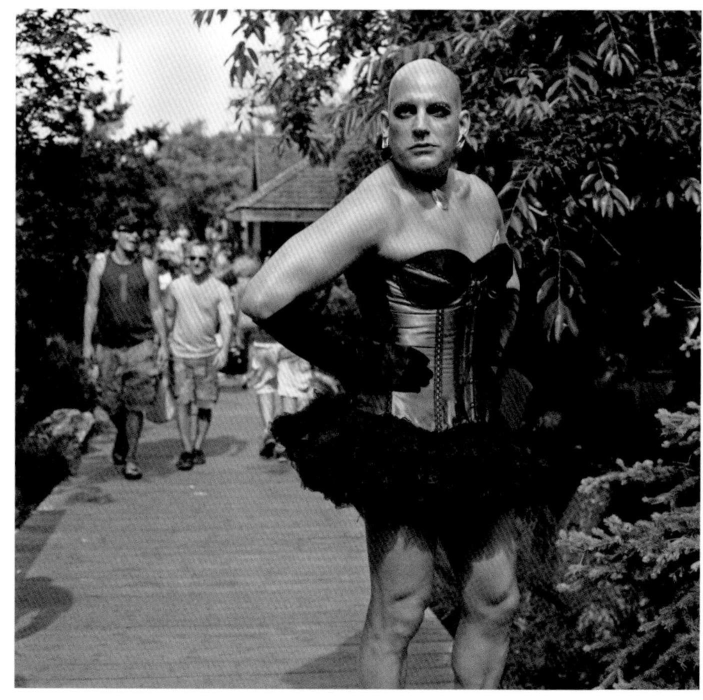

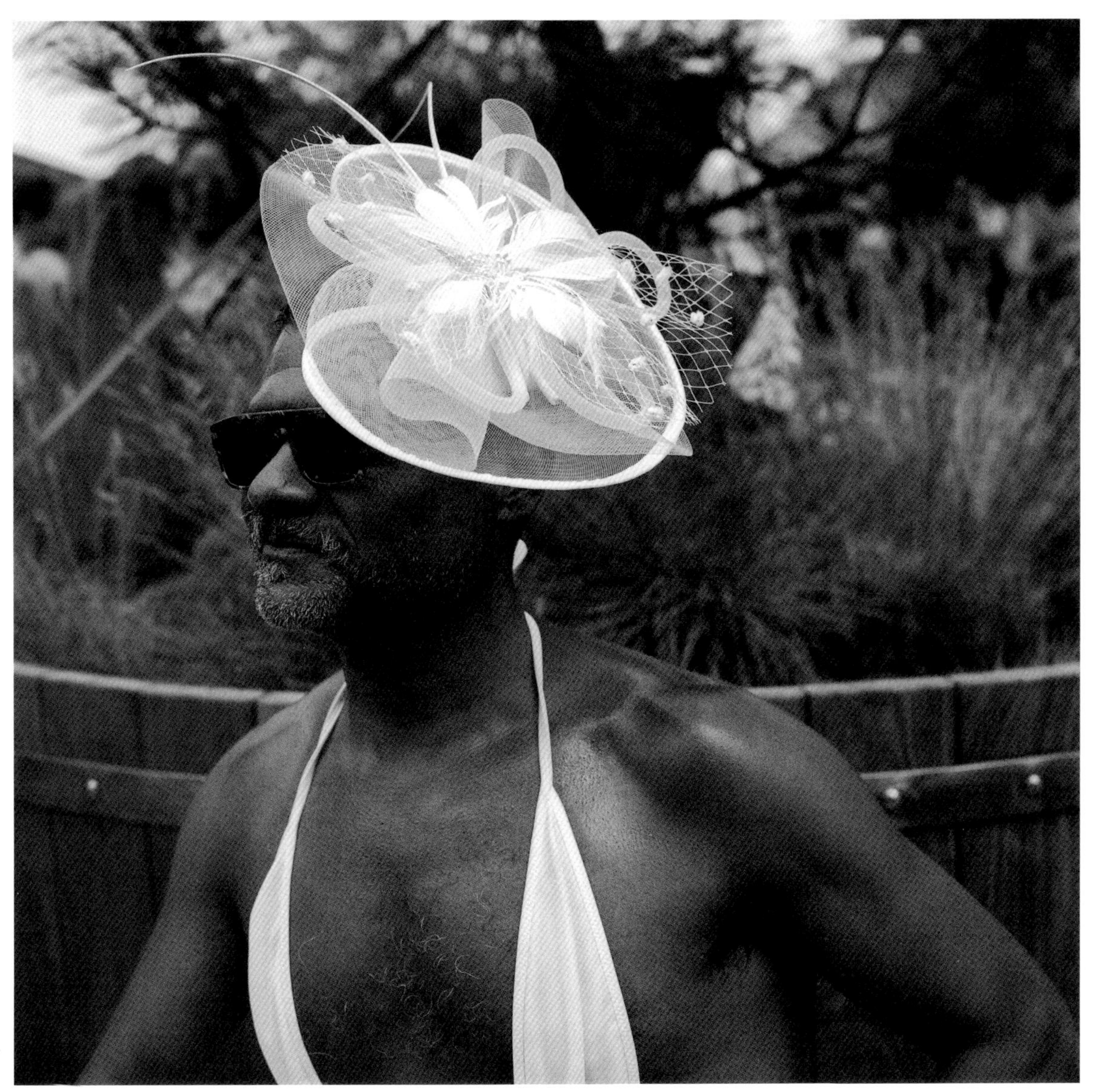

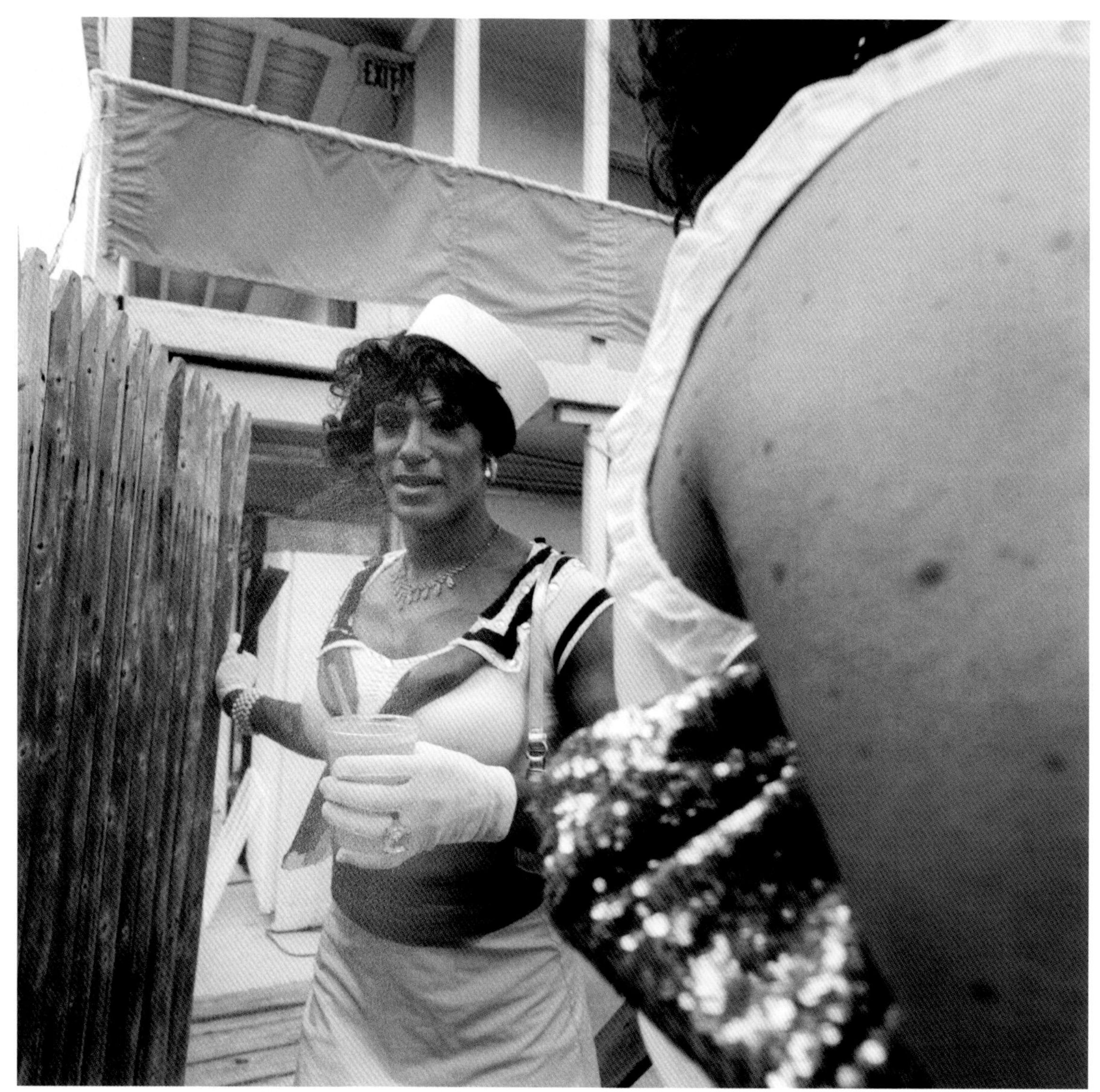
EXIT

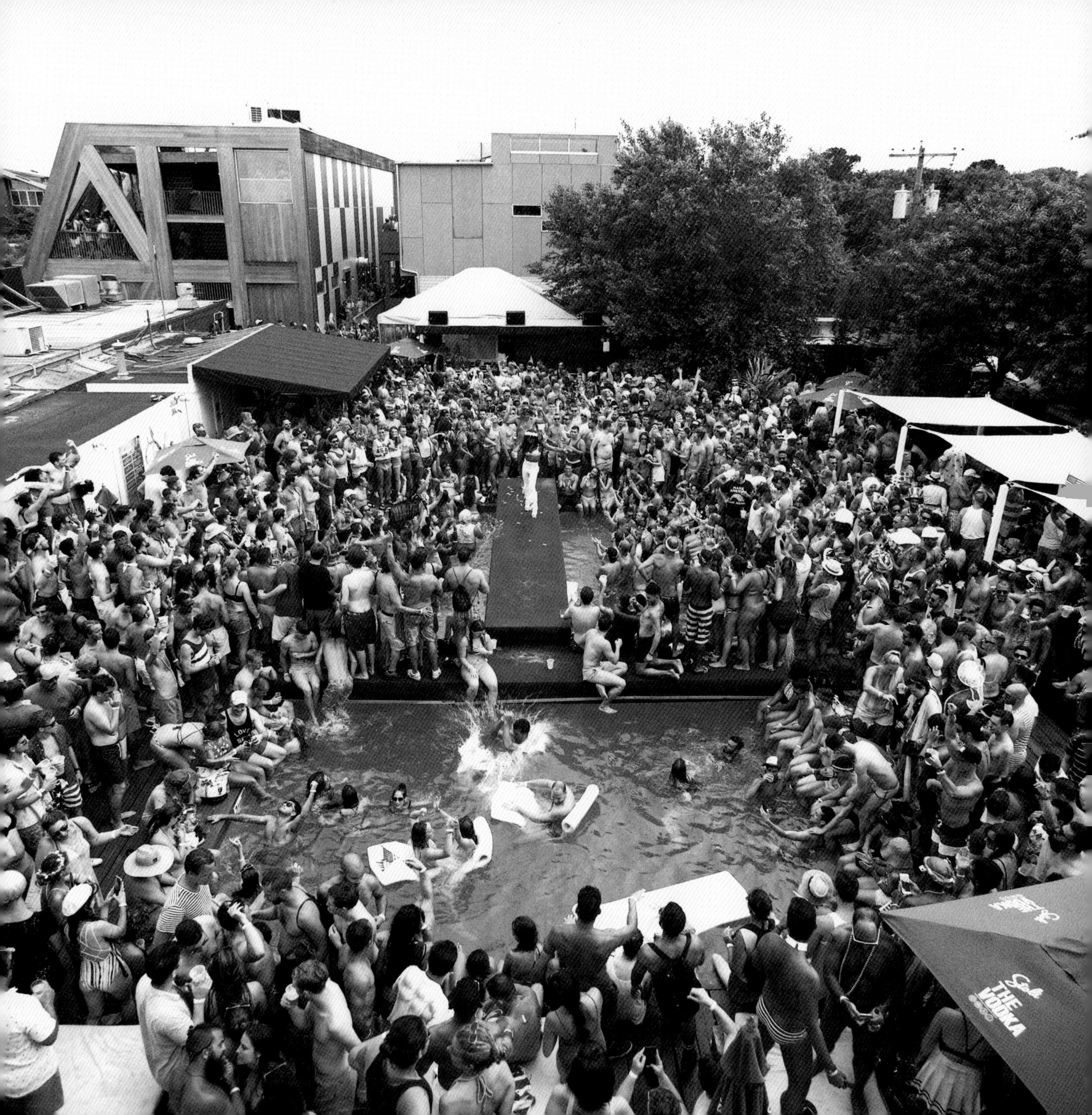
THE VODKA

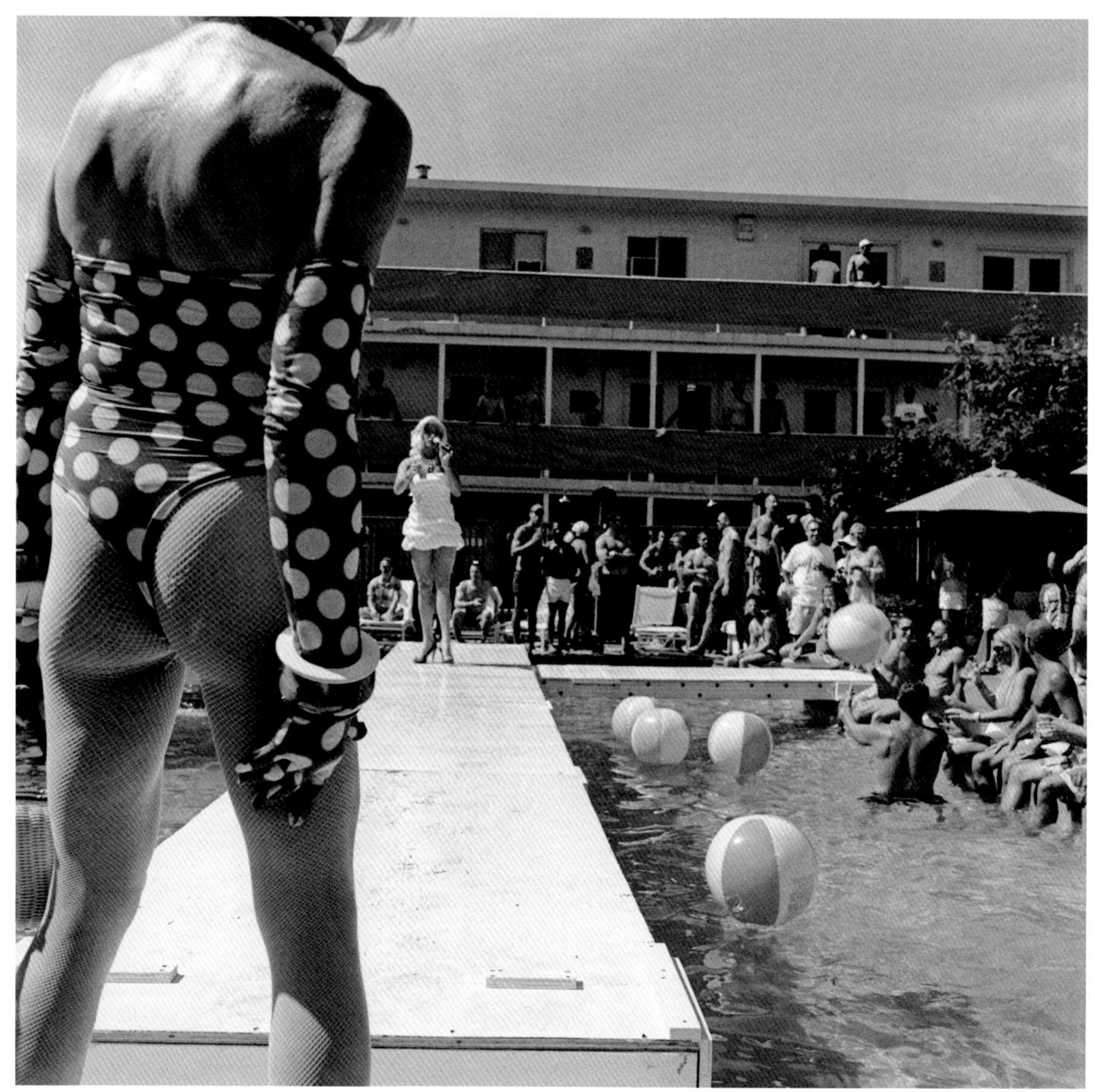

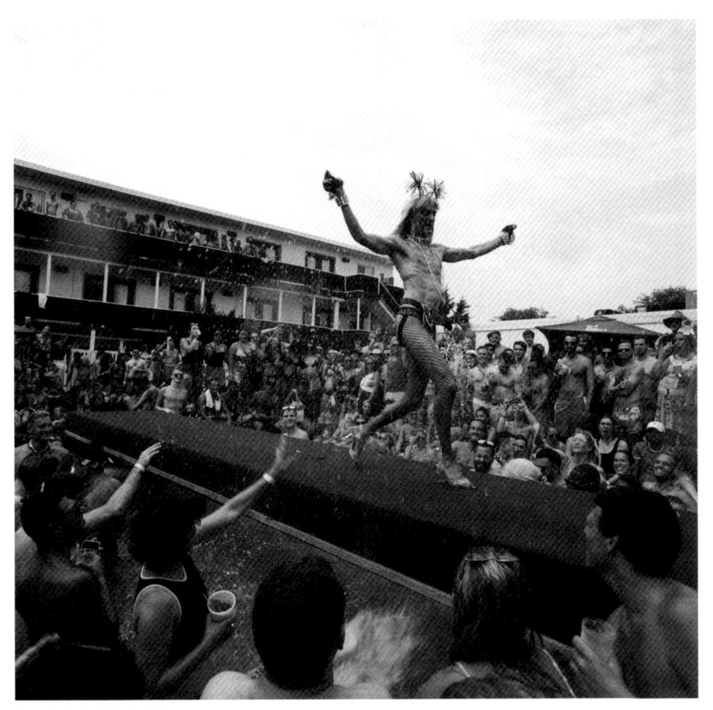

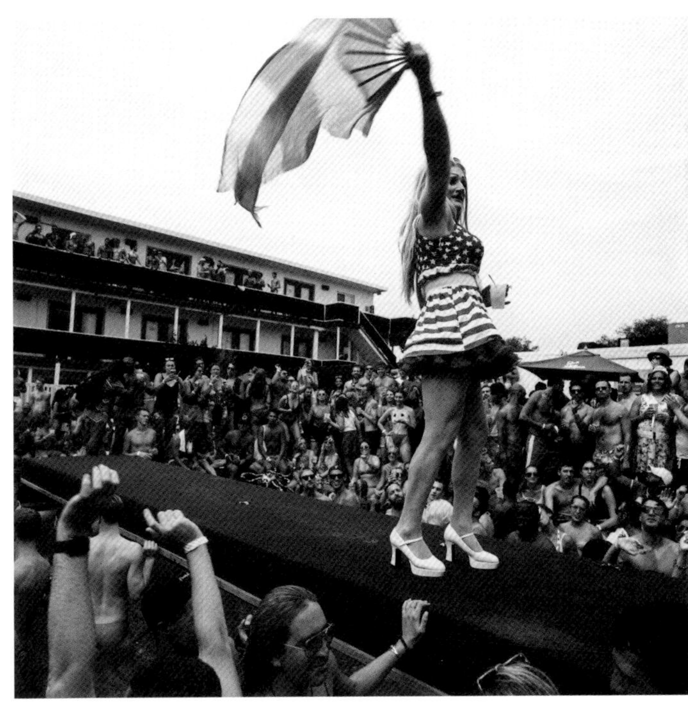

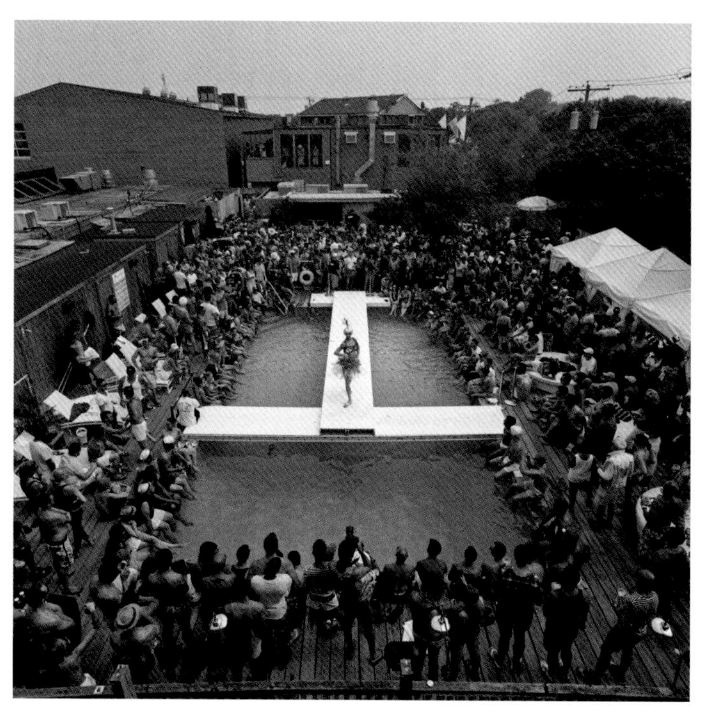

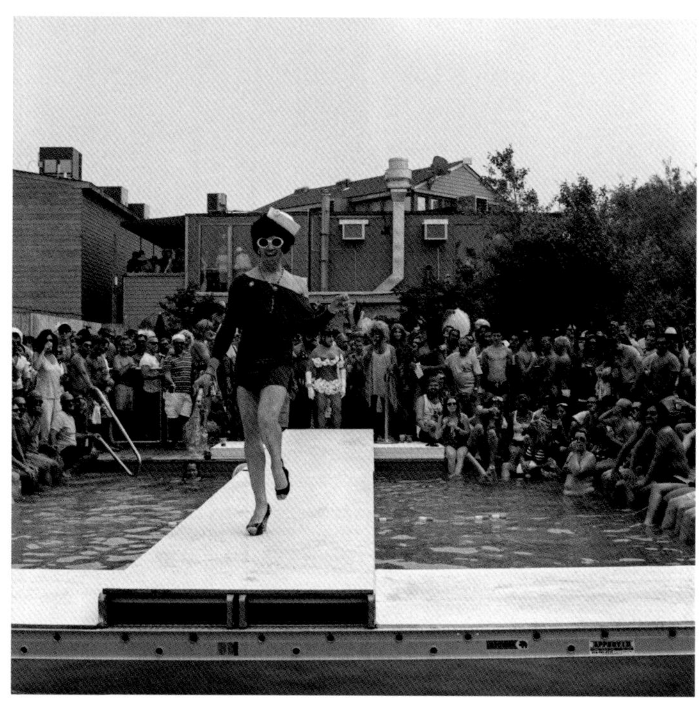

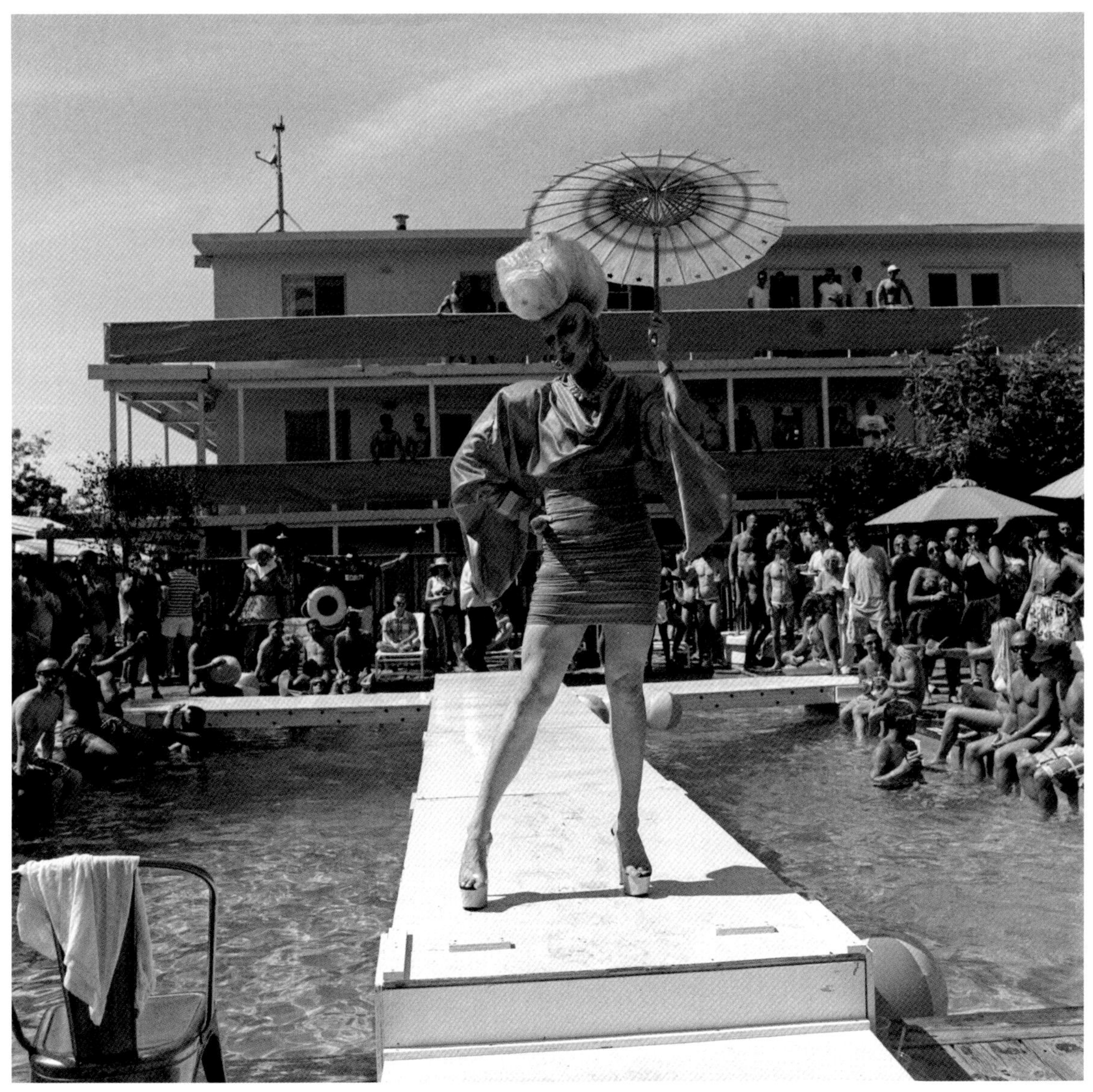

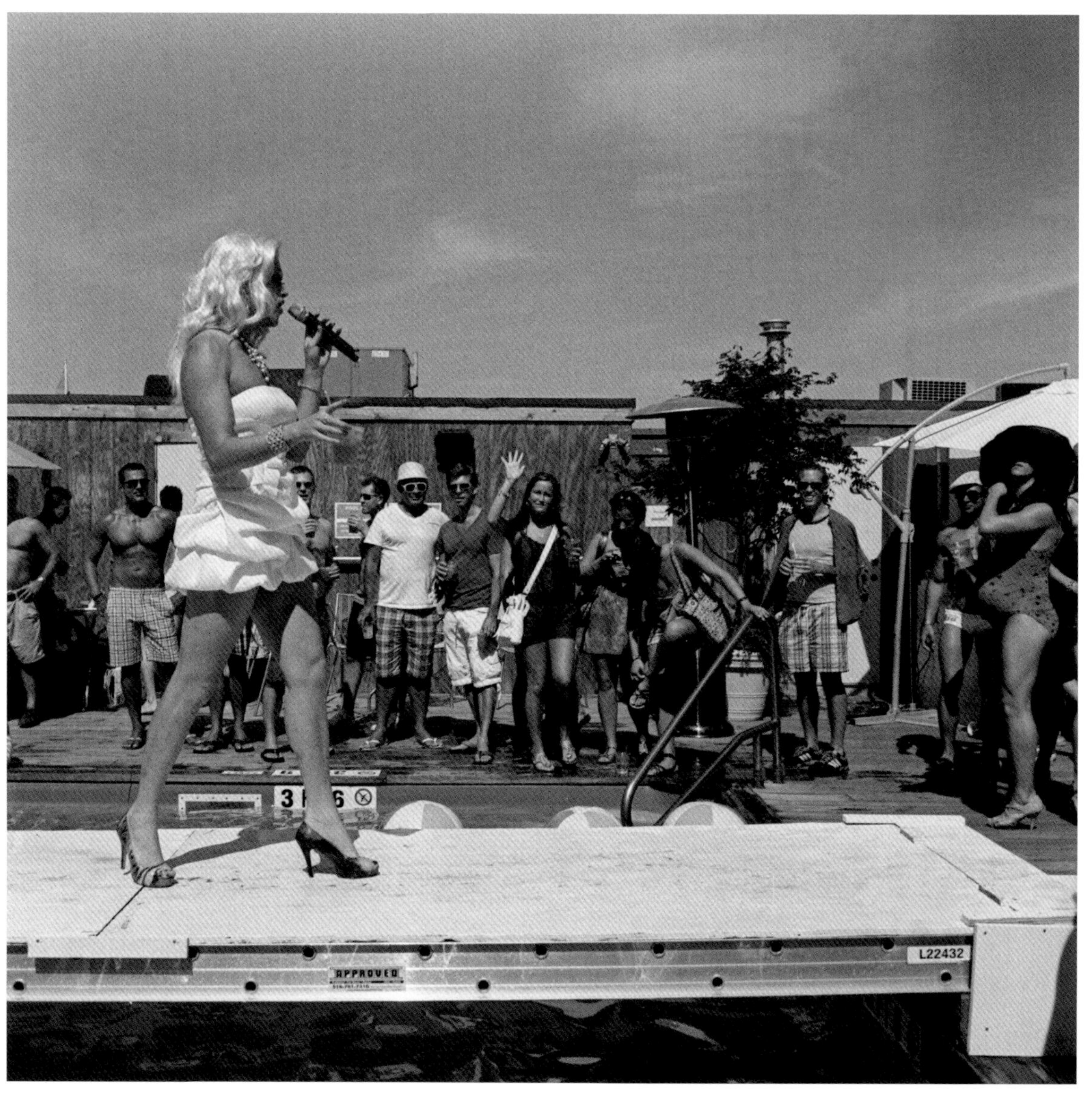
APPROVED
L22432

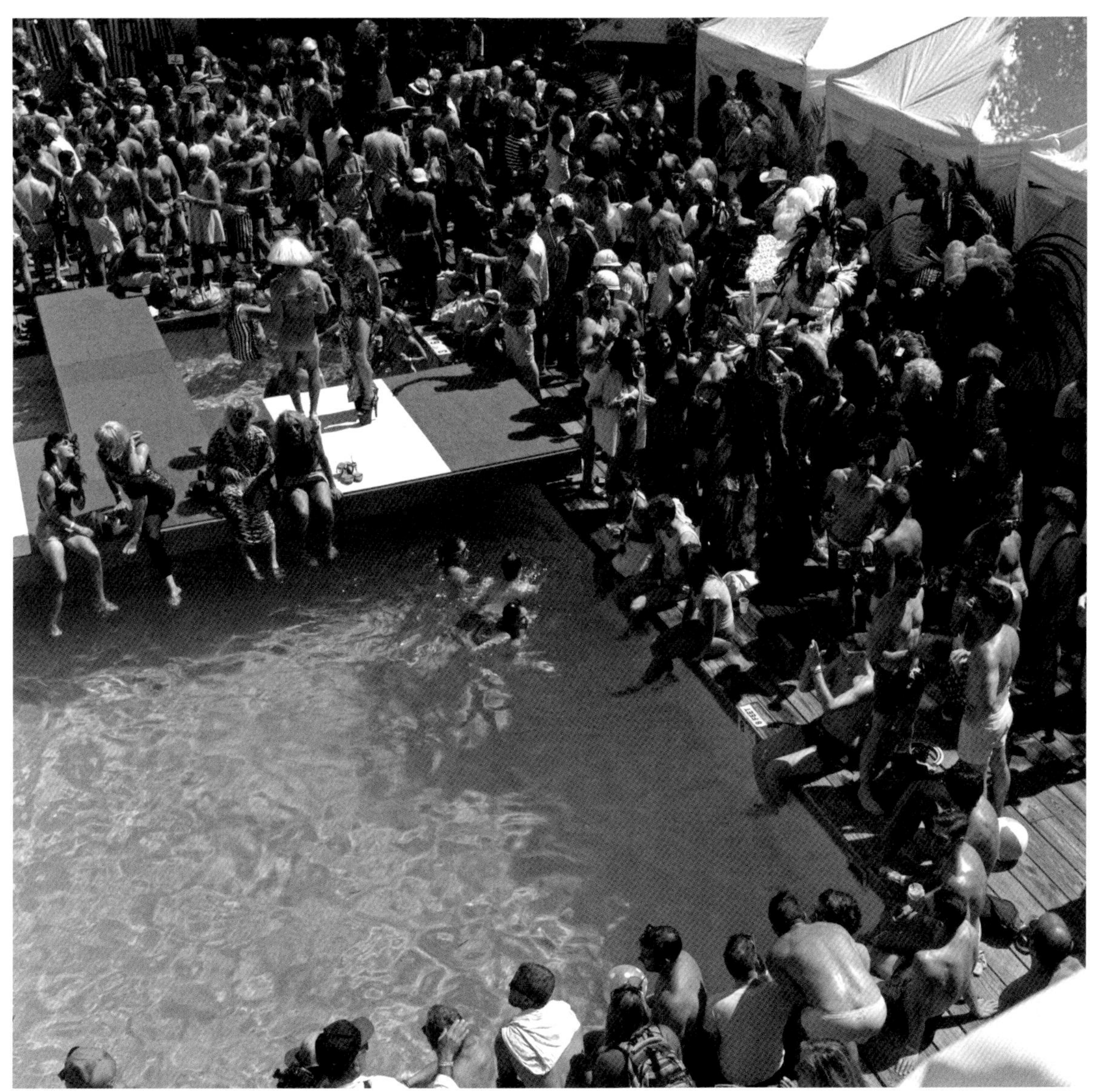

"The Invasion is a reminder of Queerness' roots breaking boundaries and transforming oppositions."

Carlo Maria Ampil

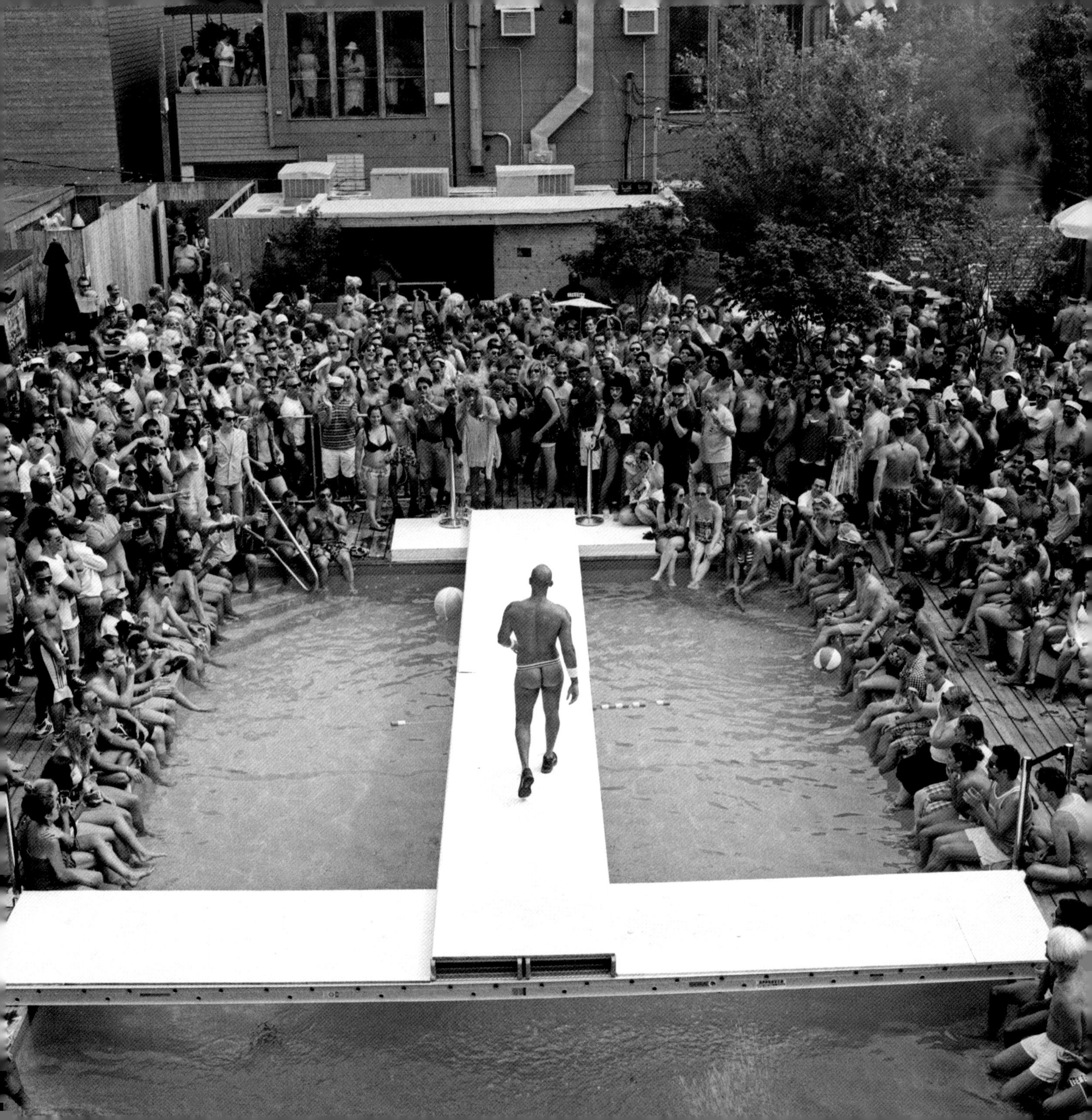

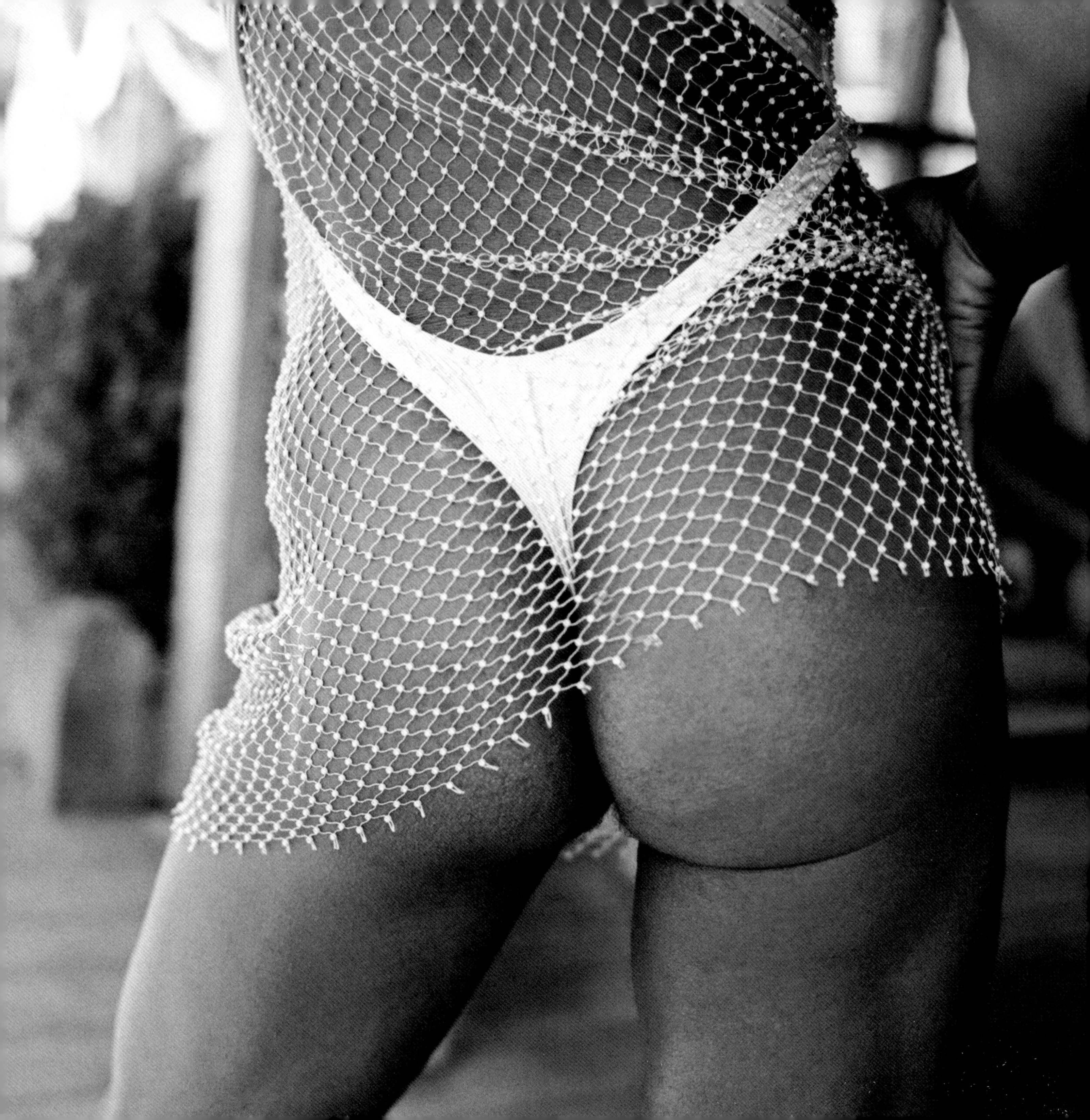

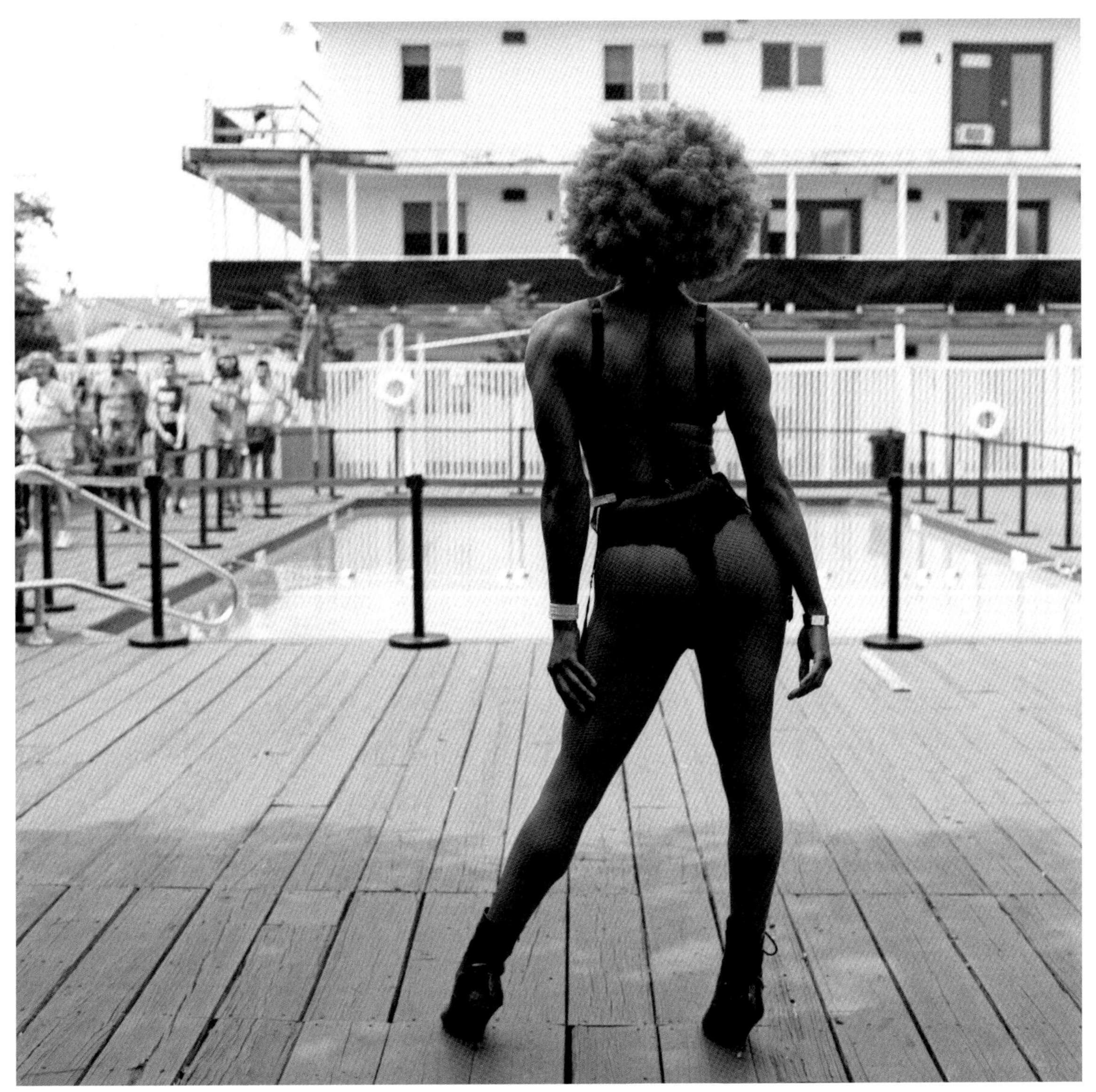

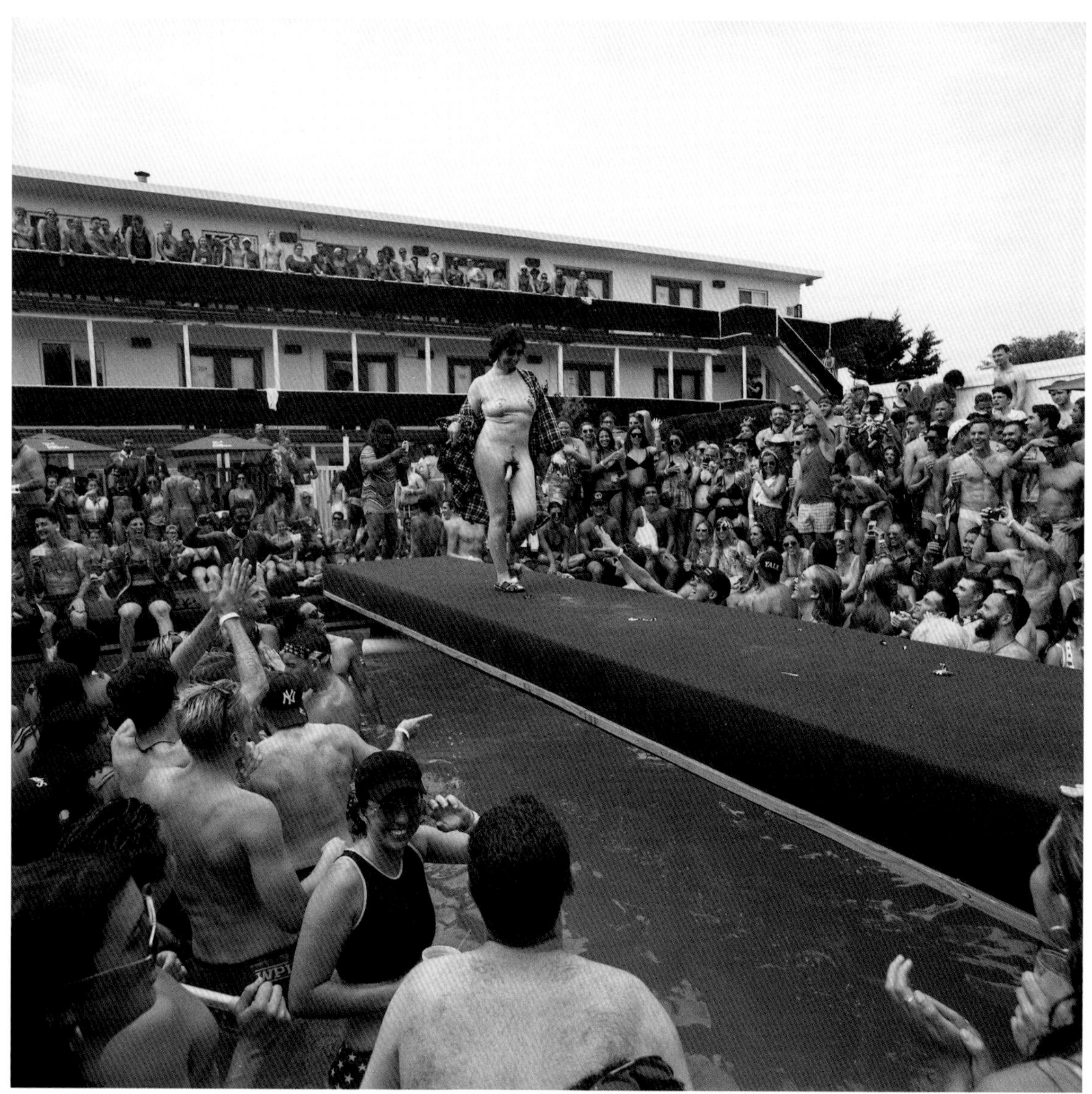

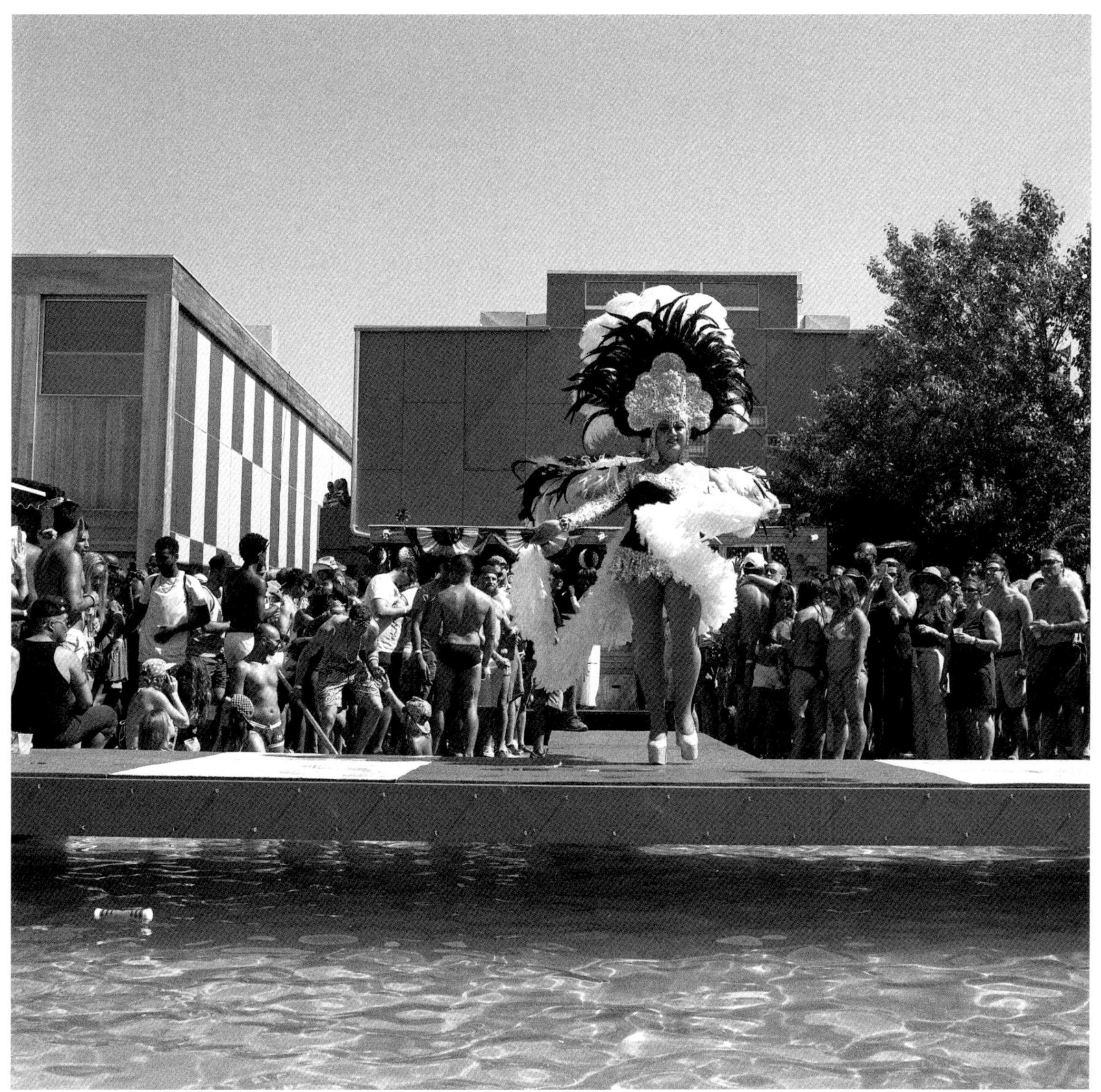

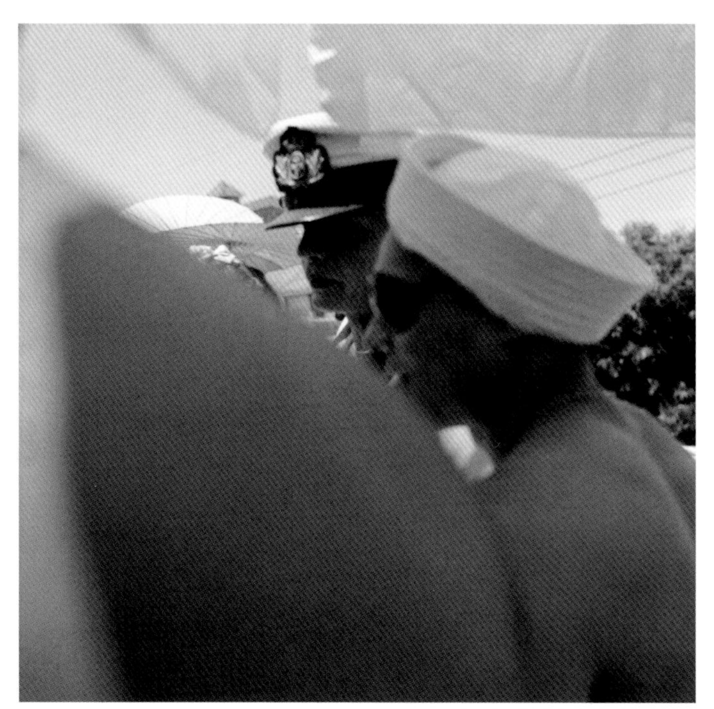

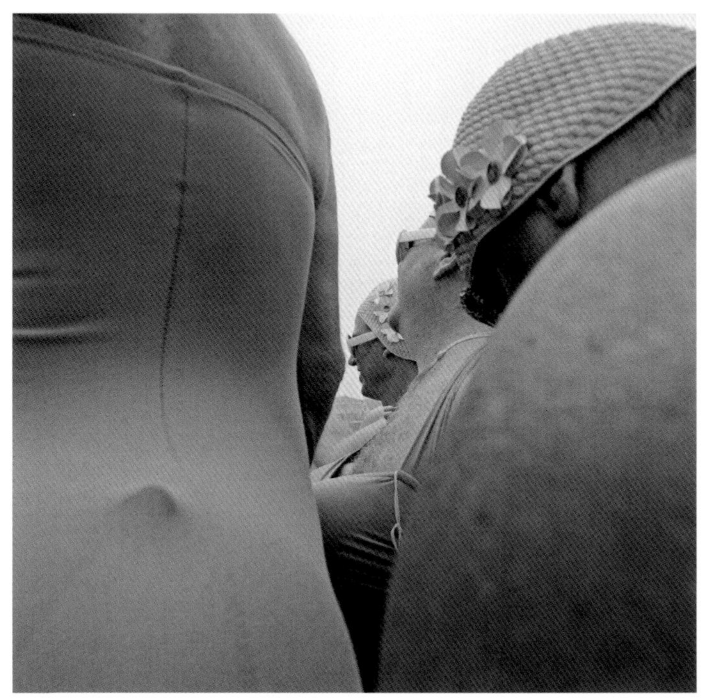

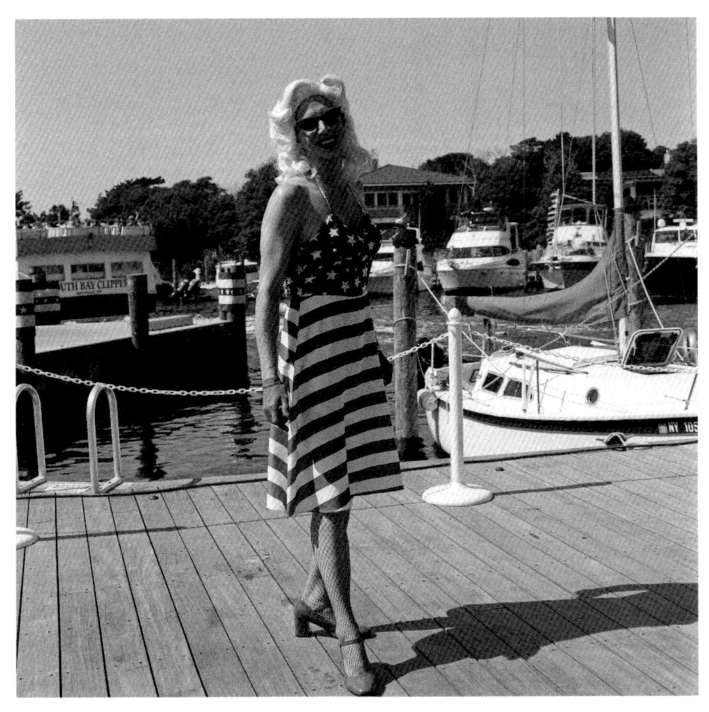
UTH BAY CLIPPE
NY 105

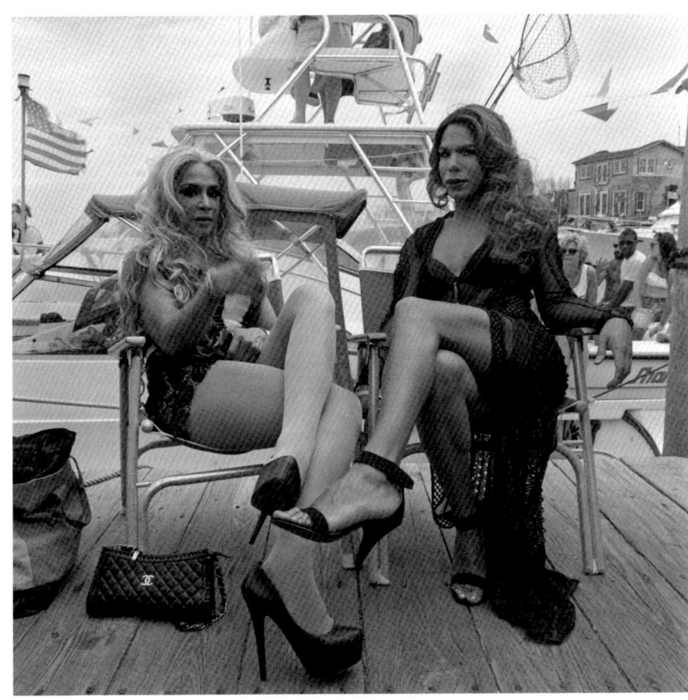

HOMECOMING

As the excitement from The Pines fades into the distance, the queens once again board the ferry, this time heading back to Cherry Grove. Awaiting their return is a local crowd, ready to welcome the year's Homecoming Queen and her entourage with open arms. The atmosphere buzzes with anticipation as the queens arrive, greeted with cheers and applause. Cherry Grove is now a sea of vibrant faces and glittering lights, and this sets the stage for the next phase of the day's festivities.

At the heart of the celebration is the iconic Ice Palace, with its shimmering pool and legendary disco. It is here that the Homecoming Queen passes the torch to her successor in a ceremony rich with tradition, emotion, and a touch of humor. From queens to Palace guests, the crowd gathers closely, all united to witness the crowning of the new Homecoming Queen of Cherry Grove. This is a moment symbolic of the spirit of The Invasion.

Following this ceremony, many of the queens finally take the chance to unwind, having been in their extravagant costumes since early morning. Some kick off their heels, remove their wigs and headpieces, and peel off lashes that have weathered hours of performances, parades, and heat. A few even make the ultimate leap and dive into the cool waters of the Ice Palace pool, a refreshing reprieve after a long day of sweat and spectacle.

As the performances continue by the poolside, the day slowly fades. One by one, queens and spectators begin to drift away, carried off by the fading light of the sunset. The air is thick with a sense of dreamy satisfaction, as if the day itself was a vivid, surreal fantasy. As the last traces of the Homecoming celebration melt into the night, nearly everyone leaves with the same sense of anticipation, eager to relive the magic all over again next year.

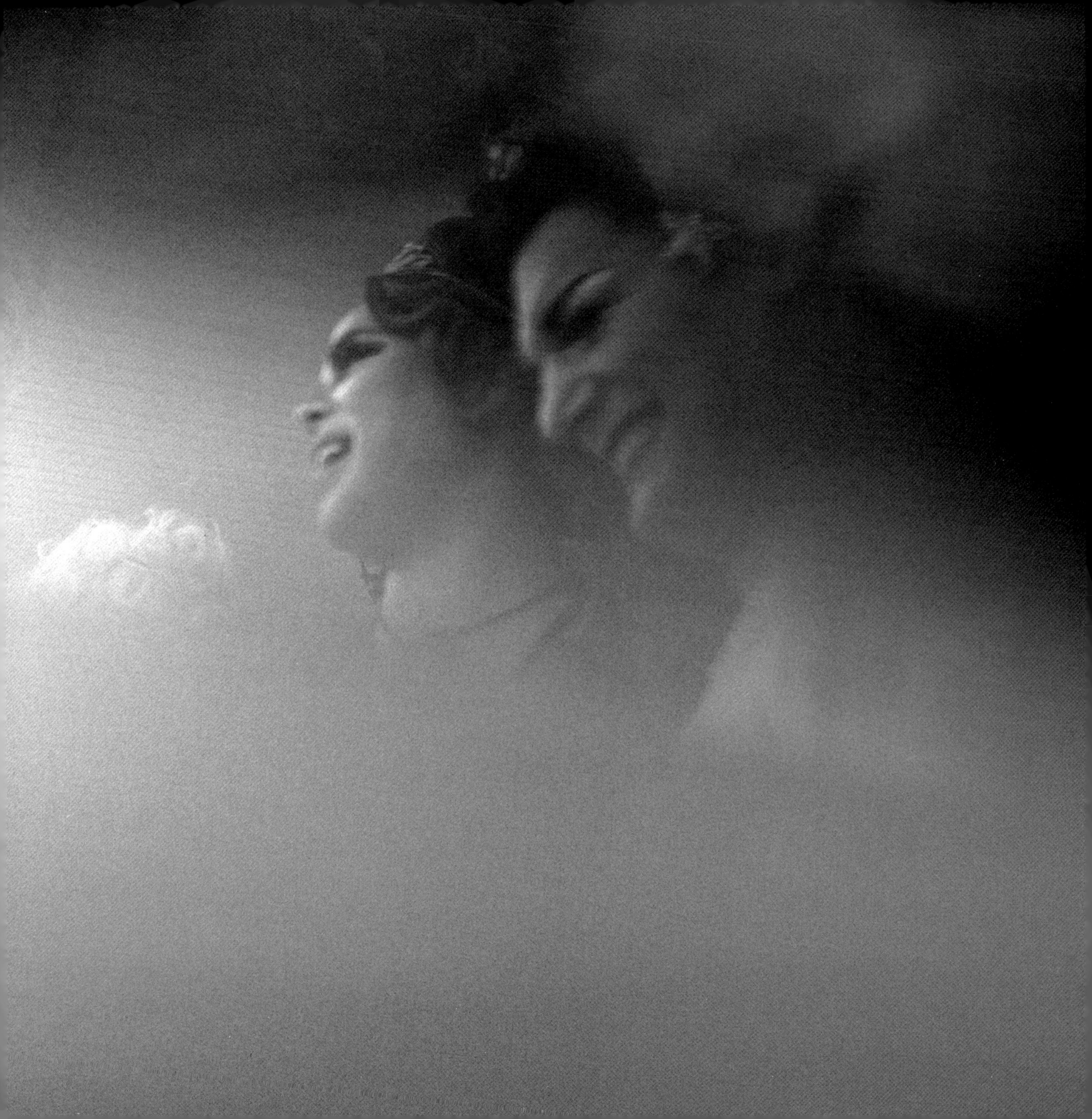

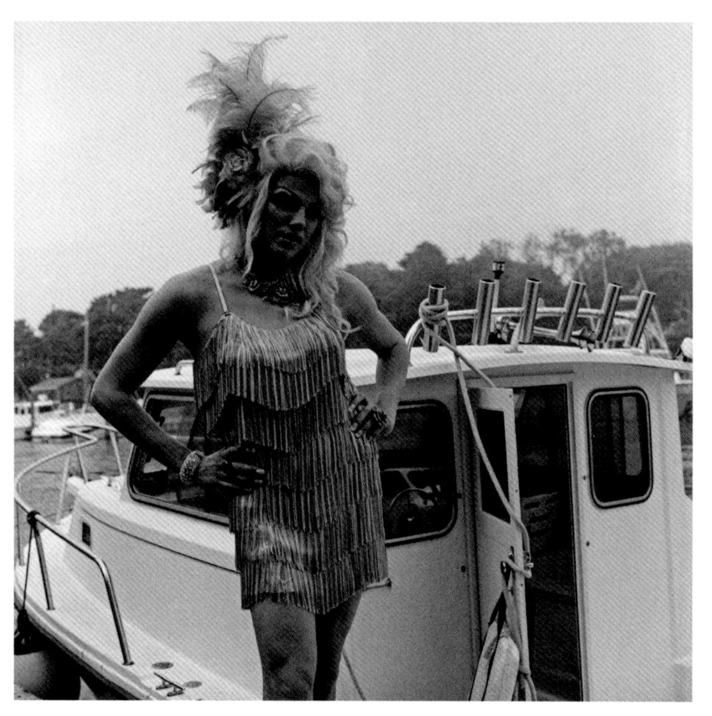

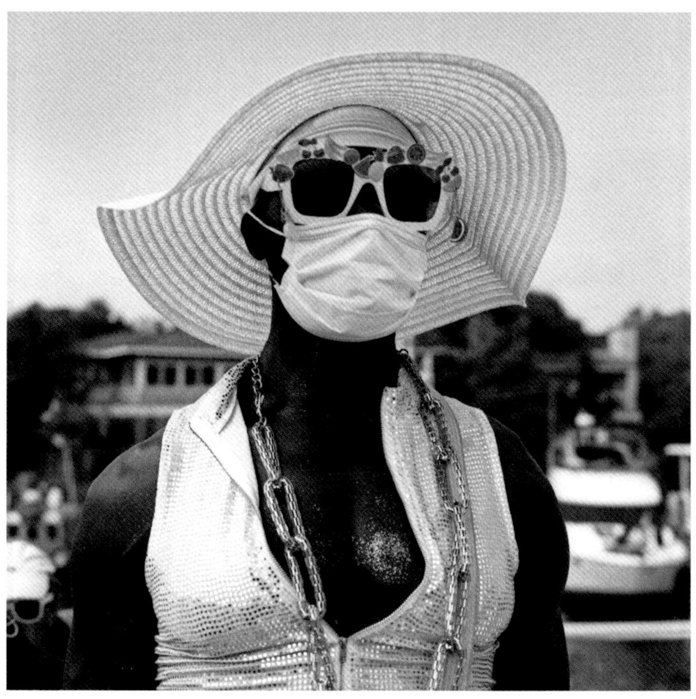

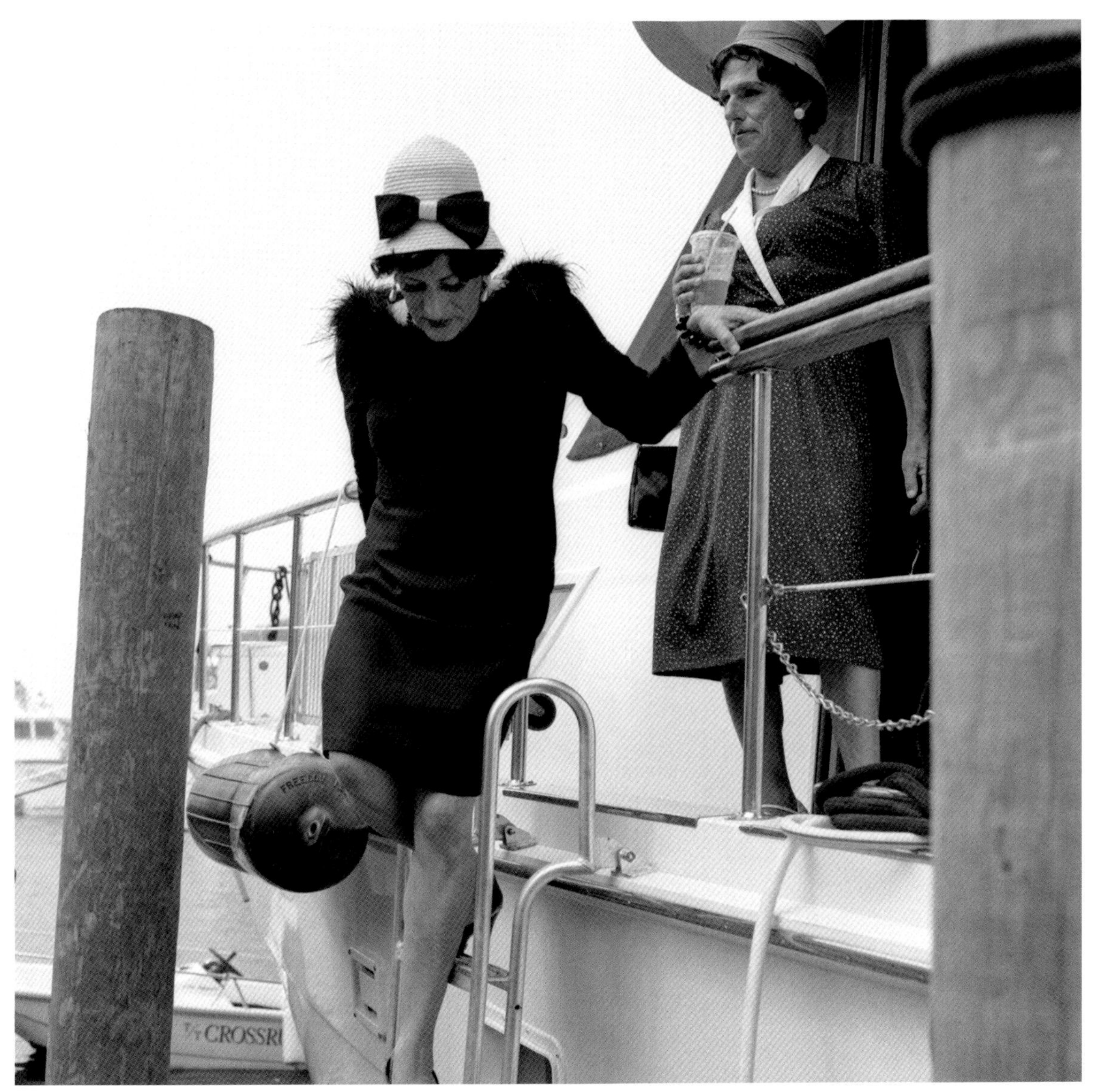

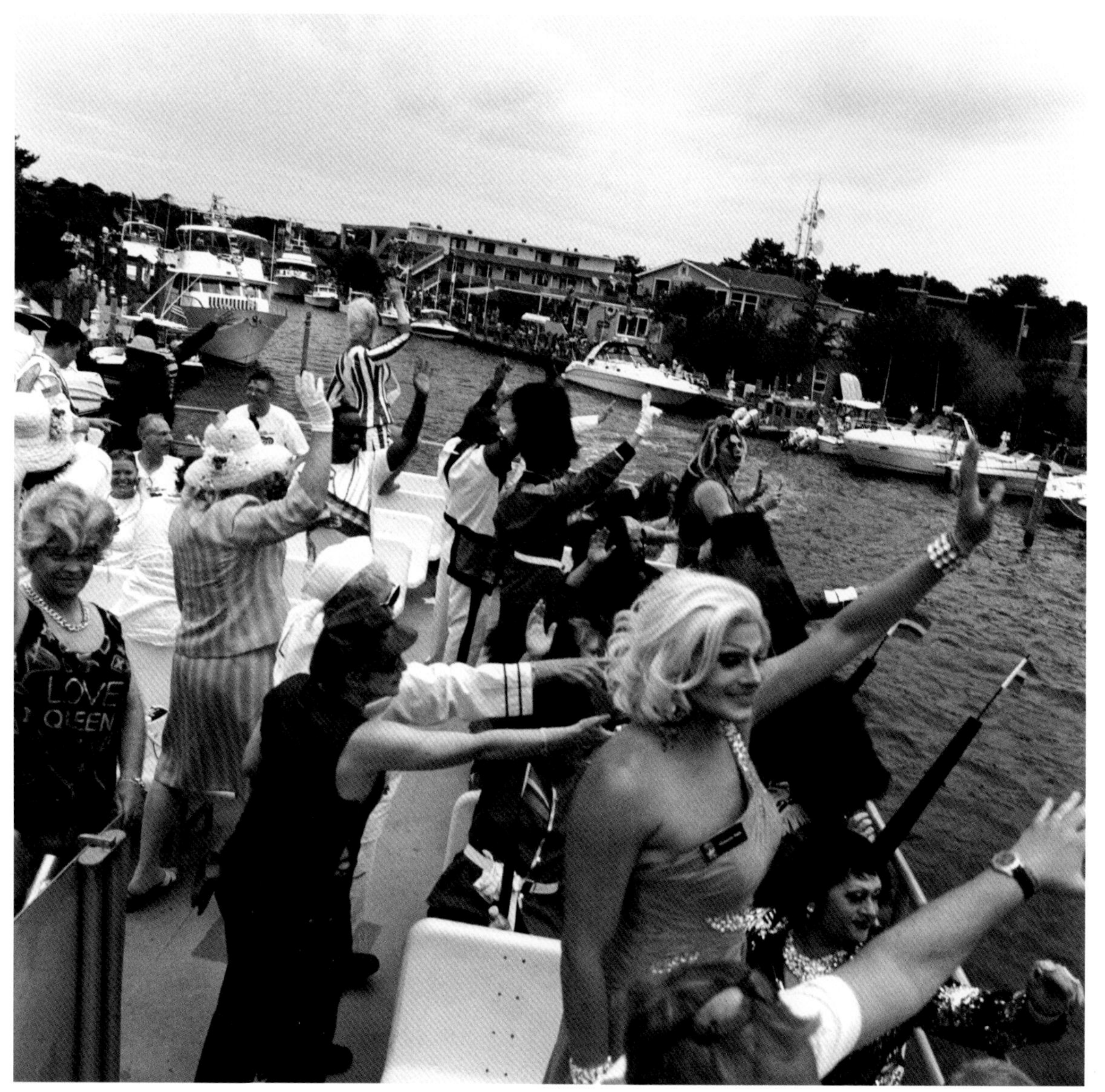
LOVE
QUEEN

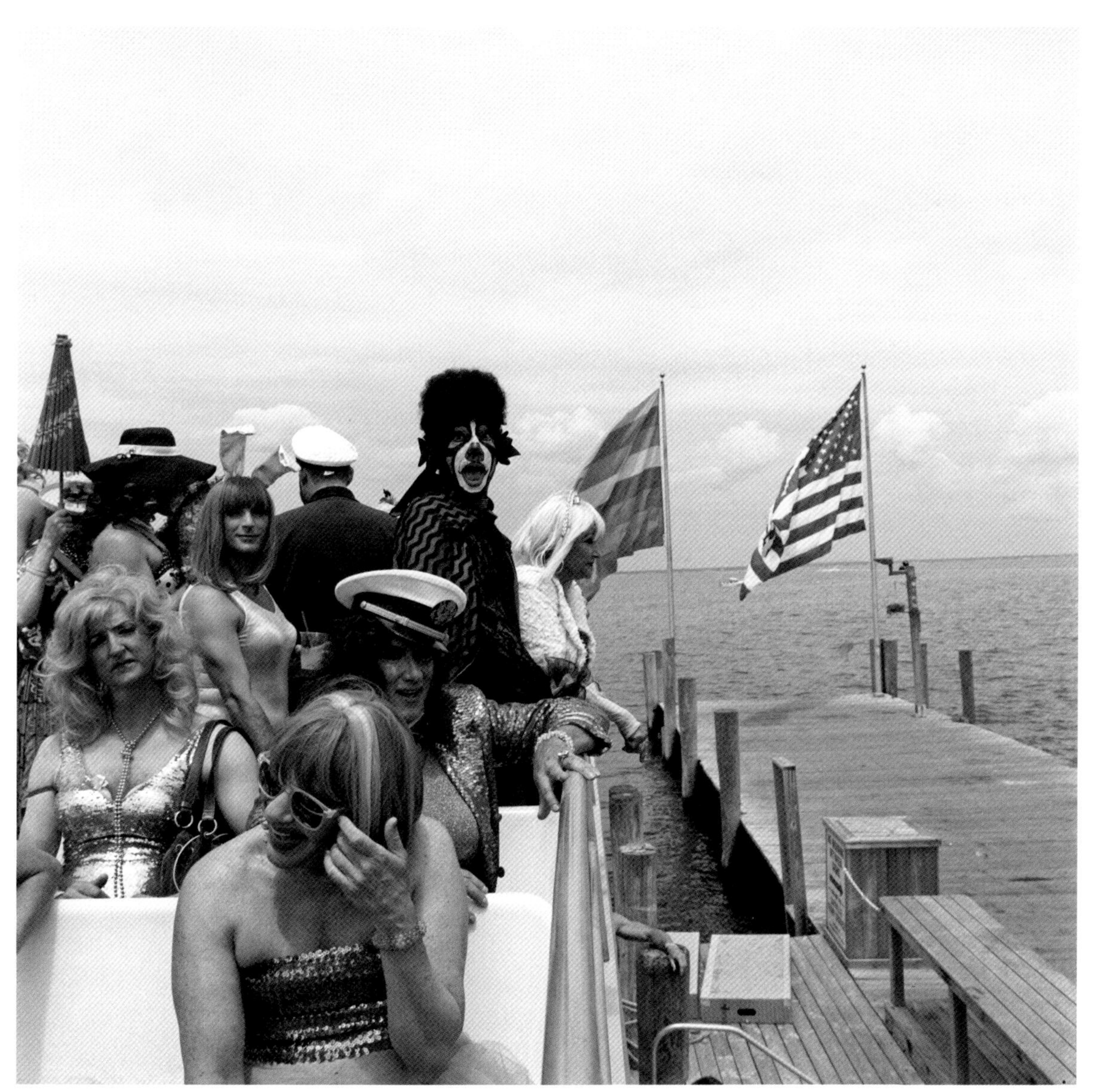

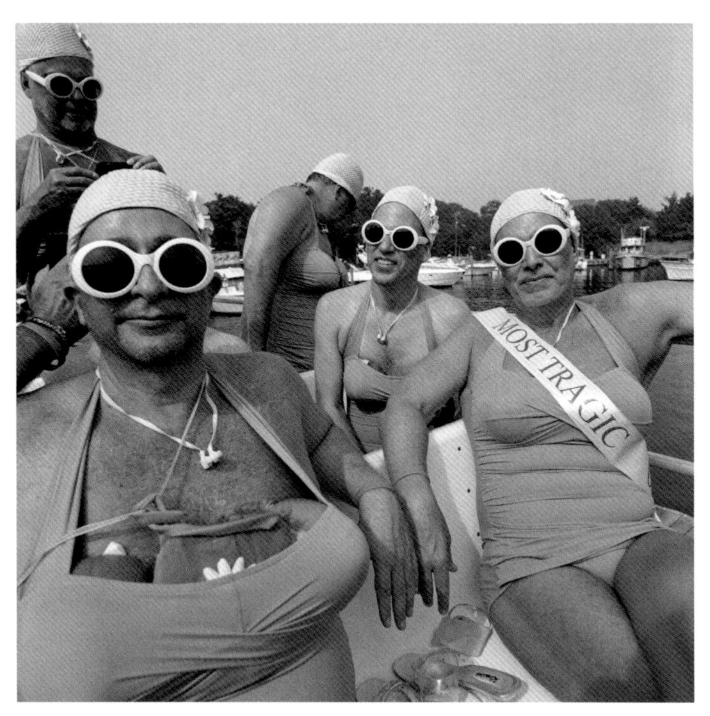
MOST TRAGIC

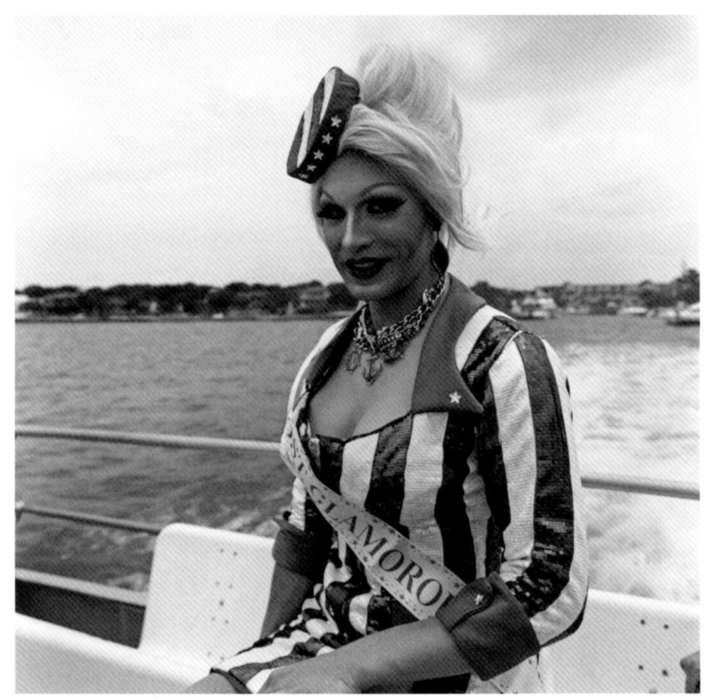

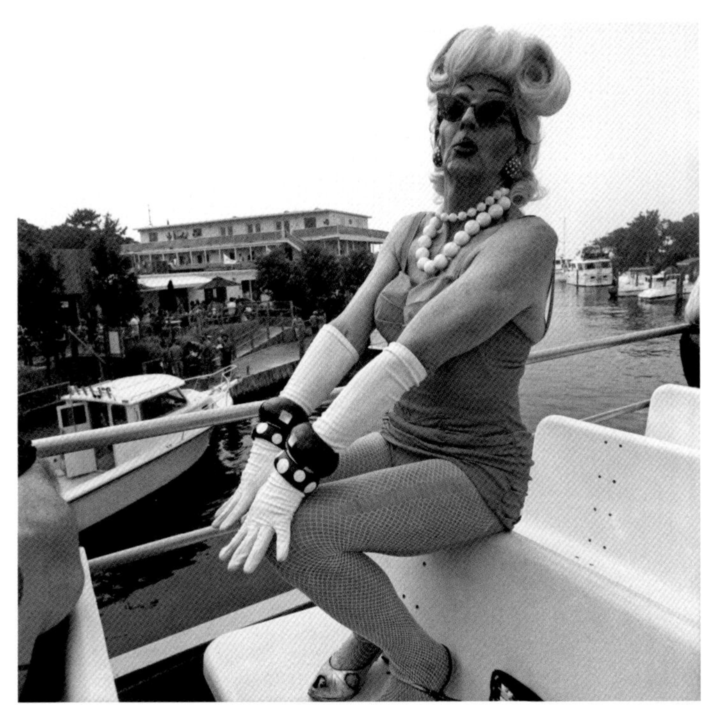

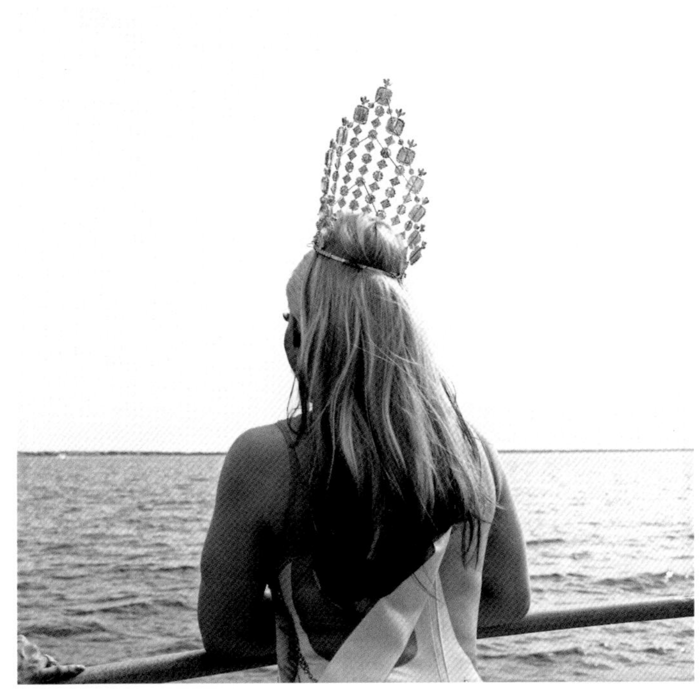

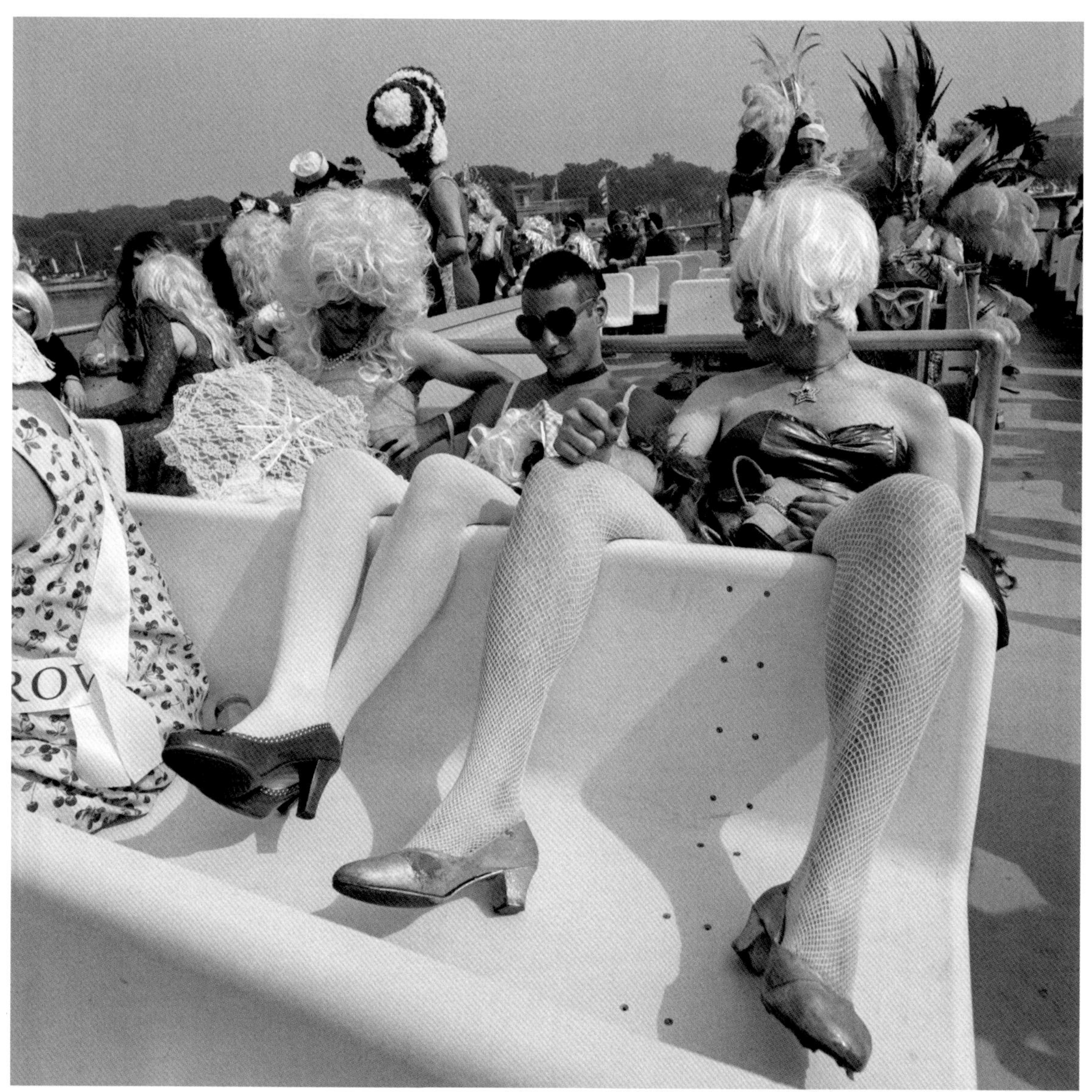
ROW

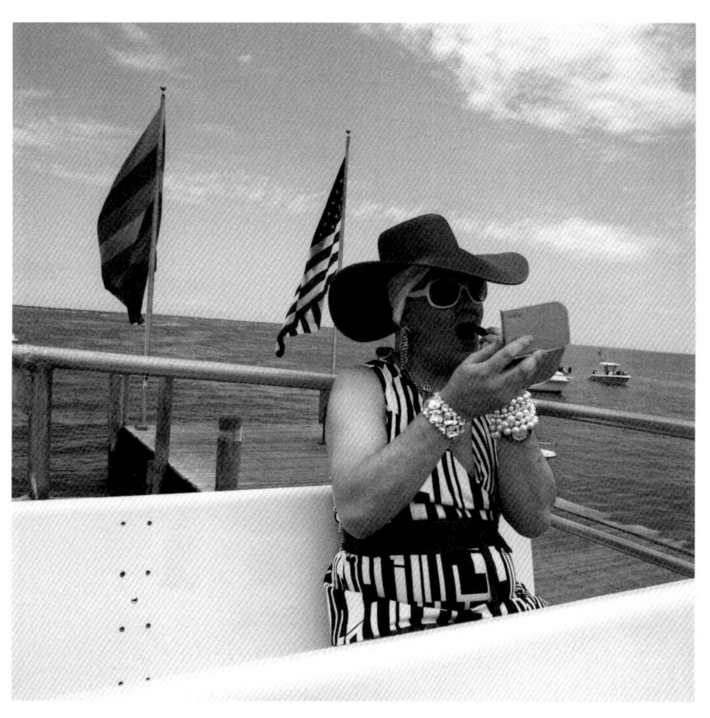

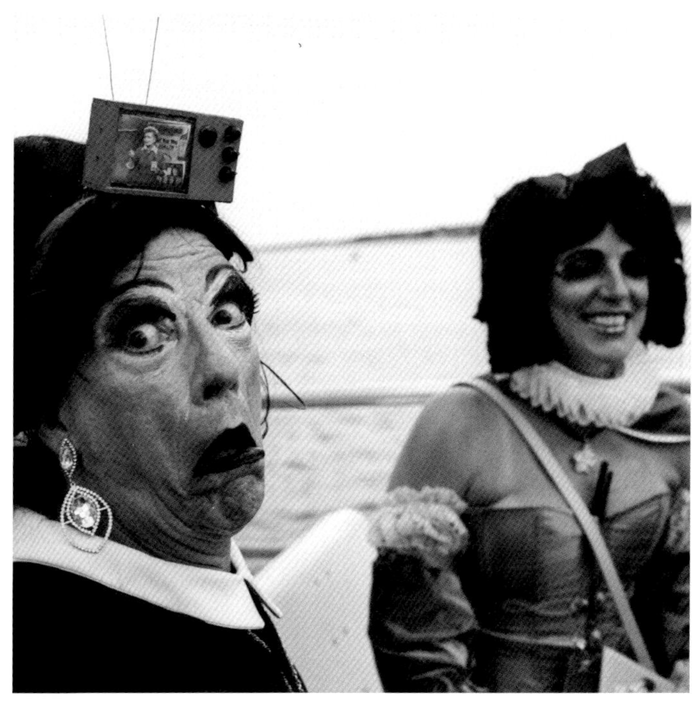

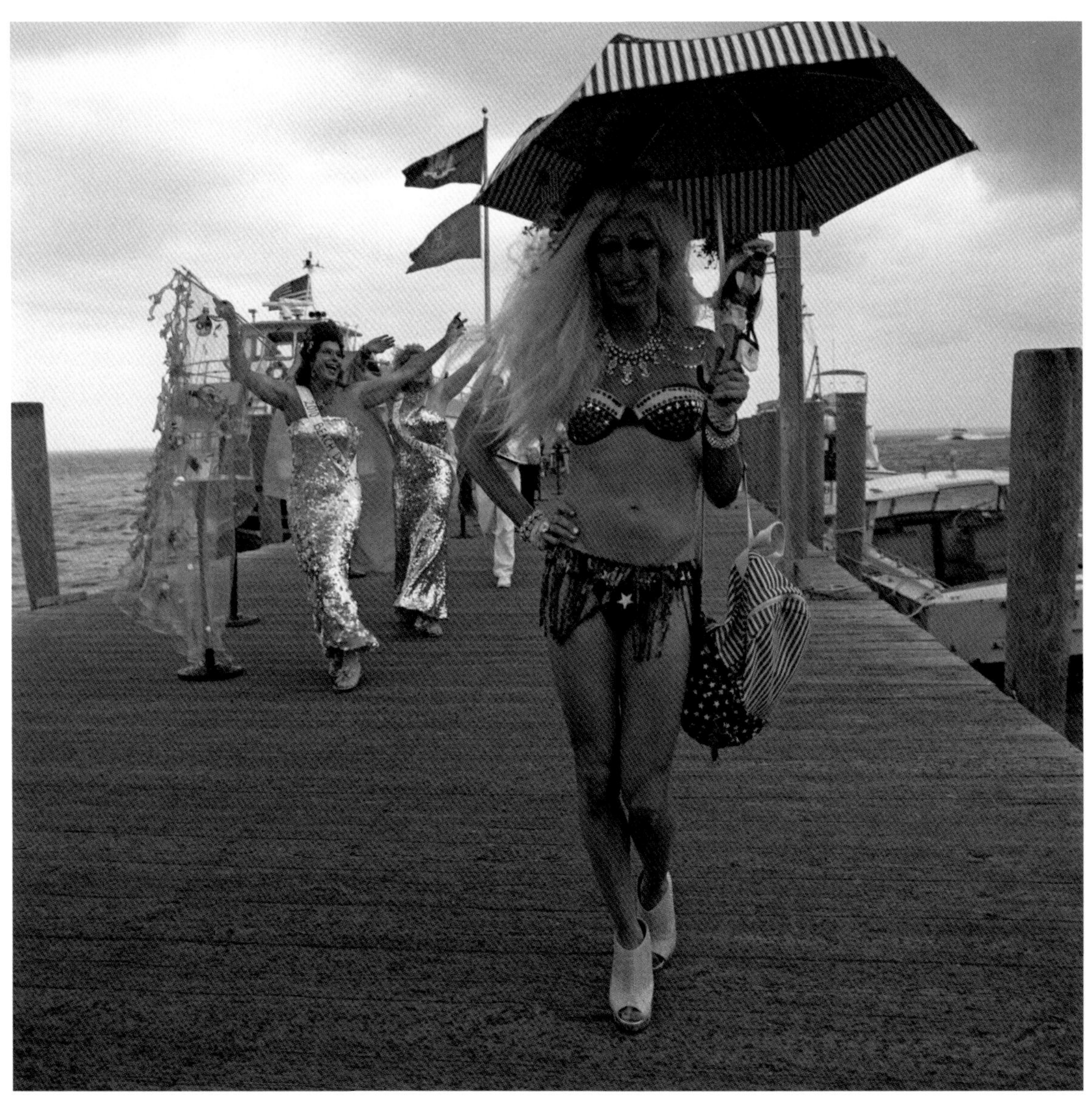

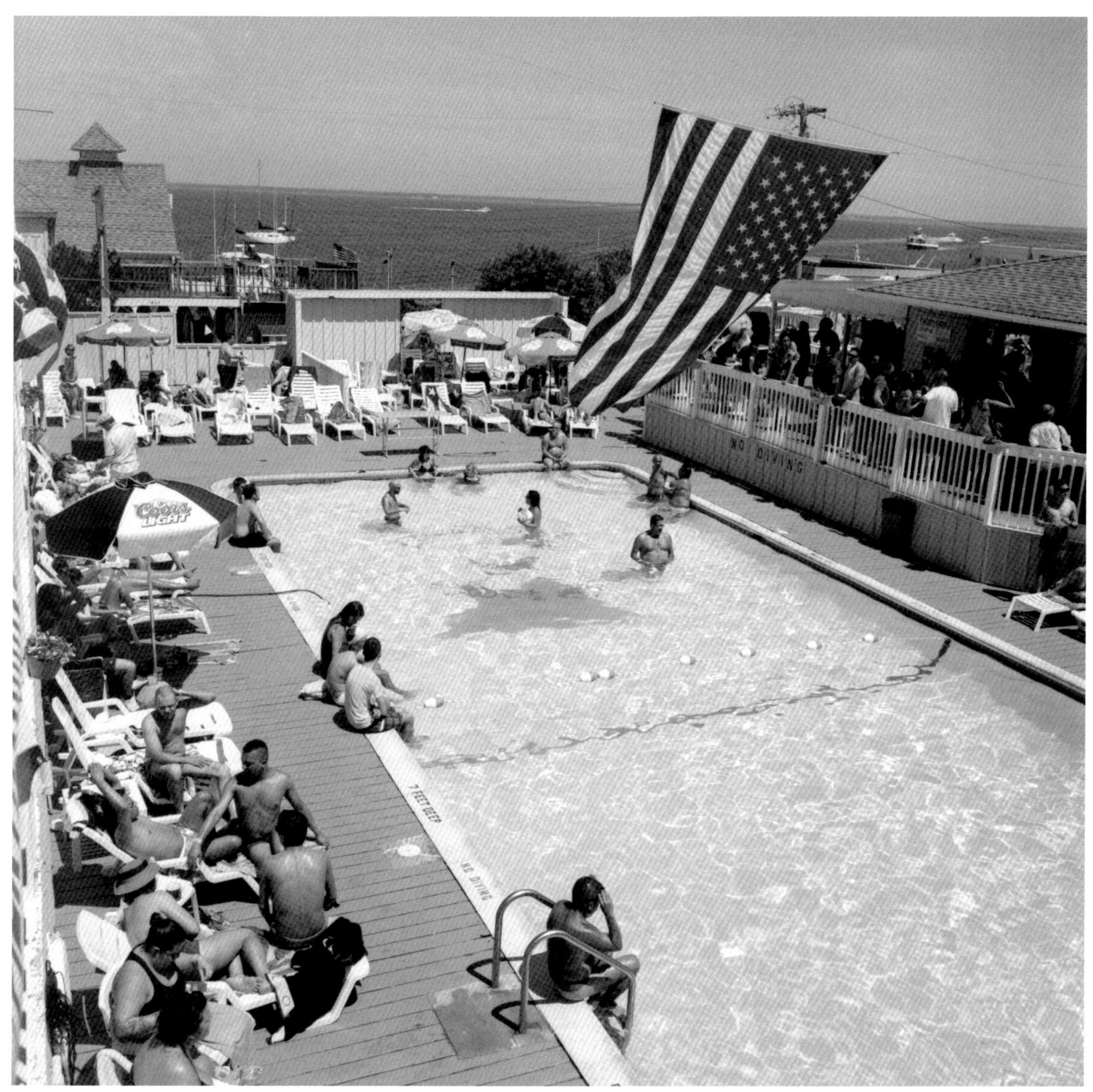
Coors LIGHT
NO DIVING
7 FEET DEEP
NO DIVING

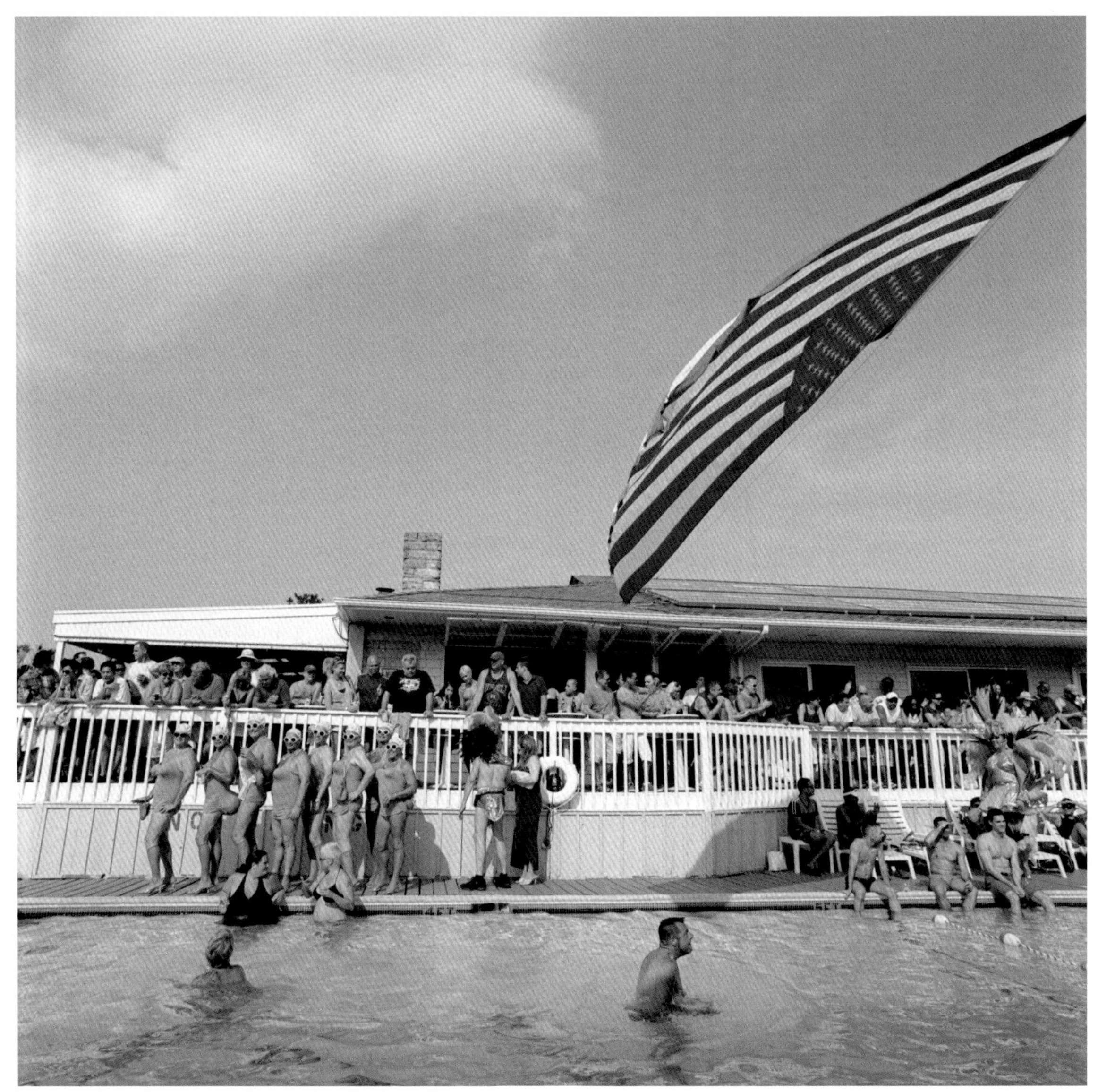

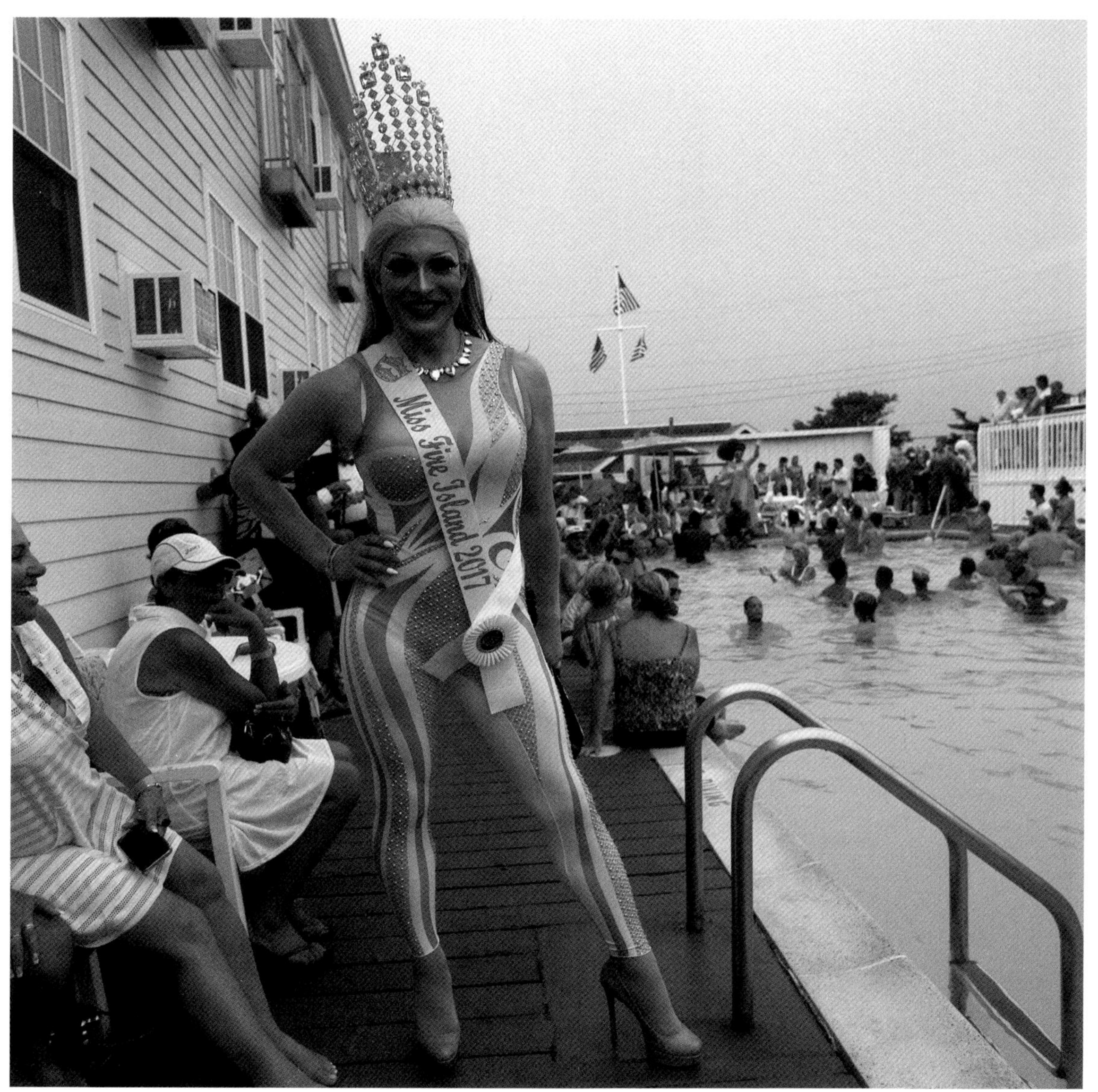
Miss Fire Island 2017

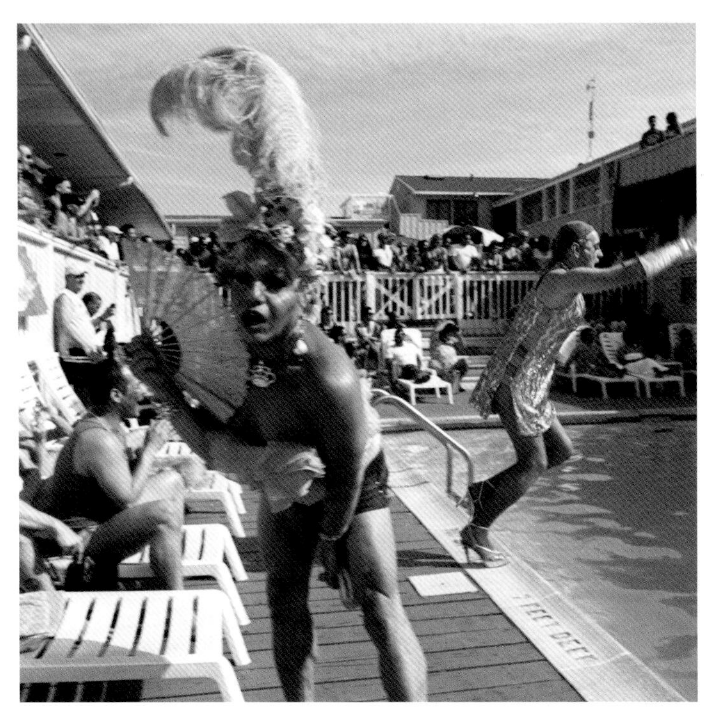

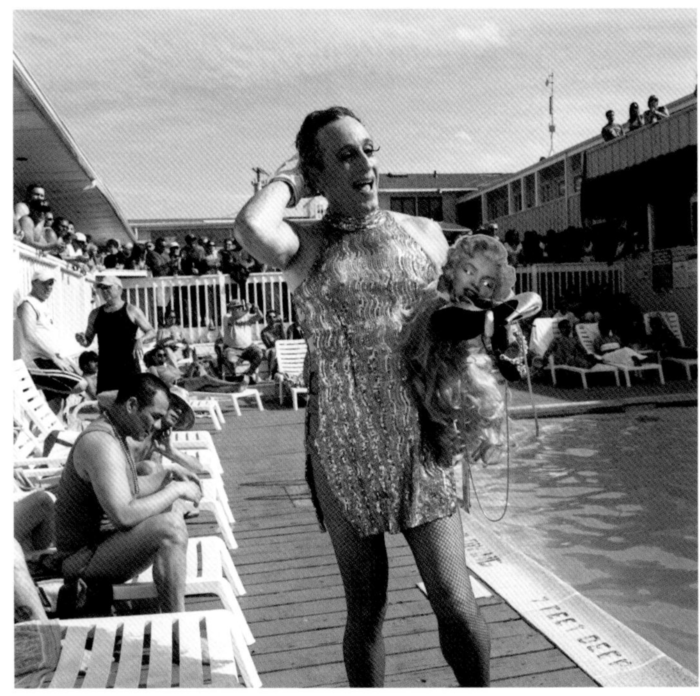

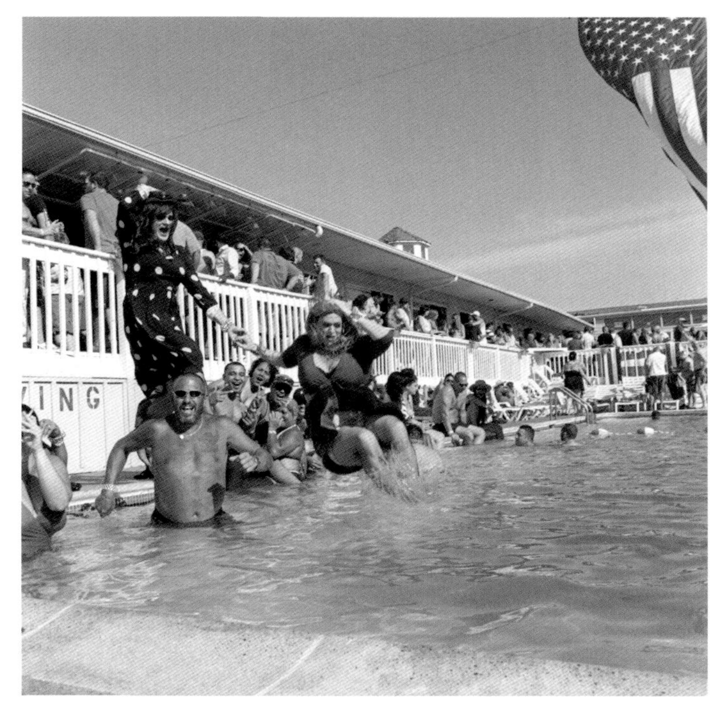

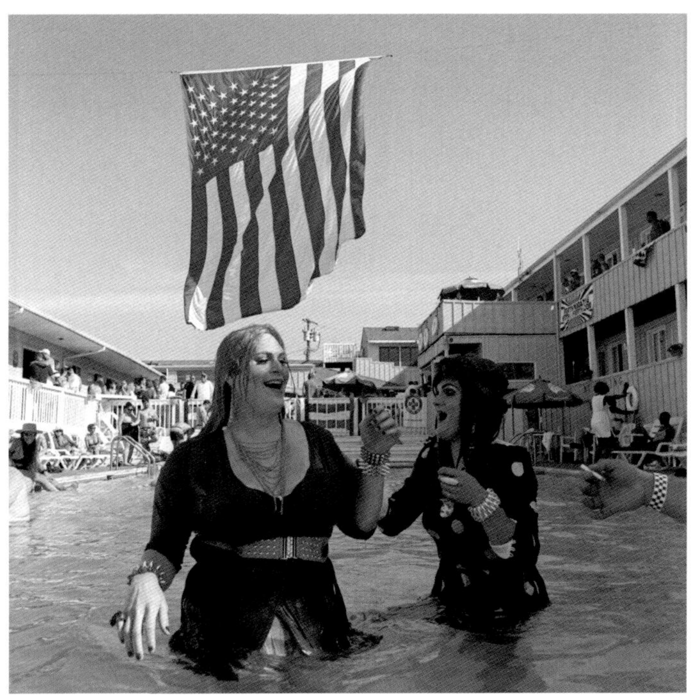

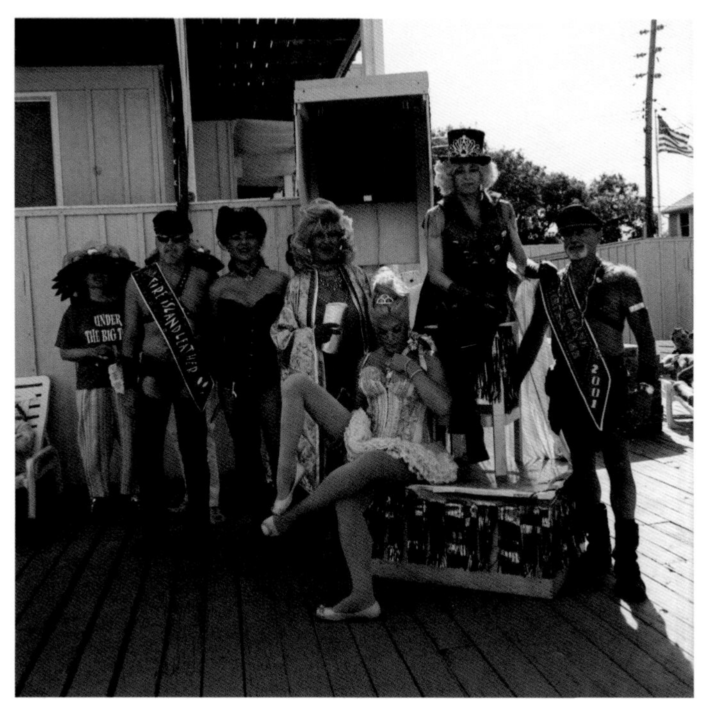
UNDER
2001

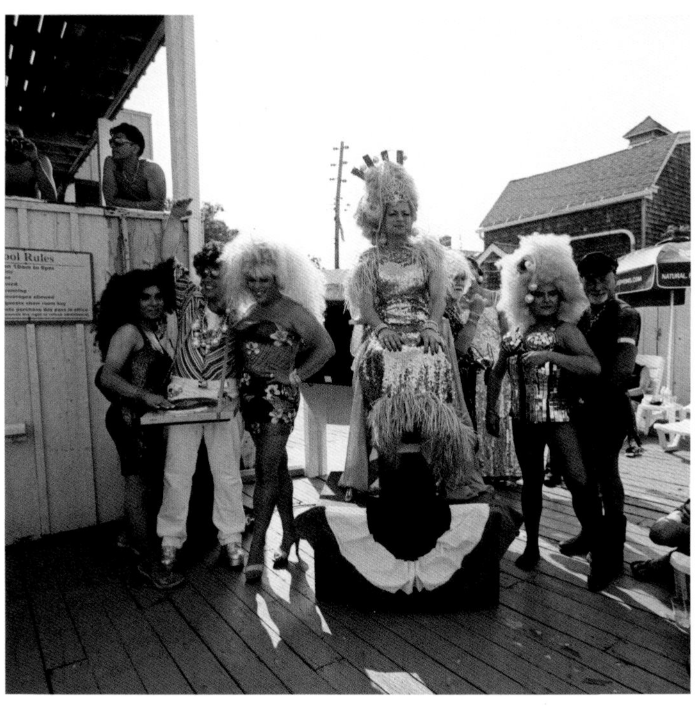

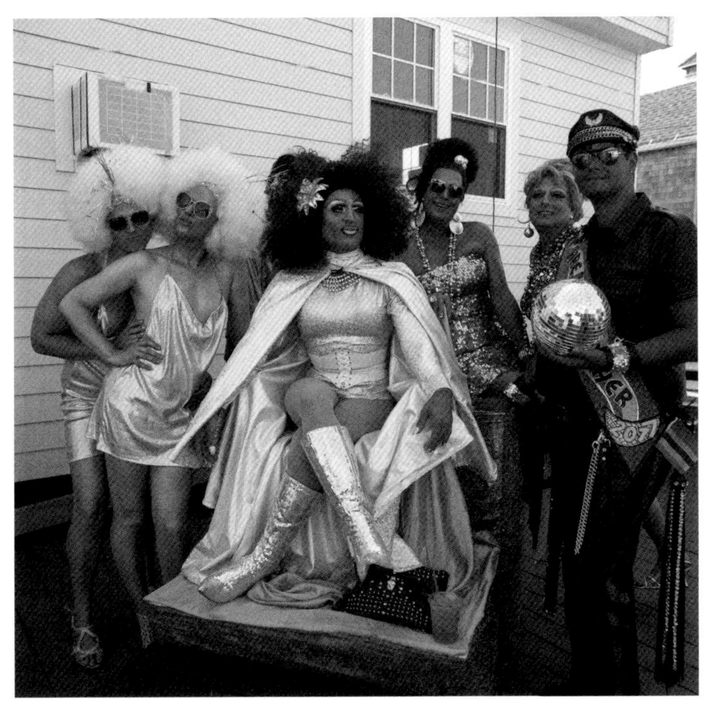

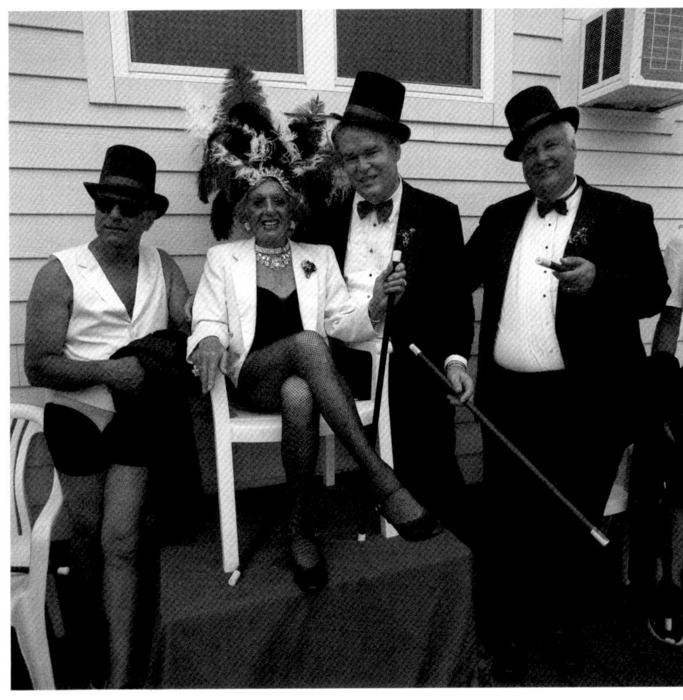

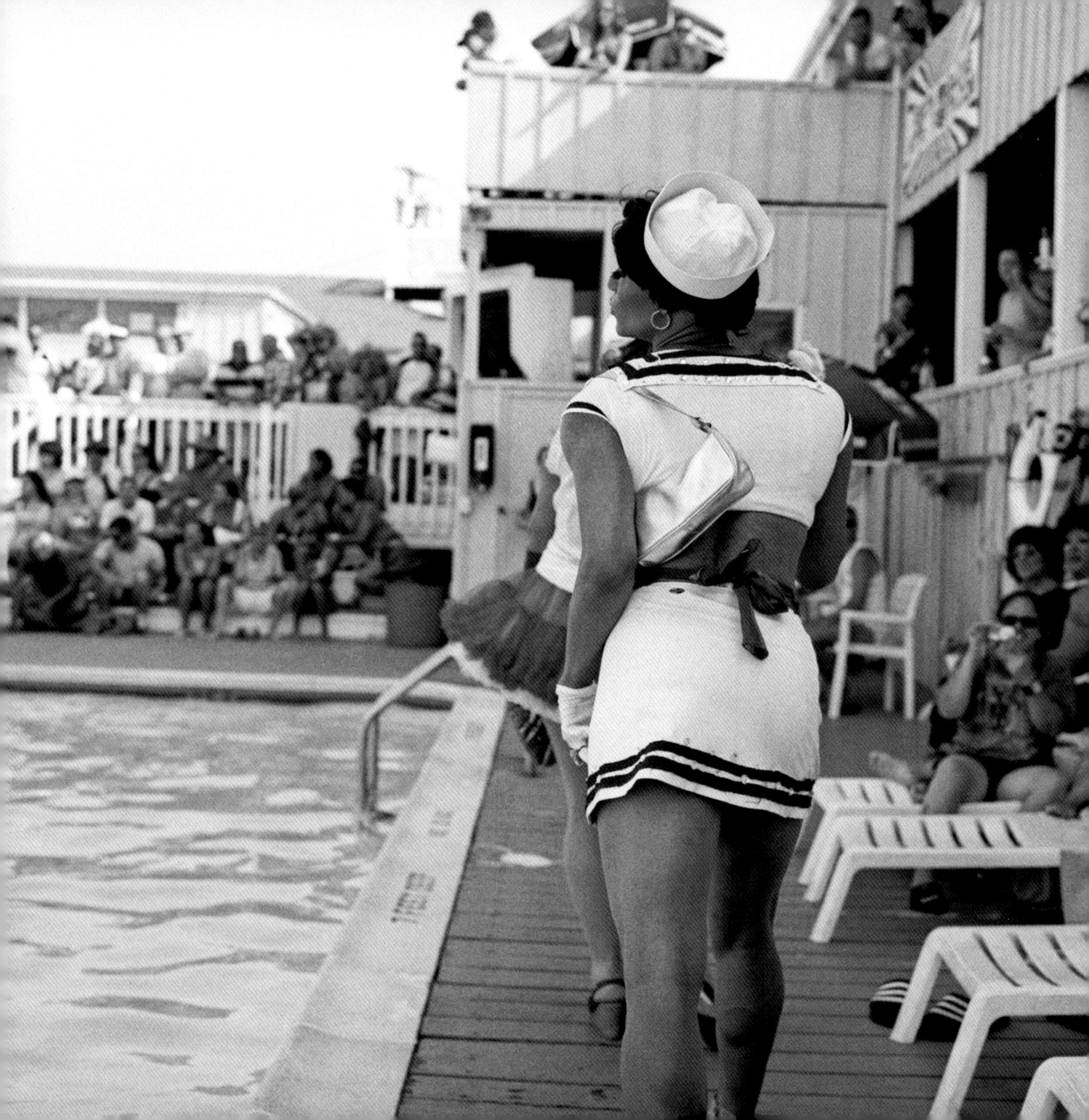

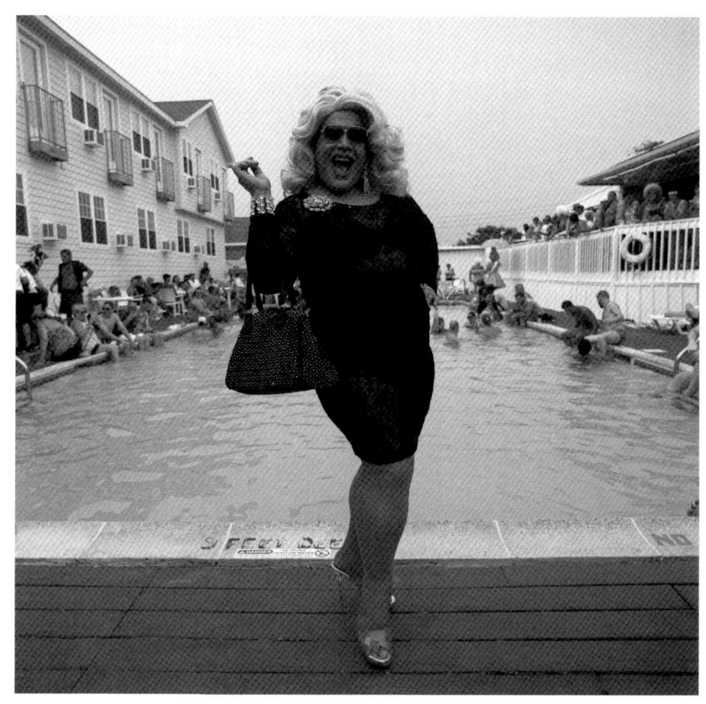

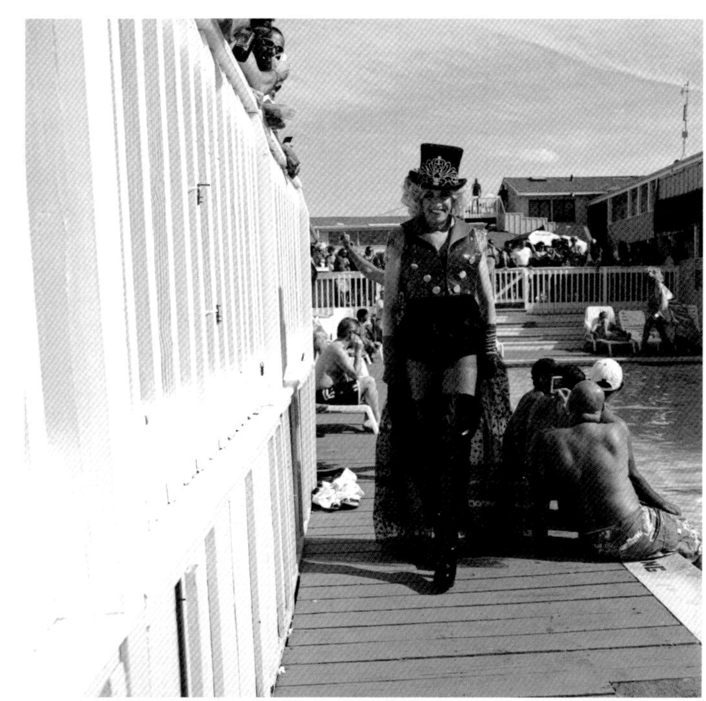

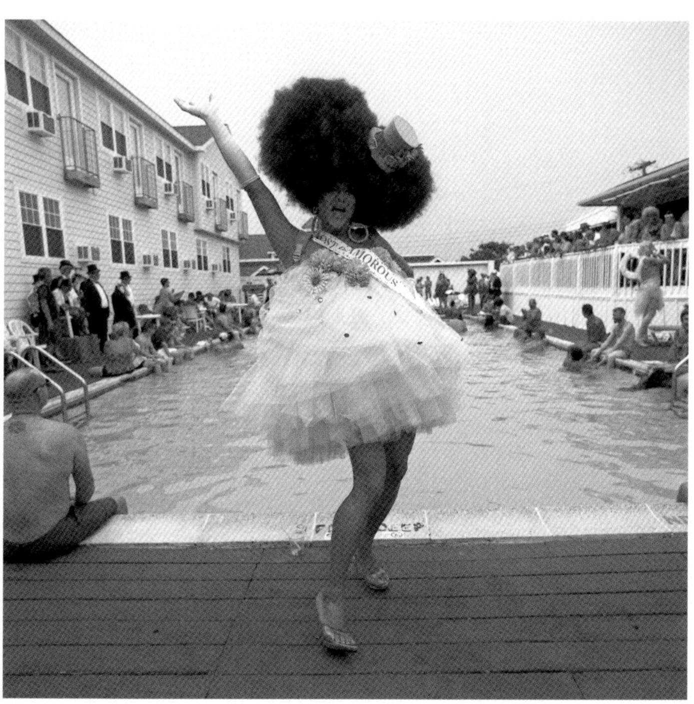

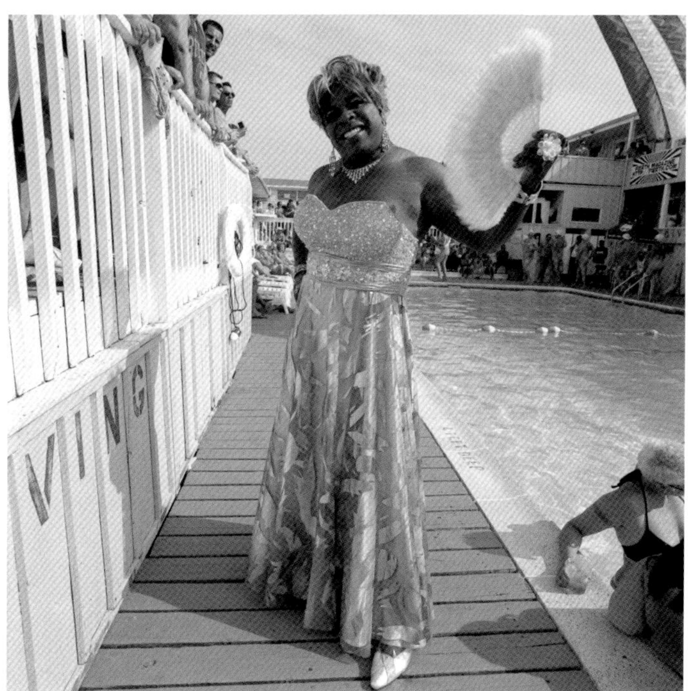

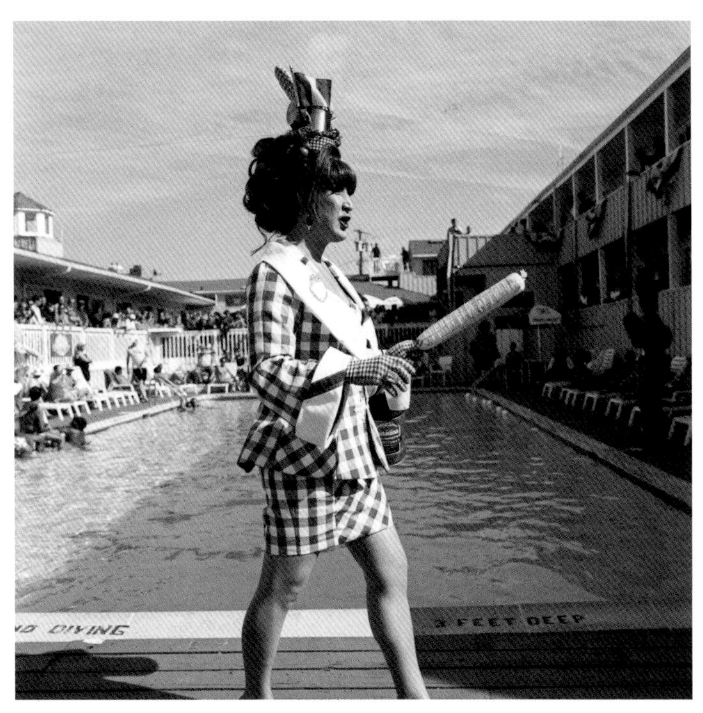
NO DIVING
3 FEET DEEP

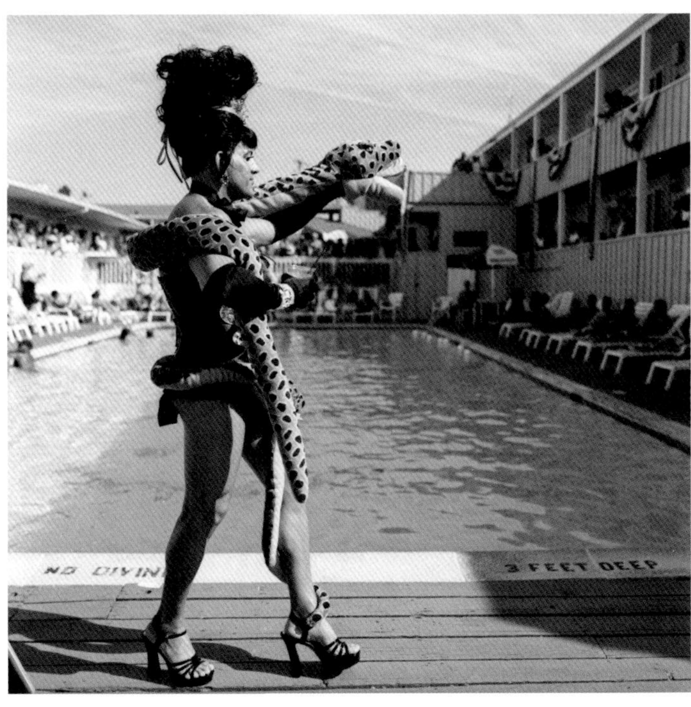
NO DIVIN
3 FEET DEEP

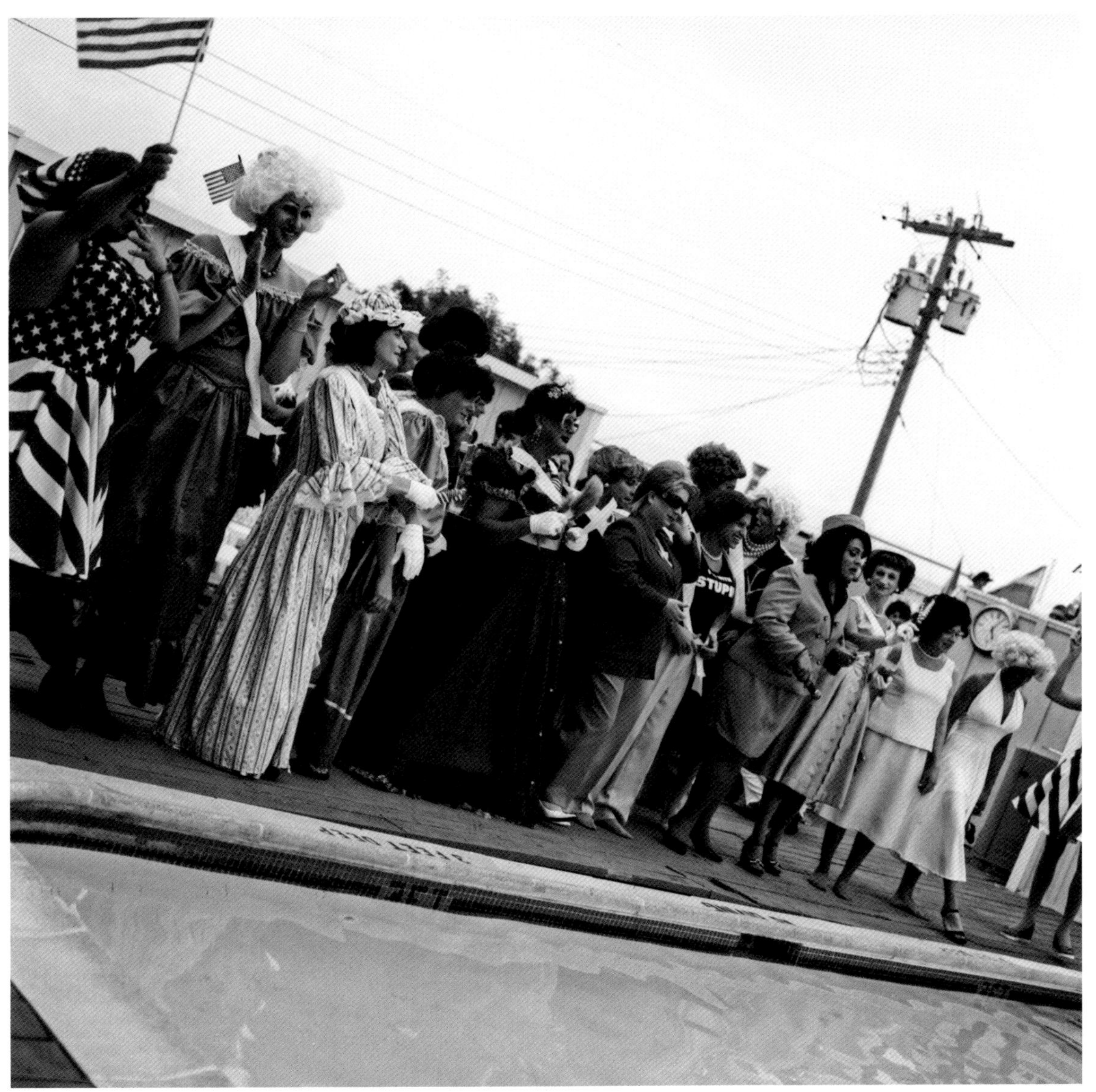

"It's a great reminder that we each have the power to change injustices."

Patty Rosado

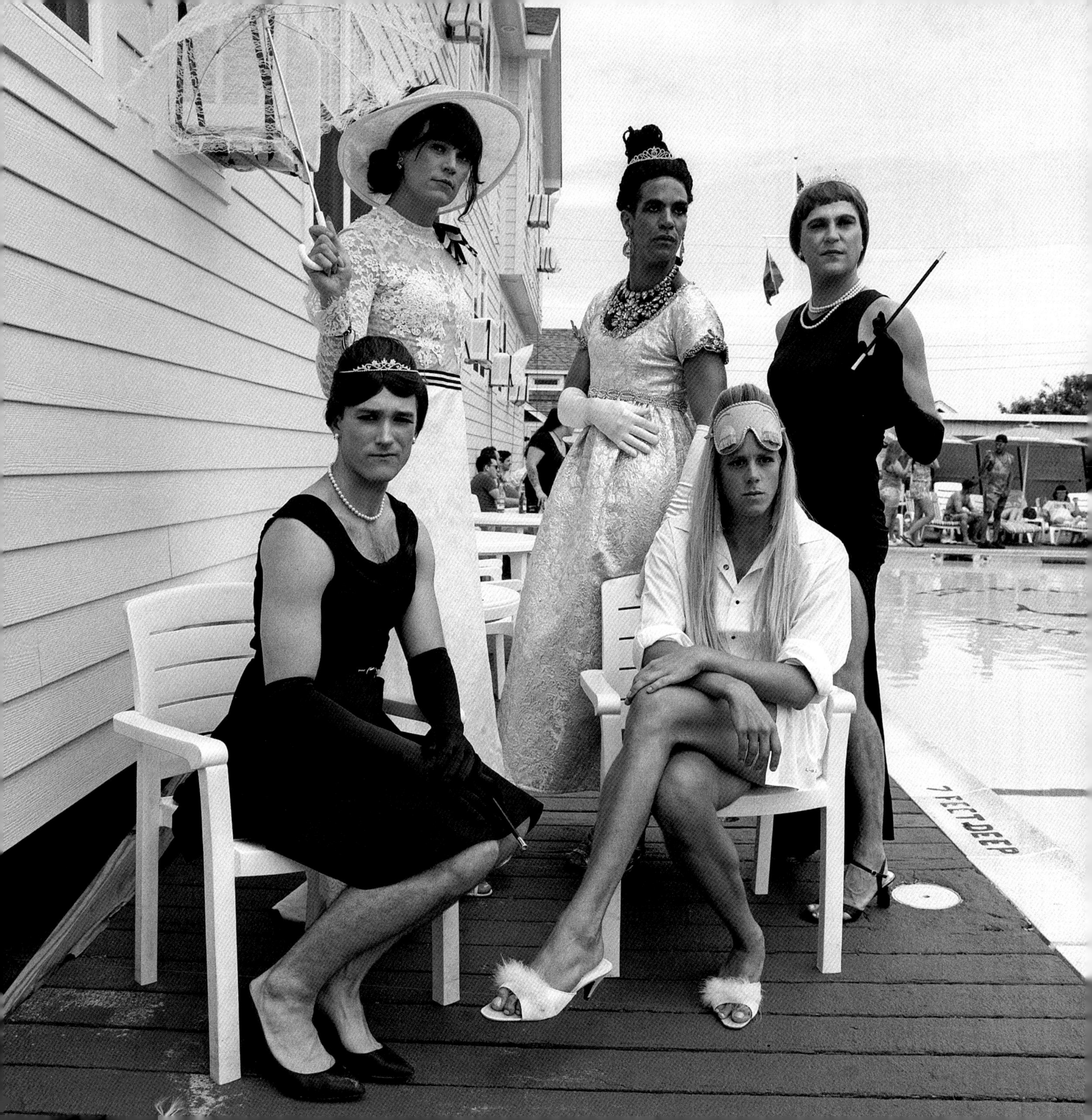
7 FEET DEEP

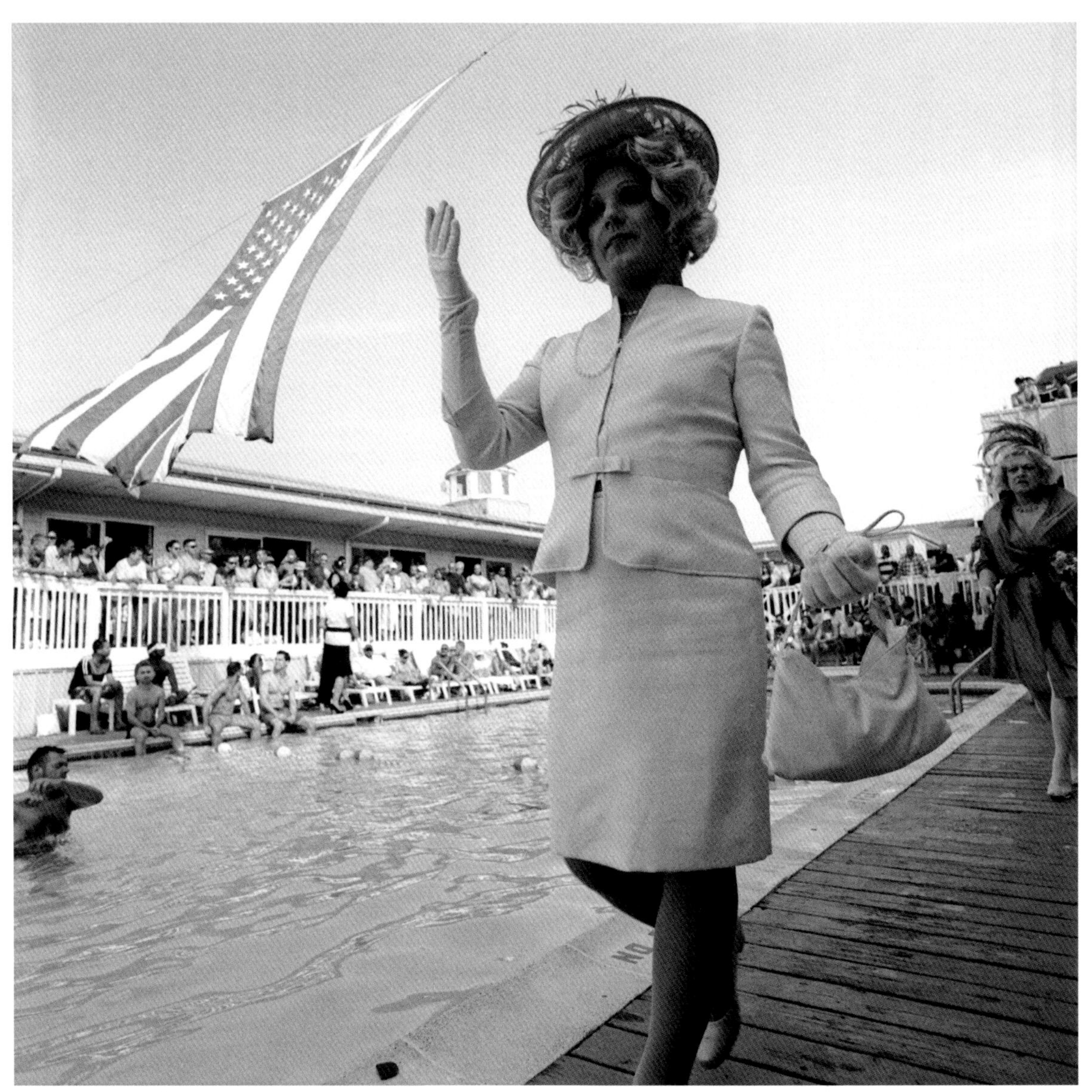

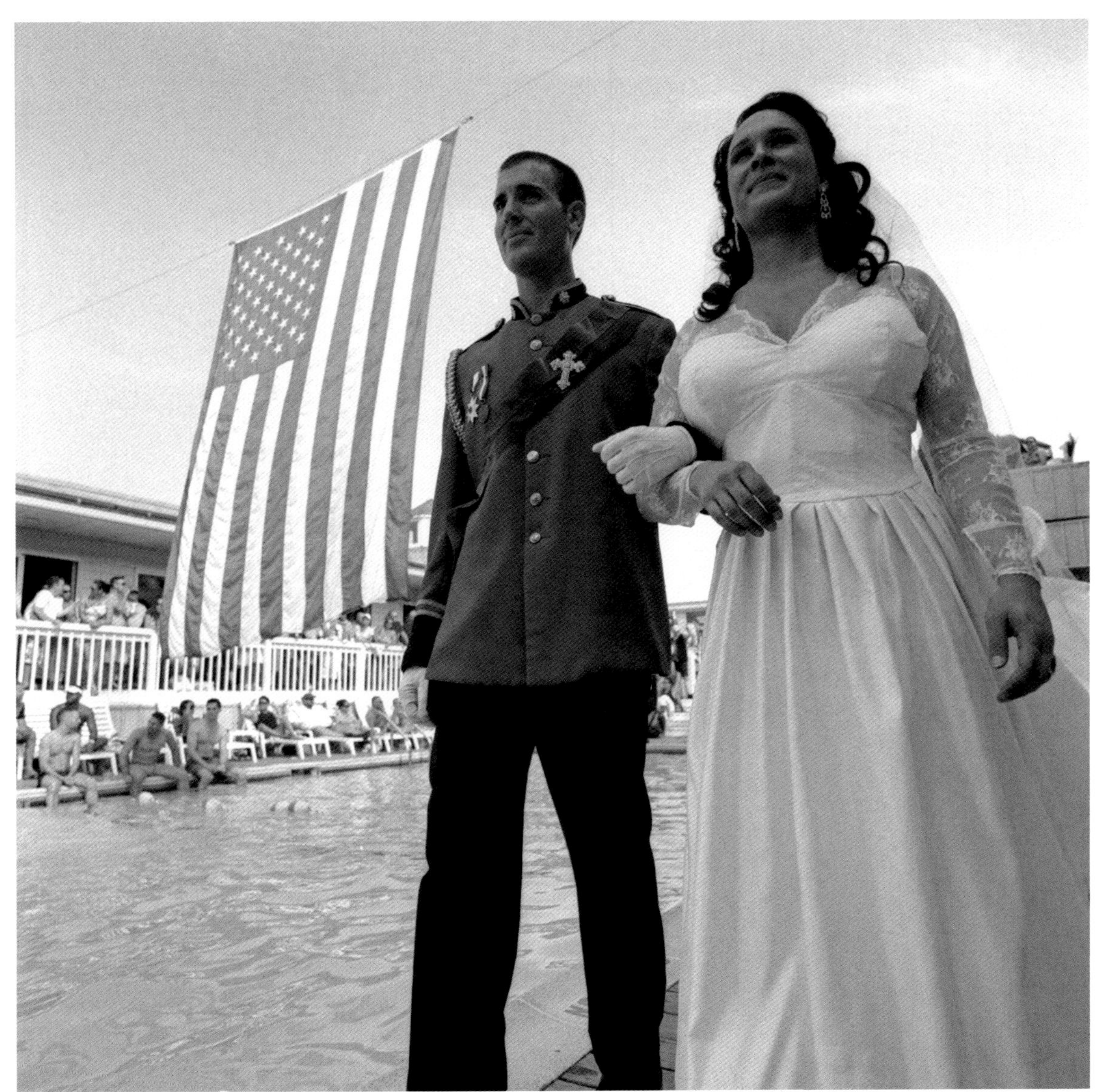

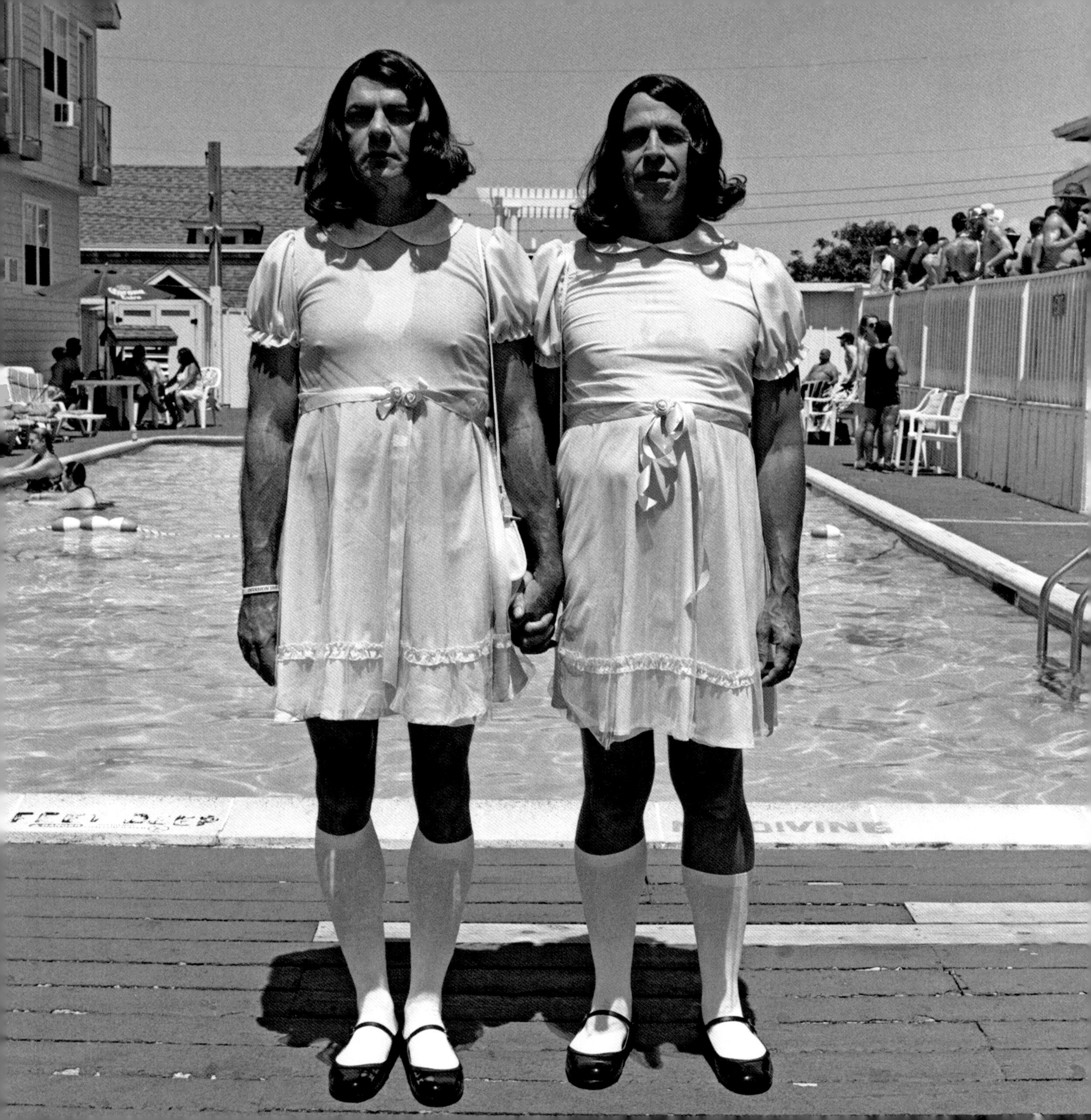
FEET DEEP
DIVING

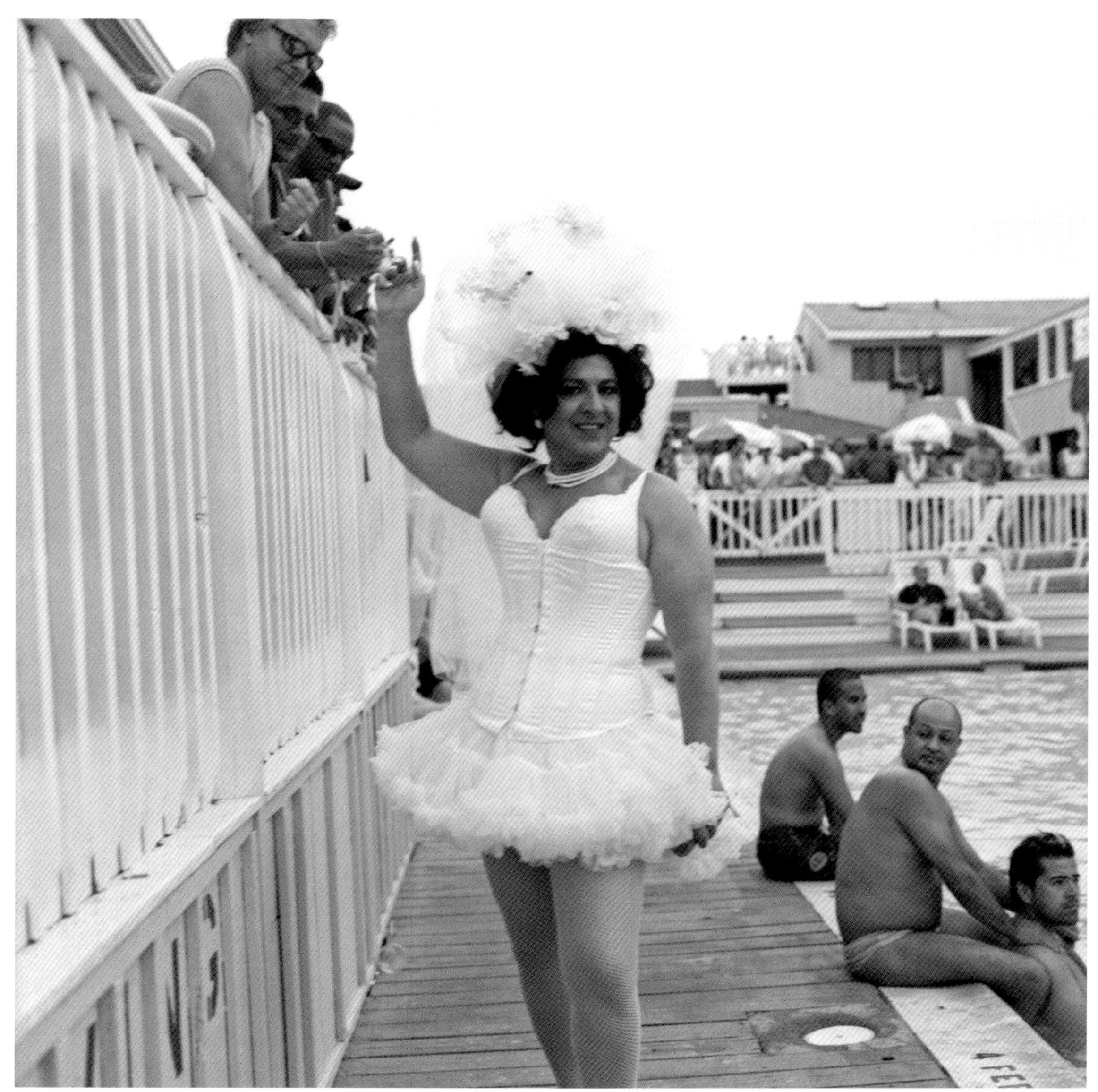

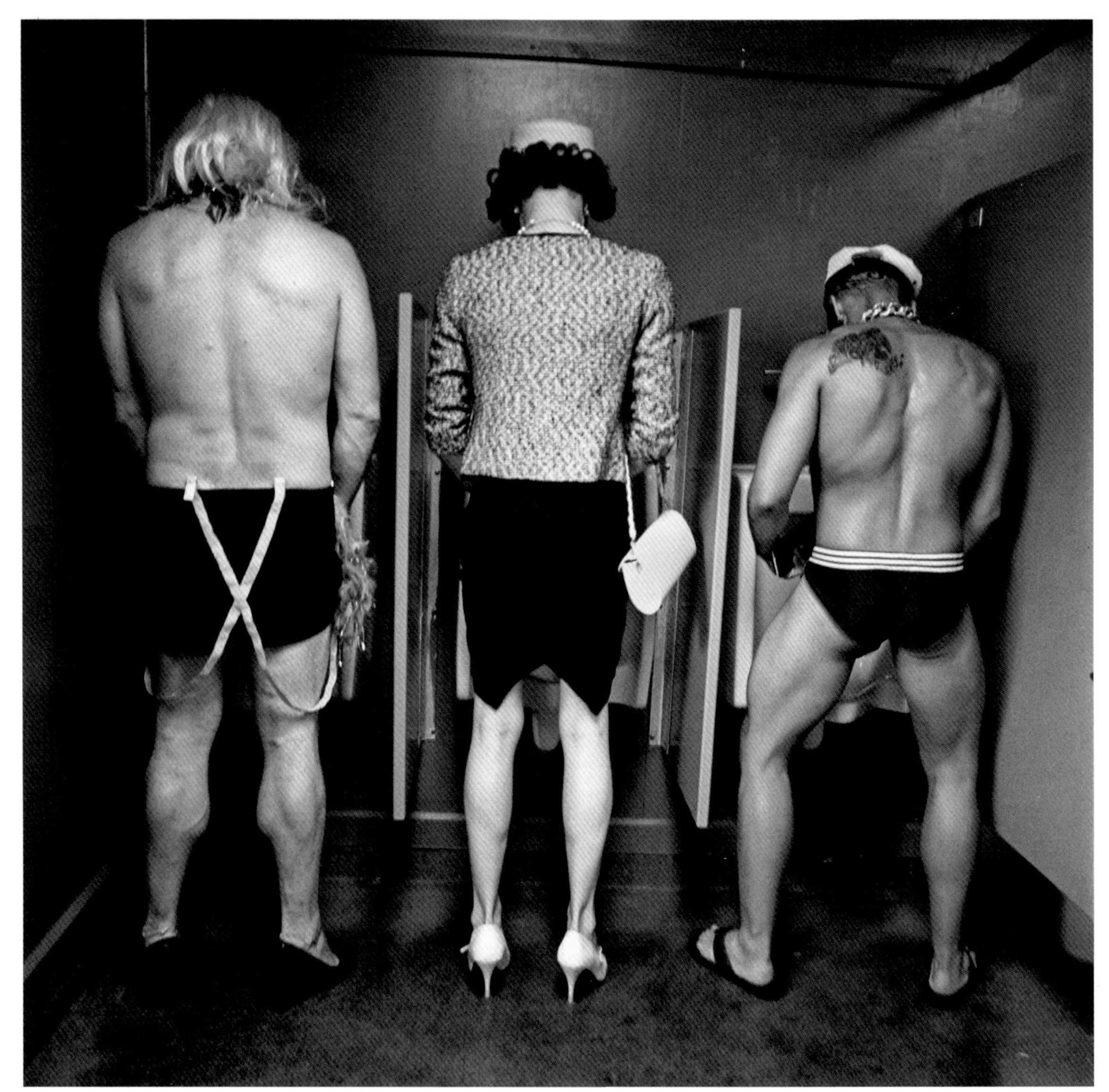

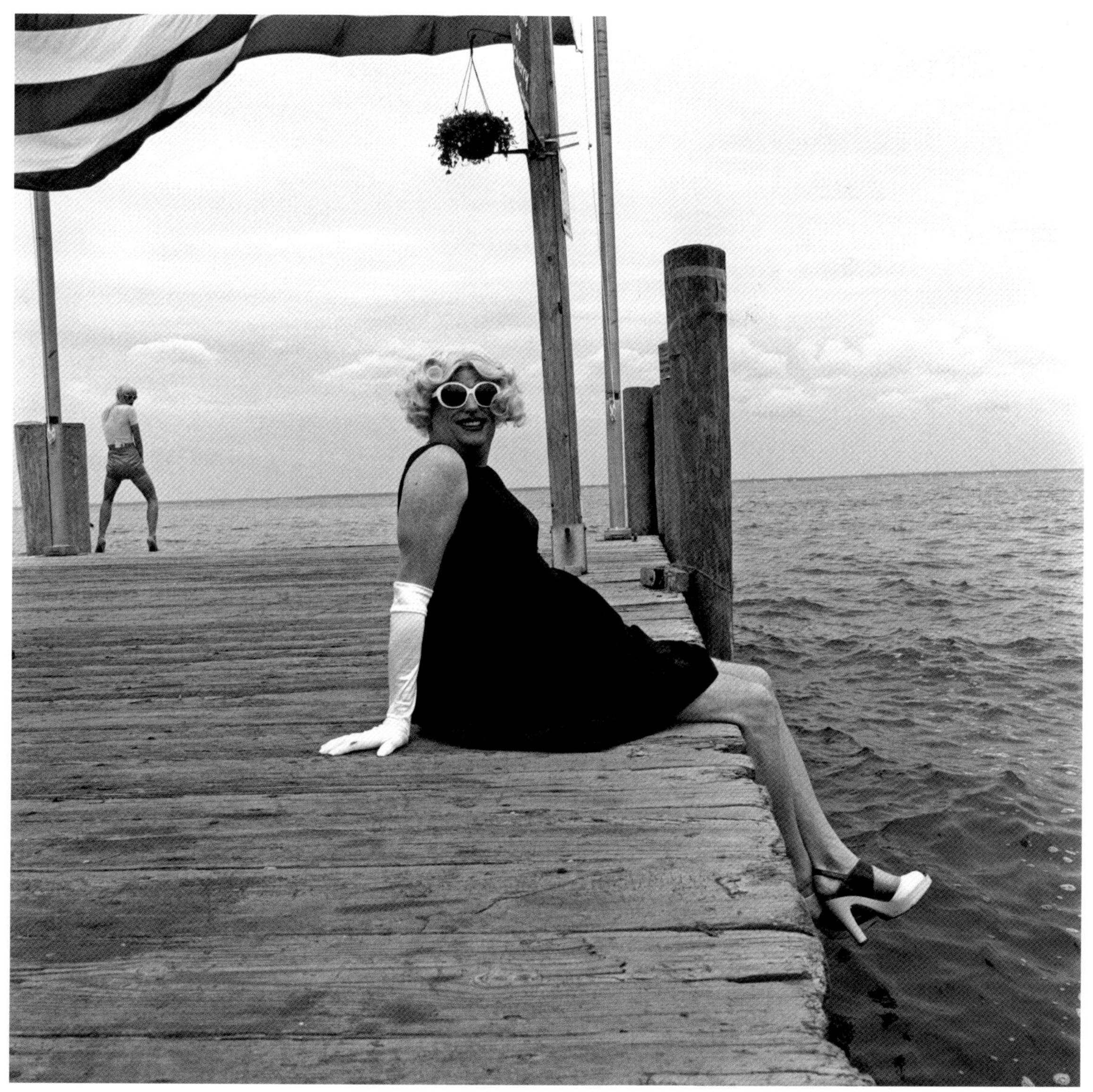

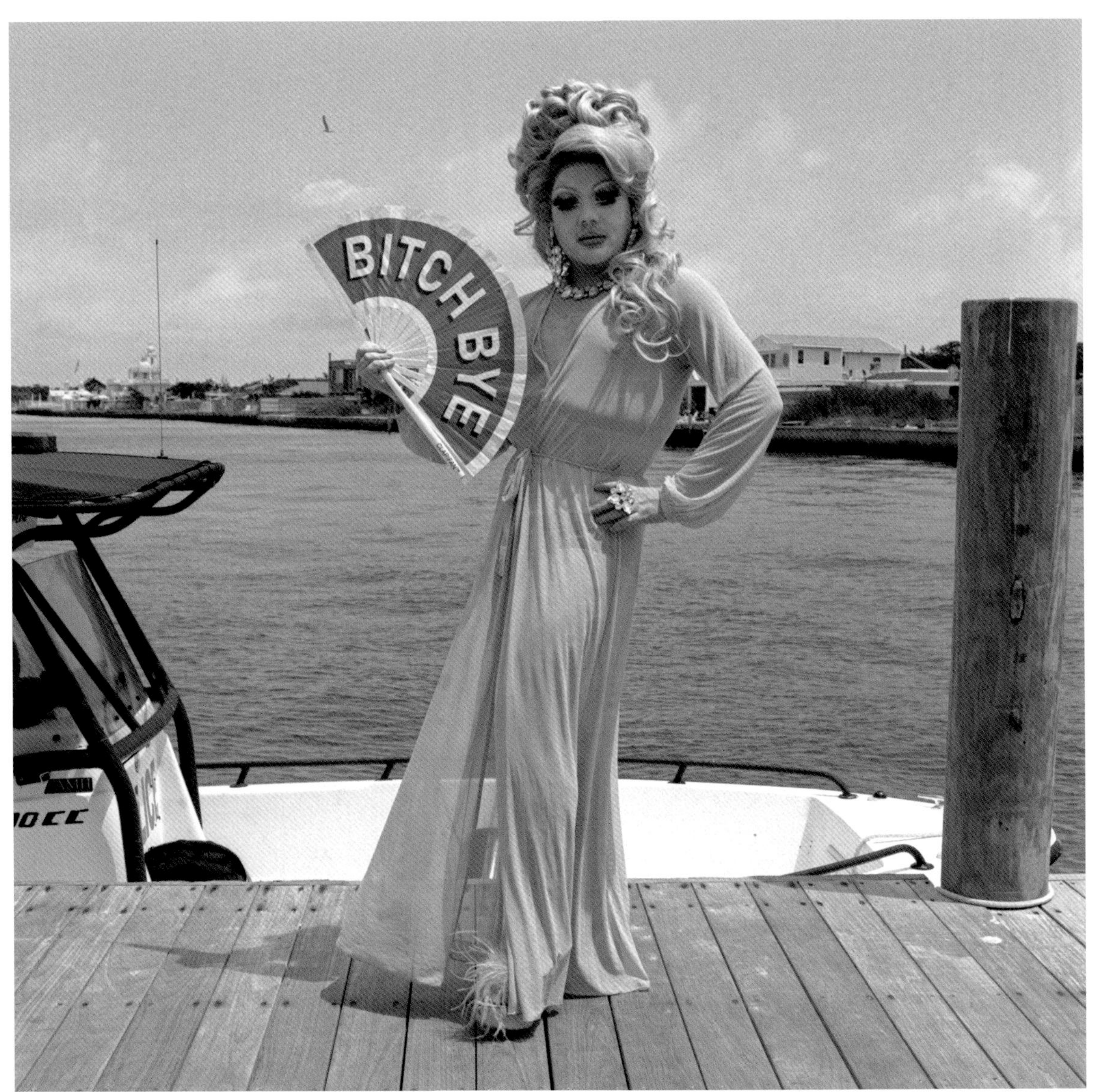
BITCH BYE

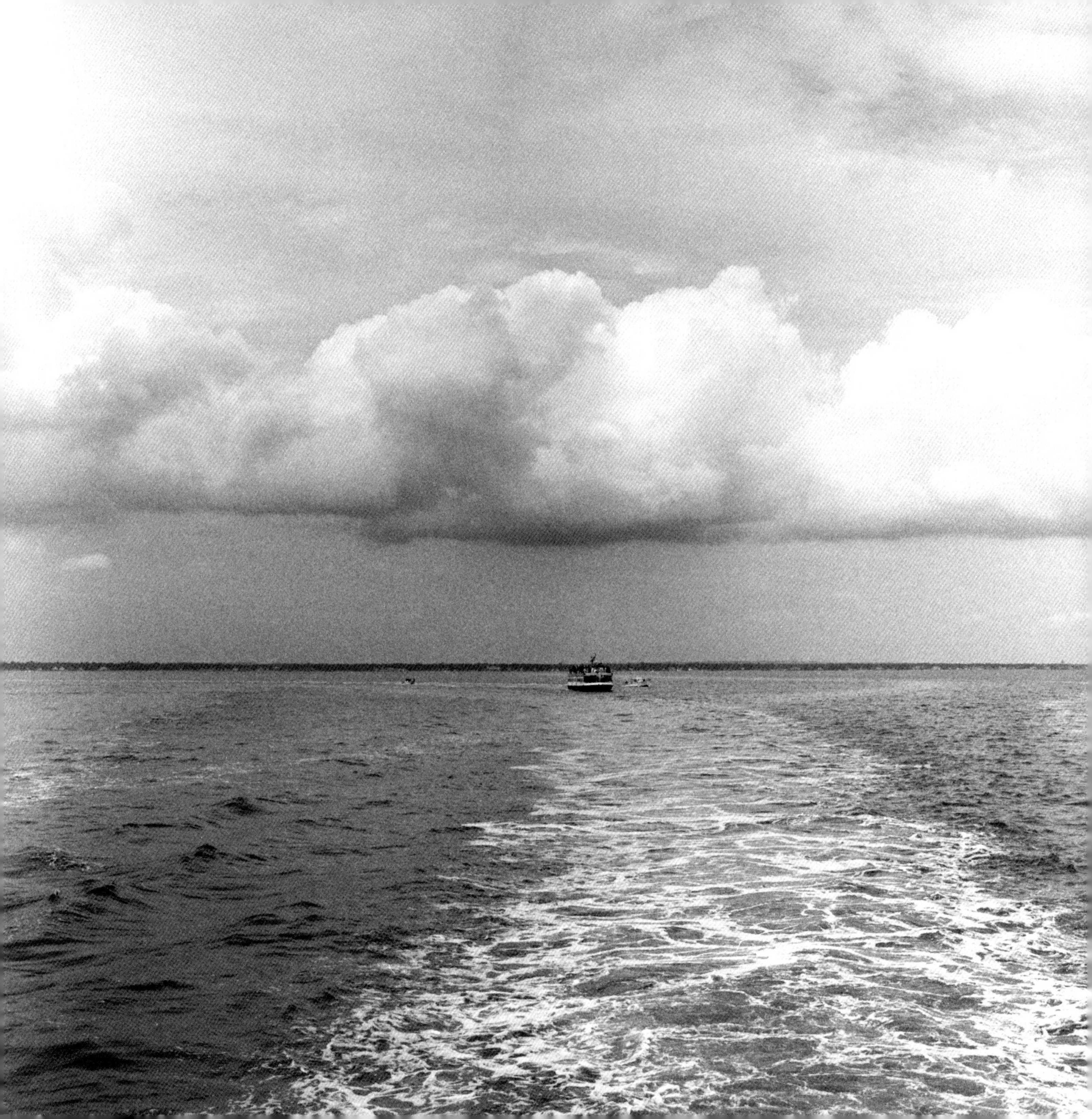

The Art of Drag Meets the Art of Photography

My journey into photographing the drag queen scene began in 2000, thanks to my friend Rosa Rosalino.

A drag performer on the weekends, Rosa knew I was studying photography in college and invited me to document the annual Brazilian-American drag ball at his bar, Scala, in Astoria, New York. The event coincided with my birthday weekend, and my friends had thrown a big surprise party for me. It was a beautiful celebration, but I was also eager to experience something unique and important. I grabbed a slice of my birthday cake and left early to head to the ball.

Walking into Scala, I was fascinated by how completely immersed each individual was in becoming these larger-than-life drag personas. As I navigated the basement where the queens were getting ready, my photojournalistic instincts kicked in. Their openness surprised me, inviting me to blend into the scene and capture intimate moments.

The backstage atmosphere was electric. Each queen had assistants, and there was fierce competition in the air. Hilarious insults flew back and forth, reminiscent of the rap battles I had seen growing up between São Paulo and New York City.

Although the main event was on the stage upstairs, I was caught up in the magic behind the scenes. Each queen came with multiple outfits, ready to compete fiercely. Once I finally made my way to the stage area, where Rosa emceed the event, I understood and felt the excitement of the competition. The crowd roared as queens took to the runway. I dashed between the basement and the ballroom, capturing every outfifit change I could. It was a whirlwind of humor and ferocity, and for me - the perfect photojournalistic challenge.

I documented the ball at Scala for several years, until Rosa eventually moved back to Brazil, and the event faded from New York City's drag scene.

By 2007, I was working on a feature documentary about drag queens around the world. Zondra Fox was the protagonist of the New York portion of the film. During filming, she invited me to come and experience a unique Fourth of July demonstration on Fire Island called The Invasion of the Pines. Intrigued, I decided to check it out. With my medium-format camera, I headed to Cherry Grove.

The inspiration that I felt as I took in the scene at the Ice Palace rocked me just as the day I first arrived at Scala. This time, the level of sophistication, motivation, and joy moved me beyond my wildest expectations. I had to restrain myself from shooting all my film too quickly, since the day had just begun. The energy of purpose was palpable, and I knew I had to capture it.

I shared some of my early photographs with the queens, and Panzi's first reaction has since fueled my commitment to see the project through: "I've never seen anyone show The Invasion with so much grace." Along the way, I have amassed a rich visual history of more than 3,000 photographs.

I offer this collection in honor of the resistance and commitment of The Invasion as well as the artistry of drag, a world that continues to inspire me.

Anderson Zaca

Photographic Archive Index 2007 – 2024

Acknowledgements

Teri Warren

"The Originals"
Thom (Panzi) Hansen
Max Killingsworth
Amelia Migliaccio
Lynn Hutton
Jack Flood
Gene Taylor
Chuck Young
Nick Sinisi
Nick Trick

Ken Stein of Sayville Ferry
Randy & Sally's Water Taxi

Cherry Grove
All Homecoming Queens for 50 years!
Dinah Stoller & Carol Gersten
Susan & Ruth Freedner
Jacques Beaulande
"The Hesters" – all of them
Phil (Philomena) Stoehr
Matt Baney & Chris Caswell
Lorraine Michels
Michael Abdis
Anita Auricchio
Joann Orfanos
Rose Levine
Craig Williams

Fire Island Pines
John Whyte
Alan Brockman
Doris Tausig
Chris Lovito
Randy Wilson
Ron Martin
Ron McKenna
Jay Pagano
Henry Robin
Ariadne Villarreal
John Wood
Gil Neary & Hal Hayes
Pj McAteer
Robert Bonanno
Robin Byrd

Thank you
Rosa Rosalino
Zondra Fox
Vanilda Zaca
Lyndsay McDonough
Ramona Ortega

Fire Island Invasion: Day of Independence

Published by Damiani Books srl
info@damianibooks.com
www.damianibooks.com

www.andersonzaca.com
www.invasionfireisland.com

First Edition
Printed in duotone in November 2024, Italy

ISBN 978-88-6208-833-6

"She's here to bless the harbor."

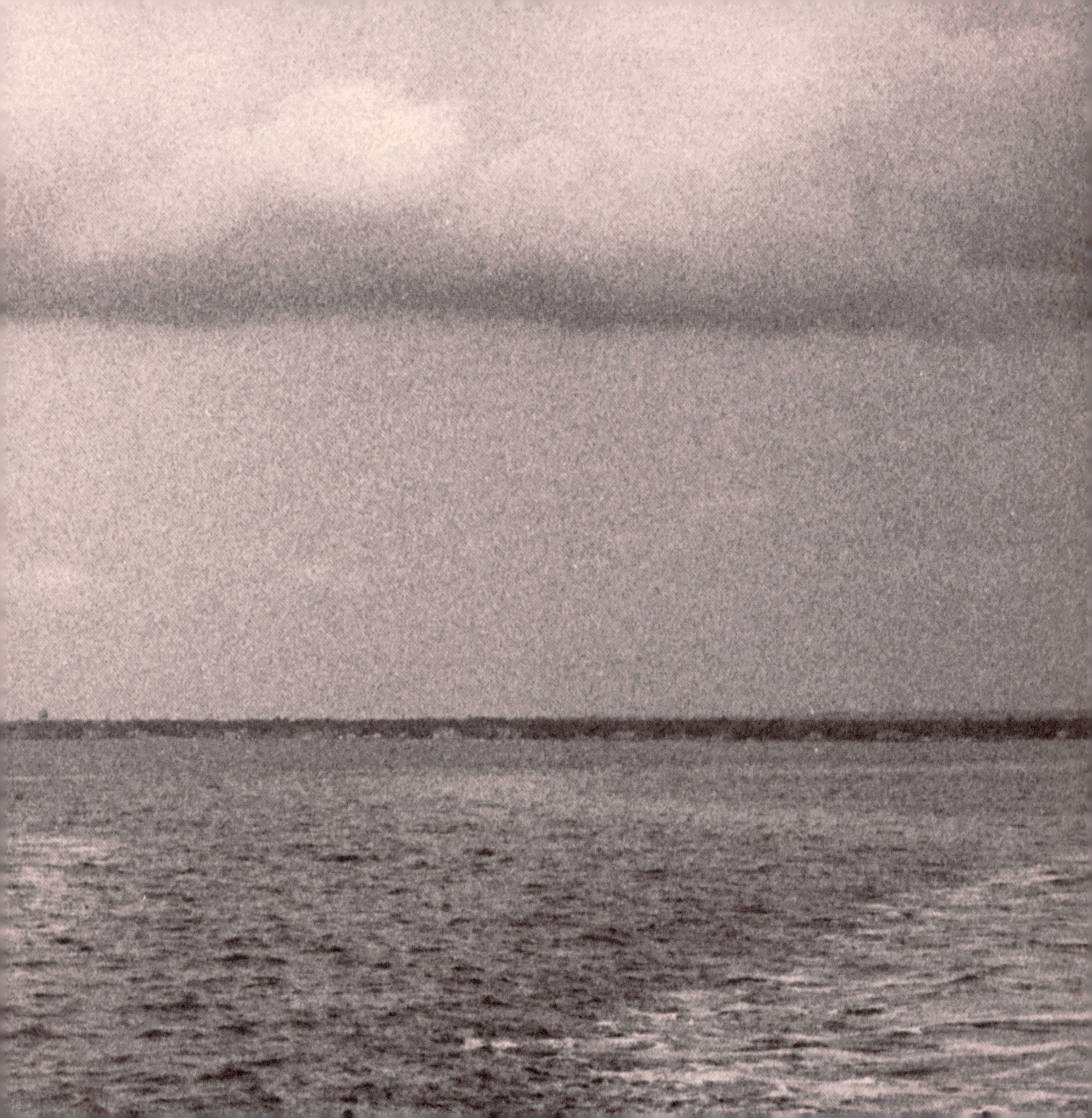